LIFE IN PARADOX

The Story of
a Gay Catholic Priest

First published by O Books, 2008
O Books is an imprint of John Hunt Publishing
Ltd., The Bothy, Deershot Lodge, Park Lane,
Ropley, Hants, SO24 0BE, UK
office1@o-books.net
www.o-books.net

Distribution in:

UK and Europe
Orca Book Services
orders@orcabookservices.co.uk
Tel: 01202 665432 Fax: 01202 666219 Int. code
(44)

USA and Canada
NBN
custserv@nbnbooks.com
Tel: 1 800 462 6420 Fax: 1 800 338 4550

Australia and New Zealand
Brumby Books
sales@brumbybooks.com.au
Tel: 61 3 9761 5535 Fax: 61 3 9761 7095

Far East (offices in Singapore, Thailand, Hong
Kong, Taiwan)
Pansing Distribution Pte Ltd
kemal@pansing.com
Tel: 65 6319 9939 Fax: 65 6462 5761

South Africa
Alternative Books
altbook@peterhyde.co.za
Tel: 021 555 4027 Fax: 021 447 1430

Text copyright Paul Edward Murray 2008

Design: Stuart Davies

ISBN: 978 1 84694 112 2

A CIP catalogue record for this book is available
from the British Library.

Printed by Chris Fowler International
www.chrisfowlerinternational.com

O Books operates a distinctive and ethical publishing philosophy in
all areas of its business, from its global network of authors to
production and worldwide distribution.
This book is produced on FSC certified stock, within ISO14001
standards. The printer plants sufficient trees each year through
the Woodland Trust to absorb the level of emitted carbon in
its production.

LIFE IN PARADOX

The Story of
a Gay Catholic Priest

Paul Edward Murray

BOOKS

Winchester, UK
Washington, USA

CONTENTS

I dedicate this book to my parents
in honor of their astonishing love

1

HERESY: AN INTRODUCTION

It came in the mail one fine morning: the accusation of "heresy." Heresy! How could things have reached this point? For a quarter-century I had been a parish priest. That was admittedly a poor fit. For the past six years I had been employed as a chaplain and college professor. Heresy was out of my league. Don't you have to publish books with radical ideas about God or Christ to be a heretic?

The word heresy stands forth in antique splendor. It stirs painful and repugnant associations from some deep recess of the Western psyche, like Black Death. Today, it is mostly a term that recalls Christian history's discarded ideas and defeated movements. Gnosticism, Arianism, Pelagianism, Donatism, and Monophysitism recall disputes from orthodox Christianity's formative period, before the imposition of definitive ways of talking about Christ, Trinity and salvation. In the Middle Ages heresy expanded beyond the doctrinal level to assume, in Catholic imagination, superstitious, even bestial dimensions. Berthold of Regensburg, an acclaimed Franciscan preacher of the thirteenth century, once expressed a preference for dwelling with hundreds of devils over enduring the perils of even a brief stay in the same house as a heretic. The blunt instruments of ruthless interrogation, torture and execution by burning were deployed against heretical movements, including the Cathars, Hussites and Lollards.

My bewilderment at the weird accusation was quickly followed by a sense of proud solidarity with fellow heretics through the ages – Jan Hus, Joan of Arc, Galileo, Giordano Bruno. But surely I am not important enough to rate this distinction. *Non sum dignus!* I am not worthy! In the accusatory letter (see the Appendix), Bishop Kevin Farrell, then Vicar General of the Archdiocese of Washington, states that I deny church teaching "that matrimony is possible only between a man and a woman." He alluded to a course I was teaching, though not by name. In this, as with the specific basis of his allegation, I was left to infer his meaning. We had never corresponded about or discussed anything relating to marriage.

He must have had in mind "Same-Sex Unions and Christianity," a course I was offering that semester at Bard College. It was organized around medievalist John Boswell's *Same-Sex Unions in Premodern Europe*, a meticulous examination of evidence regarding rites of blessing for same-sex unions that took place over hundreds of years. Were those unions marriages? Boswell argues that the answer to that question depends on the definition of marriage. Premodern understandings of heterosexual marriage focus on its *contractual* aspects and the transfer of a woman from the jurisdiction of her father to that of her husband, residually still evident in modern wedding ceremonies, when the bride is walked up the aisle by her father. During that same period, same-sex unions feature the *personal* dimensions of relationship — attraction, love and commitment — features which are certainly more central than contracts to modern understandings of heterosexual marriage. Ironically, Boswell observes, same-sex unions in the medieval period are more congruent with modern marriage than are heterosexual marriages from the same period. Shifting vocabularies and practices regarding committed relationship, from antiquity to the present, not to mention cross-culturally, make this a fascinating subject. It is also a study that provides crucial background to contemporary discussions regarding marriage, both gay and straight. My course was not, however, a platform for doctrinal assertions. Construing it as the basis for a heresy accusation is ludicrous, unless the critical examination of scholarly presentations and documents has now, in Roman Catholicism's increasingly doctrinaire climate, itself become heresy.

When I shared news of the heresy charge with a bright young colleague, her face lit up into a broad smile. "Congratulations!" she exclaimed. "How wonderful!" Her eyes, though fixed on me, looked beyond, as her mind raced through possibilities. "You know," she said, "heresy bespeaks sanctity. There must be a special aura around you, a *chi* that radiates!" We chatted about the possibility of co-teaching a course on religious sanctions – excommunication, banning, shunning, silencing.

The charge of heresy is surely meant to produce effects quite opposite to mirth and ebullience. Heresy, Kevin informed me, results in the sanction of "automatic excommunication." Excommunication is canon law's equivalent of capital punishment. Once excommunicated, one ceases to exist as a person in the church. One is cut off. But it turns out there is a sanction beyond even excommunication: "*dismissal from the clerical state.*" This is tantamount to saying, "We'll cut off your head. And if that doesn't do anything, then we'll really get serious!" And really getting serious, for the patriarchal culture of Catholic clergy, means the denial of membership in the clergy. Oddly, this sanction is theologically meaningless, since Catholic doctrine holds that ordination confers an ontological change that cannot be removed. A defrocked priest can still validly perform sacraments.

Such speculations, no doubt, elude Kevin and the recent crop of hard-line bishops, enforcers of a rigid, doctrinaire Catholicism. The older generation that ushered in the Second Vatican Council and the great opening to the modern world that it inaugurated is fading from the scene. Pope John XXIII, in a popular metaphor, "opened the windows" of the Catholic Church to the modern world. Today, those windows are rapidly being slammed shut.

In their rarefied world, Catholic bishops are so profoundly out of touch they think they are exhibiting strength and moral clarity, when they are, in fact, confusing and scandalizing by their arrogance and indifference. They take a certain pride in thinking themselves out of fashion – no "political correctness" for them, thank you very much. In fact, they are slaves to fashion: the styles of thought, behavior and self-presentation currently in vogue in their tiny, self-referential world of ecclesiastical bureaucrats.

I, on the other hand, seem to be congenitally out of step with current trends. I came of age in the midst of the counter culture's florescence, as a preppy, conservative Republican. In the late 1960s, a time of radical change in the Catholic Church, I chose to become a Catholic, entranced by romantic notions about the Latin Mass and the pre-Vatican II church. Four decades later, I found myself an avowed political liberal, during the ascendancy of radical conservatism in all three branches of the federal government. And in the Catholic Church, just as an emphatic shift to the right was taking place, during the pontificate of John Paul II, I became an advocate of progressive reform.

Mine is a story of convergences and divergences. When, in adolescence, I first became aware of "homosexuality," which gave a name to my deep attraction to males, I regarded it as utterly irreconcilable with any acceptable way of life or viable worldview. Eventually, however, what I took for opposite domains, homosexuality and "real life," converged, as I appropriated the truth of being a gay man. At the same time, this achievement of integration at the personal level ironically inaugurated a process of mounting alienation from those domains, both religious and political, where divergence between homosexuality and normality has emerged in public discourse as a defining feature.

My ordination stands at the center of the choreography of convergence and divergence that crosses through my life. In 1975 I was ordained to the priesthood together with more than three hundred fifty men from around the world. The ceremony took place at St. Peter's Basilica, with Pope Paul VI presiding. For the climactic moment, the laying on of hands, ordinands approached the Holy Father by twos. Paired with me on that occasion was Ray Burke, a fellow seminarian from the nearby North American College (NAC). A plump young man of cheerful disposition, Ray was a thoughtful, serious student. I enjoyed his company at meals and in the student lounge on many occasions. He was placid and remained largely unaffected by the moods of cynicism and self-absorption that periodically afflicted the house. There was nothing to suggest that Ray and I differed in our outlooks on world, church or theology in any fundamental way.

Thirty years later, how things have changed! Ray, now the Archbishop of St. Louis, has emerged nationally as a hard-liner. He distinguished himself in the 2004 electoral season by declaring, while still Bishop of La Crosse, that Catholic legislators who vote to protect the right to abortion may not receive holy communion in his diocese. This stance amounted to a tacit endorsement of the re-election of George Bush, whose policies on war, national security, capital punishment, and the economy are replete with moral deficits. As a strategy to protect "life," this attempt to sway the electorate was utterly myopic.

The following year, Ray placed the lay directors of a parish in St. Louis, St. Stanislaus Kostka, under interdict, because of a dispute he was having with them regarding control of parish resources. Yes, *interdict!* The denial of sacraments to an entire group, a sanction that most of us know only from histories of the Middle Ages.

Where does this authoritarianism come from? What happened during the past thirty years? But there is not only Ray. Other NACers, now bishops, from my years at the "seminary of baby bishops," are demonstrating similar proclivities. One issued a warning against the theological work of his recently deceased and somewhat liberal predecessor. Surely this was a slight that served no compelling doctrinal or pastoral necessity. Another ordered priest signatories to an interfaith clergy declaration of support for gay, lesbian, bisexual and transgender persons to recant. And what purpose can such a recantation serve beyond a display of the naked power of a bishop over his priests? Does such a public humiliation convince anyone that the purposes of reason and moral witness have prevailed?

The authoritarian, rightward march of men with whom I have lived and studied bewilders me. How could our paths have so diverged? Where did we separate? How did I come to be in the place where I find myself today — openly gay, socially progressive, proponent of a democratically reformed Catholic Church — while much of my sacerdotal cohort moves toward rigid authoritarianism based on a pre-Vatican II model of church as a pyramid ruled from the top down? How is it that I find myself accused of heresy, while my contemporaries, now moving into positions of power, are enforcing a rigidity of doctrine and practice that was foreign to the dynamic theological environment of our youth?

When the divergence began is clear: the election in 1978 of Pope John Paul II. His pontificate, from the start, was marked by a mood of "restorationism." From the restorationist perspective, following Vatican II the church lost its bearings. From liturgical practice to theological investigation there had been too much accommodation to modern sensibilities. In a word, too much "freedom."

Homosexuality emerged as a powerful marker of the divergence between reformist and restorationist versions of Catholicism. Post-Vatican II reformers hold that faith finds its complement in reason and experience. For restorationsts, faith must stand in spectacular, defiant isolation against the new. The struggle over homosexuality – the moral relevance of modern scientific insights regarding sexual orientation; reassessments of the scriptural and theological bases for asserting the sinfulness of homogenital relations; the moral claims of gay and lesbian persons regarding their identity and place in church and society — is not just about homosexuality. It is about the meaning of Catholicism. I have engaged this struggle intimately.

Homosexuality and Catholicism provide the texts and contexts of my life's story. Both domains are appetites, attractions and forces whose signals I seek to decipher. They are texts from which I draw terms and concepts to construct and reconstruct identity and purpose. My investigations of these texts take place within environmental and social contexts that interlace them with meanings and histories. Homosexuality, in my youthful world, pertained to shame, sin, abnormality, fear, hiddenness, risk, rejection and rebellion. Catholicism was a domain of mystery, antiquity, holiness, the sacred, the pure, the forbidden and, for an American Protestant boy, the exotic. These contexts shift, as church and society change, over the course of my life, as well. This book glances back and forth to track that shifting. Following the story's movement may be akin to watching a tennis match, as I move between domains. Both, however, are profoundly implicated in each other. Homosexuality underscores my choice of Catholicism. Catholicism informs my commitment to being proudly gay. But paradoxically, the process that promotes healing and integrity in my life, the convergence of domains, marks the path of my divergence – my "heresy" — from official church structures.

I find it impossible that I leave either domain aside. Both are central to my journey, describing the core from which it begins and the goal toward which it tends. Both provide the means of encountering God. When, finally, the creator receives me back into eternal embrace, will it not be the fulfillment of my yearning, expressed in the Eucharist, for communion, and will this communion not encompass and fulfill the attractions and passions of my homoerotic nature? Eroticism, whether homosexual or heterosexual, is sacramental, a means by which to encounter God in yearning and reaching for profound connection with another person.

In sharing my story, I hope to shed light in an area where there is still much darkness. Homosexuality and its metonyms — coming out, gay rights, gay community, gay marriage, the ordination of gay persons — embroil church denominations on a scale that has not been seen in the United States on any issue since the Civil War. Roman Catholic leaders, to my dismay, have invested resources and prestige in organized campaigns to deny rights for gay men and lesbians in society, even in the absence of a single word against homosexuality from their purported master, Jesus of Nazareth.

Homosexuality and the Catholic priesthood strike many, whether Catholic or not, whether gay or not, as categorical opposites. Along the lines of: sin and righteousness; fire and water; heaven and hell. If a priest has homosexual inclinations, some claim, he cannot acknowledge or act on them in any positive way and remain faithful to his vows. That would be hypocrisy. If he lives a double life, his ambivalence will result in disastrous relationships. If he openly acknowledges his homosexuality, he will surely face rejection and punitive sanctions.

Since the start of my coming out in 1976, a year after ordination, I have encountered reactions to my identity as a gay priest that range from nonchalant acceptance of a seeming commonplace to indignant anger at what simply cannot be. Both ends of this continuum include gay and nongay persons, practicing Catholics and former Catholics, highly religious and proudly nonreligious individuals.

This memoir tells about how I came to be in this realm of contradictions and have long remained there. I shall not characterize it as having only one, specific meaning that can be grasped by its poignantly triumphant or fatalistic conclusion. For one thing, the story is unfinished. I am still living it. This book traces parts of that story's process: journey, struggle, coming out. It presents, I know, fodder to those who seek to drive gay men from the priesthood, as well as to those who disdain Catholicism for its structural homophobia and sexism. Although I am unambiguously and proudly gay, some will be dissatisfied that my story does not conclude with the renunciation of Catholicism. Others, conservative Christians, will be incensed that I have not had what, in their view, would be the integrity to seek laicization.

Why, then, have I written it? Why disclose these tales of my ungainly Life in Paradox? Throughout my work on this book, I have been driven by the desire to reach the many, of whatever sexuality, gender, religion, philosophy or way of life, who are trying to find their way through thickets of similar, if not identical, circumstances. My story, while presenting no shining example of success, nevertheless offers, I believe, a few hopeful moments. Moments when contradictions reconcile. Moments when perplexing paradox yields to luminescent clarity. Moments of some normally obscure dimensions of our world brought into vivid relief.

Whatever clarity emerges here radiates from irreducible mystery, an energy that I encounter at the core of my existence. I call that mystery God. God is neither personal nor impersonal. Perhaps better: God beyond thought, beyond categories, beyond personal/impersonal, though certainly not less than personal. God beyond God. The flood tide of clashing categories that I have lived and sought to navigate has delivered me to a rich and fertile soil of new life and fresh meanings.

The antagonists in my story are church officials — pastors, church bureaucrats, bishops, a cardinal. While I relate here the sometimes-bitter truth about their attitudes and treatment of me, especially with respect to homosexuality, I hope that I have succeeded in crafting their portraits along sympathetic, if not flattering lines. While I hold that we are responsible for our choices, I find in church officials a frequent, even an expected, lack of congruence between personal conviction and actual conduct. At times, they even say as much. That is, as office holders in the Catholic Church, they find themselves constrained to uphold "church teaching." The positive spin that some of these "Company" men put on this is that they have elected to adhere to church doctrine and discipline, even if they personally disagree, because they recognize the importance of obedience to a truth that is greater than themselves. Here precisely is where I disagree. What "truth" is it that we witness, when it is not what we know in the heart? I find such a stance to be not ennobling or selfless, but unfree and bureaucratic. As such, it cannot impart liberating truth, but only confusion and fear.

What troubled my antagonists, years before homosexuality surfaced as an issue between us, was that I did not fully join them in their unfreedom. I was in but not of the clerical matrix. In subtle ways, at first, my mind and heart declared independence by questioning what should be beyond question and disassociating myself from The Company's expectations. Above all, I suspect, I failed to conform, in their view, to the appropriate image of a priest. A prayerful and compassionate man, I believe, is what people saw; but yet, I was somehow not *homo clericalus*, a priest who understands and enjoys the privilege that flows from the clear distinction between clergy and nonclergy.

With this self-description it may seem that I crown my own head with laurel leaves of victory. Far from it! I was slow, painfully slow, to understand why I was unable to find in the Archdiocese of Washington a home. I twisted and turned in my efforts to find the right fit there and, not finding it, sought solace in self-indulgent and self-defeating behaviors, before choosing productive ones. But at the bottom of it all: a stubborn will to freedom.

Could my constitution really be so different from that of my clerical confreres? Do I dare to claim that I am free while they are not? The implications of such questions extend beyond my tortuous history with the Roman church. It is a question that pertains to people in all kinds of organizations: governmental agencies, corporations, armies, hospitals. It is the question of what it means to be a person within a social structure that organizes itself hierarchically for the fulfillment of a stated purpose.

Freedom and power necessarily and famously conflict in bureaucracies. The crushing of personal expression beneath the impersonal demands of organizational life is in many respects the story of modernity. It is also the story of church polities in the modern age. In Roman Catholicism, with its impressive edifices, colorful garb and antique customs, precisely where one expects to find governance that combines pastoral warmth and wisdom, one encounters instead the familiar flaws and tensions that typically exist in bureaucracies from armies to banks: executives with little practical experience of work in the trenches; choirs of sycophants eager to tell those in power what they want to hear; the inability of those at lower levels to make their voices heard by higher-ups; indifference and hostility to new ideas. Though gilded and stretched across an exquisitely baroque stage, these patterns thrive in the Roman Church.

Freedom commences in the act of questioning the givens. Freedom looks under rocks, thumps walls in search of hollow spots, and peels away surfaces. Freedom is impious and impertinent. Some of us are constituted in such a way that this is fundamental to who we are. In itself this penchant is not virtuous. It is simply one of the ways of being in the world. All people, of course, share this characteristic, but in some it is lodged in a central, defining way, especially if their experience of life has set them somewhat apart. Whether out or not, gay persons know that prevailing heterosexist assumptions about the direction and meaning of a fulfilled life do not work for them. This affords a stance at some critical distance from society, where freedom has a bit more space for development.

Freedom is no mere indulgence. It is the act of intimate encounter with meaning. It looks beyond foundational myths, legends, official histories, popular aphorisms, slogans, and inviolable rules to the very sources of meaning. Upon such intimacy, which one famously finds in poets, prophets and visionaries, rests the ability to imagine and construct alternative ways of life. Indeed, productive change, which is crucial to every society's survival, depends on the existence of this capacity. Even the Catholic Church needs its freethinkers.

But freedom perplexes bishops. Not knowing it experientially, they are not sure with what they are dealing when they come across it. They rely on an intuitive sense that informs them: "this guy is not one of us." Yet it may be tough to nail down the problem. It may be, as it was in my case, that there is nothing overt, nothing objectively wrong: no serious misconduct, no flagrant disregard of church law, no blasphemy. No *real* heresy. Usually it is subtler: hints of a disturbing disengagement from familiar ways. A vague disregard for ecclesiastical fashions. Strangely, bureaucrats often harbor a tinge of jealousy toward the free. In some cases, such as mine, they may even demonstrate remarkable tolerance. With time, however, unfree elites, such as the higher clergy, will move to suppress, silence and expel subordinates who challenge their interpretive dominance, even if they must violate their own, stated principles in doing so. Bishops shield their hypocrisy from view, by appeals to "church teaching" and "tradition," which are their own ongoing creations. In short, they make an idolatry of their own power.

I might have been there myself: an ensconced bureaucrat uttering occasional doubts behind the safety of closed doors. Even daring to think myself enlightened. I might have been in that position, but for the intervention of love.

Love first enticed me into Catholicism and the priesthood. Love also enticed me into the gay community. And deep in my soul I know these are not two loves, but one. Catholicism – at its best – reveals the sacramentality of the world. Gay life – at its best – testifies to the sacredness of human sexuality. Quiet words behind closed doors are not an option for me. Filled with a burden of love, gifted with the liberating word, I find myself compelled to declare:

In being gay, I give glory to God.

My catholic spirit rejoices in God's boundless love.

What is hidden and rejected, God raises up,

while those who control and manipulate are toppled.

God satisfies the hunger for justice,

but sends away those who deny truth.

From the days of Abraham and Sarah

to those of Jesus the Christ and myriad saints,

this has been the constant

of God's encounter with humankind:

liberation, when least expected.

11

PART I

THE POWER OF TRUTH

CHAPTER 1

TENSIONS

I

In the year that king Uzziah died, tenors and bases intoned the anthem's somber beginning. An adolescent, I was one of five boys in the Senior Choir of St. George's Episcopal Church. Sopranos and altos joined the next phrase, paralleling the men, one octave above: *I saw also the Lord, sitting upon a throne.* Pause. *High!* We reached D-flat. *Hi-iiigh!!* I pushed for an E-flat. *And lifted up, and his train fiiii-iiii-iiii-lled,* we broke into four parts, filling the church with ponderous, disturbing chords, *the tem-ple!*

I did not know who King Uzziah was, but his exotic name stirred my imagination with thoughts of a distant time and place. Based on the call of the prophet Isaiah, this anthem by David McKinley Williams kindled lofty images. This must be what it is like to see God, I thought. People in white, middle class, suburban Arlington County, Virginia did not have such experiences. My world was quite different from Isaiah's. We had televisions, refrigerators, and automobiles. Our world was neat, clean, scientific. We lived in brick houses — or, at least, the newer ones, the ones built after World War II were of brick. We believed in God, but outside of church were squeamish about religion.

God belonged in His house. At St. George's we worshipped in a building that was completed in 1952. Like the homes in our neighborhood, it was built of red brick. It was a bright, sensible building, topped by a tall, pointed roof. It said church clearly and obviously, but in a manner modulated to modern sensibilities. I could not envision God's train filling St. George's.

St. George's was a warm, kid-friendly parish that was founded in 1909 by English immigrants. Theologically and liturgically neither "high" nor "low," under the sober leadership of its rector, the Reverend Hedley J. Williams, St. George's was part of the Parish Eucharist Movement that emphasized community participation and more frequent celebration of the Eucharist than most Episcopalians had known. Sunday services were marked by a solemn dignity, without being stuffy or precious.

Music played a crucial role in our worship. For the new church, the parish invested in a fine, rebuilt Moller pipe organ. We also maintained two choirs ("Junior" and "Senior") to lead the congregation in hymns and chants. During my early teens I sang in the Senior Choir, after being singled out by Mr. Zabory, the choir director, for having a strong, soprano voice. Every week the choir performed an anthem, usually selected from the English choral tradition. Music, prayers and Mr. Williams's thoughtful sermons provided rich nutrients for my imagination.

As a member of the Senior Choir, I participated in the adult services and found myself steeped in the imagery and stirring, but ever decorous Elizabethan English of the *Book of Common Prayer*. From it the officiating minister prayed: "Oh God, the Creator and Preserver of all mankind, we humbly beseech thee for all sorts and conditions of men; that thou wouldest be pleased to make thy ways known unto them, thy saving health unto all nations." I relished such language, which firmly established church in my mind as a high-minded endeavor that outweighed everything about the everyday world and its pedestrian discourse. The very scope of our prayers ("saving health unto all nations") indicated that there could be no higher purpose.

I first began to read the Bible at the age of fourteen, when I was waiting, one day, for my parents in the parish library. There I came across a copy of the recently published New Testament of *The New English Bible*, one of the Bible's first modern translations. It looked and read like a real book, unlike my copy of the Authorized King James Version, which was printed in two columns of small typeface on thin, gilt-edged India paper.

I read the Sermon on the Mount. The clear words of Jesus were fresh and challenging. For the first time, the teachings of Jesus captured my attention: "Put away anxious thoughts about food and drink to keep you alive, and clothes to cover your body. Surely life is more than food, the body more than clothes." "Pass no judgement, and you will not be judged. For as you judge others, so you will be judged, and whatever measure you deal out to others will be dealt back to you." The directness, the logical simplicity, the pure idealism drew me in.

II

I began to understand Christianity as having to do with life in its totality, everyday life, even life at Williamsburg Junior High School. Religion fortified me and gave me hope as I went into that world every day, where I somehow did not belong. Whereas St. George's was a second home, a place where I felt safe and comfortable, school was altogether another matter.

Since the age of six, when I began first grade, I recognized that I did not always fit in well with groups of boys, long before the awakening of the sexuality that gave a name to some of the difference. It was not so much that I noticed that I was different as it was that my peers called attention to it: less physically aggressive, less interested in competitive sports and models of fighter planes, more likely to include girls among my close friends and more interested in conversing with teachers.

At the age of ten, two classmates, Buddy and Bill, organized a virtual posse to repeatedly chase me home from Nottingham Elementary School. I was not only frightened by their behavior; I was bewildered. What cosmic thing had happened that made me such an obvious target? What was wrong with me? What was "wrong" was that I failed to fit into some of the masculine role expectations of my social world. Even if I did not feel myself deficient in any way, my peers were adept at sniffing out the weak link in their cohort's claim to masculine power.

When I reached puberty, homosexual attractions and spiritual aspirations both began to press vigorous claims on my attention. Both introduced difficulties, because being overtly religious (which, for me, was what it meant to be spiritual) was not much more socially acceptable in the suburban neighborhoods in which I grew up, than being homosexual (a "fairy," in masculine parlance). My interest in religion focused primarily on a sense of mystery and the sacred, on the God whose train filled the temple. Sexual feelings did not, at first, seem to have anything to do with religion. As an Episcopalian, I did not pick up the negative messages so familiar to Roman Catholics and fundamentalist Protestants that associate sexuality with sin. I did not fear that I had offended God or fallen into mortal sin, because I had fantasized about guys.

What I did have, however, was shame, the sense that society's rejection of homosexuality is so profound that I dare not disclose the existence of such feelings to anyone. I learned at an early age to maintain a strict custody of the eyes, lest I be accused of being a dreaded "fairy."

On the one hand, I found in myself spiritual urges which, if channeled toward religion and ministry, could be translated into a socially recognized and honorable profession, namely, the priesthood. On the other hand, I found in myself sexual and affectional urges and attractions which, if acknowledged, could lead to personal disaster. The solution at which I arrived during adolescence was to suppress sexuality and pursue my religion.

At the age of fourteen I sought a "calling" from God for the priesthood and more or less satisfied myself that I received it, during a week of summer camp at Roslyn. Roslyn is an Episcopalian camp in Richmond set on a serene, grassy acreage, where rolling hills dotted by occasional willow trees reach toward the James River. One night, as I lay on my bunk, I conjured in my imagination a convincing image of Christ calling me to the priesthood. It was, notably, not a comforting, healing or loving Christ. It was Isaiah's fierce, demanding, regal figure, a foreshadowing of my pursuit within a few years of a more rigid, authoritarian and ceremonious version of church than what St. George's offered.

Mr. Williams seemed to me a thoughtful and studious priest, but amiable to the point of weakness. If Christianity was to mean anything, I felt, it should challenge people to pay more attention to God and the demands of the gospel than we seemed to be doing. Mr. Williams often included amusing anecdotes in his sermons, for example, about a child who began the Lord's Prayer, "Our Father, who art in heaven, how do you know my name?" This anecdote, which he repeated in several sermons, invoked a few predictable chuckles, before he continued on to explain that the child's unintentional mistake actually raised a profound question. I wondered what had happened to the God whose train fills the temple. These sermons, like the building's architecture, were bland. They were too much suited to the tenor of life in the suburbs, where religion is all right, in its place.

Mr. Williams's associate, Reverend Al Clark, did raise some sparks, by his firm support for the civil rights movement. One Sunday evening, after the Young People's Group meeting, Mr. Clark and I remained in the parish kitchen talking for two and a half hours about civil rights, the social gospel, and what I thought was wrong with St. George's. Our discussion had been prompted by a sermon in which he praised Martin Luther King. We leaned against the stainless steel counters of the recently completed kitchen. Mr. Clark was in his late thirties. His appearance was neat and clerical, although he removed his collar.

"Martin Luther King is not someone we should be praising in church,"

I insisted.

"Why not?" Mr. Clark asked.

"Because he has Communist affiliations. Also, he's getting people to march in the streets and I think that will lead to violence. He's telling people that they can solve their problems by going to the streets. Maybe things need to change. But taking people to the streets is not the way to do it."

"Well, how would you bring about change?"

"Through prayer. People all over the country should be praying about the question of racial integration."

"Prayer? Just prayer?"

"There is no greater power than God. All we need to do to change things is to turn to God."

"Is that what Jesus told his disciples to do, to just pray? What about the parable of the good Samaritan? It was the priest and the Levite, in spite of their prayers, who passed by. The gospel calls us to action, Paul, not just prayer."

"Yes, we need to be charitable, but let's not forget what God has given us. In the Eucharist we receive Jesus Christ himself. What more do we need?"

"Paul, I know you want to go into the ministry. But God is not calling you to be a 'Mass priest.' That's what they do up the street, at St. Charles. They celebrate Mass every day. They have several Masses on Sundays. That's what Roman Catholics do. But there's more to church than that."

Episcopalianism is a balancing act between Catholicism and Protestantism. I was raised with a Protestant emphasis, but began to gravitate toward the Catholic end of the spectrum. I was looking for transcendence, an experience of church that would lift me above the tedium and dull materialism of the suburbs. I longed for spiritual experience, for direct contact with God. It was Catholicism, not Protestantism, that evoked mystery, history, saints.

At the age of sixteen, I wrote in my journal: "For over two years I have wanted to be an Anglican priest. In only this have I been vaguely consistent. Even so, I vary greatly in imagining what type of priest I want to be: a monk? a pastor? a professor at a seminary? I don't know." Church provided an exciting set of possibilities. My sense of opportunity was nurtured by the Washington Cathedral, a great gothic church that had been under construction since before I was born and, my father told me, would continue to be under construction after the end of my life. It spoke to me of the medieval church, of a time when monastic communities chanted the Divine Office in church choirs. I frequently pored over the bookstore's merchandise, especially books on gothic architecture and medieval abbeys. There were also theological books, from which I gleaned something of current, liberalizing trends in the church. Bishop John A. T. Robinson's *Honest to God*, which provoked enormous public attention at the time, disturbed me as an effort to reduce Christianity to something dull, tepid, and safely modern.

Seminarians from the nearby Virginia Theological Seminary reflected this intellectualistic, demythologizing trend. Every year, two were assigned to St. George's, where they preached, prepared candidates for confirmation, and supervised the Young People's Group. They were thoughtful, mature men, most of them in their thirties, who were entering the priesthood after some experience in other careers. Most were married, and while they pursued their three-year program of study, their wives often worked to finance their endeavors and cultivated the embroidery and needlepoint skills that would enable them to equip their husbands and parishes with decorative stoles, linens and cushions.

Under the supervision of a seminarian, the Young People's Group went on an annual weekend retreat to Shrine Mont, a rustic, Episcopalian retreat center in the Appalachian Mountains. Our conferences took place in a large cabin, where the seminarian would sit pensively in his easy chair by the fireplace and begin by lighting his pipe. All seminarians, it seemed, were pipe smokers. A brisk fire licked at a stack of logs that would dwindle during the course of our discussion. I often found the tone of these conferences disconcerting. The seminarians spoke of the social gospel, the Christian's vocation in the secular world, and situation ethics, the notion that moral choices must be modulated to the demands of specific circumstances.

I argued passionately against these liberal, secularizing trends which were dismantling what I understood Christianity and church to be. Nevertheless, during the course of my many discussions and arguments with these thoughtful pipe smokers, something fundamental was being modeled for me about what it means to engage theological truth. The seminarians were showing me that being church does not mean having all the answers. Often, the best that we can do, given the strains and confusion of modern life, is to throw a few logs on the fire, light our pipes, sit back and talk things through, understanding that our conclusions are always tentative and subject to revision. Truth is not simply given; it is what we strive together to discover. The words of the clergy are not definitive. Even the opinions of a fourteen-year-old boy must be taken seriously. In my impatience, however, I imagined I should be getting meatier stuff from my religion. St. George's was too comfortable.

Through a high school friend, Michael, I discovered the "high church," when I was sixteen, and started attending Sunday services at two high Episcopal churches in Washington, Ascension and St. Agnes (the name of *one* of them) and St. Paul's. Both seemed very "Catholic," compared to St. George's. The priests were addressed as "Father." The Sunday Eucharist was called "Mass," instead of "Holy Communion," and Mass, especially "High Mass," was a colorful, glittering, and aromatic affair that bespoke solemnity and mystery at every turn. These were places where one might sing and believe the words of Williams's anthem: *And the posts of the door moved at the voice of him that cried, and the house was filled with smoke.* The solemnity of these liturgies drew me in and, by their ancient echoes, stirred my imagination.

At seventeen, I became a member of St. Paul's. On mornings when there was no school, I would rise at 5:30 to take the earliest bus into the city so that I could attend Matins and Mass there. Afterwards about ten parishioners would remain for breakfast, which was lovingly prepared and served in the parish hall by an elderly parishioner, Mildred Milburn. On Fridays, Mildred would grill smelts for us, a dietary sign that we were true Catholics. I admired the four priests who rotated the role of celebrant among themselves at these morning Masses, but was especially impressed by the rector, Father Richards, an older man with close-cropped hair and a mild speech impediment that produced, when he celebrated Mass, a hypnotic drone that was somehow reassuring. Thus began my journey into the Catholic tradition.

Sexuality was a subtext to these sojourns. My attractions to men never felt anything but perfectly natural. I noticed the guys around me in school. In the ninth grade, I was mesmerized by David, whose face and body were prematurely toughening into a compelling manhood. In High School there was Jonathan, whose blonde hair, milky skin, and lean body quickly imprinted themselves into my memory banks.

I always assumed that the attraction could not be mutual. It never occurred to me that any of these youths, whom the gods had favored, could possibly return my interest. I assumed all of them were heterosexual. Moreover, I was skinny and my muscles were hopelessly puny. In phys ed I was routinely outclassed by my teammates: in wrestling, pinned to the mat instantaneously; in basketball, hopelessly awkward. I was always among the last chosen for any team. The one sport where I showed some promise was soccer, but we spent little time on that.

An unmistakably homoerotic tension overhung the locker rooms. There were jokes about who was a fairy, especially when anyone began to get an erection. A good measure of curiosity about one another's bodies and maturation into manhood pervaded much of the talk and interaction. I was too nervous, too ashamed of my body and too concerned about disclosing my feelings to just be one of the guys. I therefore developed a pattern of shutting down and avoiding communication on these occasions: shower and towel off quickly, dress and get out. The locker room symbolized how I felt about myself in the world of men — exiled from my own gender. It was not that I felt myself to be anything other than a man — certainly in no sense female — but somehow, always, a different man, the odd man out, not a man who enjoys camaraderie and approval in the world of men. Thus the pattern developed of tamping down and subordinating my feelings for the sake of presenting the world some carefully crafted version of self.

III

During my first twelve years, home was a dark, red brick, "Cape Cod" house on Twenty-seventh Street, where I lived with my parents and sister, Reba, who was four years older than me. What I most liked about our home were the yards and trees. The backyard was dominated by an extraordinarily tall, thick-trunked weeping willow. Beyond it, near the honeysuckle, was a black walnut tree. The driveway was lined by tall locust trees. My parents complained about the locust trees, which, they insisted, were simply "weeds." I liked them, however, and enjoyed the yellow, oval leaves that they rained down throughout the summer. The garage, separate from the house, was a dank abode of spiders. It had containers of tools and, for some unknown reason, barrels of coal (we had oil heating) that were ripe for a young boy's explorations. I dreamed of discovering a way to pressurize the coal so that it would become diamonds.

Until the age of five, Pete O'Sullivan, my best friend, lived next door. Pete was Catholic, I learned from my parents. One day, when we were talking near the back porch, I said to Pete:

"You're a Cath-lick." I don't remember that Pete said anything in response. The statement was neither accusation nor inquiry. It was just something that I said. Information heard and repeated. I doubt whether I even knew that this word had something to do with church. After I went back into the house, however, my Mother held me tightly by the arm and instructed me sternly:

"Never, never say to Pete again that he's a Catholic!"

I wasn't sure whether this was because being Catholic was a bad thing. What I learned from my Mother, however, was that it was the sort of thing that should not be talked about.

I remember those years as though they were one endless summer. Pete and I ventured onto a small farm across Twenty-seventh Street that provided an inexhaustible site for exploration. It was owned by Roscoe, who was "part-Indian and part-Negro," I heard. Pete and I helped ourselves to the blackberries from the bushes that lined his gravel driveway. Behind Roscoe's house was a well that seemed unimaginably deep. Pete insisted on climbing along the edge, inside its protective cover. I was disinclined to take such risks myself, and I was terribly frightened for Pete whenever he would perform this stunt.

Pete and I had a secret. We put our pee-pees together sometimes. We enjoyed it. In fact, we enjoyed it so much that I suggested we glue them together. Pete said he would think about it. Then, one day, on my back porch, he asked:

"Do you have some glue?"

"What? Why do you want glue?"

"You know, to glue us together."

"Ah, why don't we go play in your house?" I suggested.

I was afraid of being overheard. I don't remember being told not to talk about pee-pees or sticking them together, but somehow I knew this was not the type of conversation in which one engaged within earshot of others. I also sensed that gluing our parts together was hopelessly impracticable. Pete and I could not live being joined like that.

After Pete and his family moved away, I knew that the sex play between us was something I had to keep to myself. In fact, I thought of it as a secret I would take to my grave. It must never be repeated to anybody. How I came to have such a fearful notion I do not know. But by the age of six, I took up what I assumed would be the lifelong burden of concealing a shameful secret of same-sex indulgence.

My parents are both natives of the Washington area, something of a rarity in an urban area dominated by politics and the military. My father sold insurance, an occupation that suited his independent spirit and restless drive to move about. He worked long days, often going out again in the evening to meet with prospects. Due to the poor health of my widowed grandmother and my mother, who suffered from a thyroid condition during their first years of marriage, he was deferred from military service during the Second World War. Since many military families lived in our neighborhood, I often compared my father with other Dads, who were Captains and Colonels. They were more interested than he was in sports and physical activity, which at times made me envious. But those Dads were also stricter and steered their sons toward military careers.

My father was raised in a stern, southern Baptist household. He refused his parents' offer to finance his college education on their terms: no dancing, drinking or gambling — not that these were ever of more than passing interest to him. The strictness of his upbringing was recalled and lamented in our family. I was thankful to be raised in a more lenient, sensible household.

Behind his serious demeanor lay a fundamentally playful heart. He loved to read me stories. He particularly enjoyed puns and verbal games, which inevitably elicited moans and groans from his audience. One of his favorite responses to my frequent questions was to tease me with the words, "Horses, want to buy a mule?" For a long time, I had no idea what he had actually said, because he would say it so rapidly. When I finally got it, I still didn't get it, and so would interrogate him about the saying, to his inexhaustible amusement.

My father had very strong beliefs. He would tell me about them, as I sat, watching his progress on various household projects — painting the basement, rolling out the summer carpet, raking the leaves. The Communists were our enemies, he explained. They wanted to take over. In Russia countless numbers suffered under their oppressive regime. Many people had been placed in prison and forced labor camps. The House Un-

American Activities Committee issued reports, which he sometimes brought home, about Communist subversion in the United States. What made the United States different from Russia, and, in fact, better than any country on Earth, was *freedom*. We were free in this country to worship, read, write, and live as we chose.

I was an eager pupil. I found it comforting that my father knew all of this. When the fathers of two of my friends died suddenly of heart attacks, I wondered what I would do if my father died. How would I know what to think about world events? When I reached adolescence, he took me to a few meetings of the John Birch Society, where we watched films about the Communist menace. The Soviets' plan, forged by Lenin, was to take over the world country by country, until finally the United States, like an overripe fruit, would simply drop into their hands. The prospect was horrifying. What would happen to our family? Would I be tortured? What would I do in prison?

My mother left the field of political analysis to my father. Her domain was the home, which she kept as a meticulous, yet comfortable environment. Before I started school, she often fixed my favorite lunch, a grilled cheese sandwich (American cheese on white) and chocolate milk. A point of discussion often was whether the crust should be cut away from my sandwiches. I wanted them crustless, but she believed the crust contained nutrients that I needed. Once a week we journeyed into the city by bus, to shop at Woodward and Lothrop's, an elegant "downtown" department store. A highlight of these forays would be lunch in the top floor restaurant.

My mother was raised in a close, loving household that struggled, it was often recalled, through the Great Depression. At the age of eight, she decided on her own that she wanted to go to church. Her parents were Christian, but not regular churchgoers. She chose St. George's, which near her elementary school, because she enjoyed the services and was impressed by the kindness of the parishioners. After marrying her, my father converted, not having found much solace in the moralistic, Biblical literalism of Fort Meyer Baptist Church (later, Open Door Chapel) where his family worshipped.

When my mother read me stories, she often held me on her lap and looked at the book over my head. She read in a tone that was completely different from that of my father. He liked to have fun with the stories, to use them to tease my sister and me. My mother was a thoughtful, careful reader, who conveyed the text faithfully, without joking, except where the story was supposed to be funny.

A few weeks before I started school, my parents were working on the front yard and my mother began to cry.

"Boys are rough," she said.

I did not understand what she was talking about, but could not get her to explain. My father spoke up:

"Your Mother's worried about you going to school. It's going to be all right," he reassured her.

The moment left a vivid impression. Just what was I in for, when I would start first grade? I was about to leave the haven of a comfortable home and endless summers for something very different.

My sister was already in school. Reba would be entering sixth grade, when I entered first, at Nottingham Elementary School. Since she was four years older than me, she would normally be in fifth grade, but because she had skipped third grade, she was a year ahead. Reba and I played together sometimes, but she deemed me too young for inclusion in her activities with her friend, Susan. When my sister was excluding me from some game — pick-up sticks, go fish, Chinese checkers — Susan often made an appeal on my behalf. She was sympathetic, because she also had an older sister and had suffered the humiliation of exclusion.

From early childhood it was clear that Reba and I had quite different temperaments. I was introspective, intellectual, quiet and shy. Reba was outgoing, sociable, and assertive. Despite her efforts to exclude me, we often played together.

In truth, I preferred my own toys and activities. After Pete moved away, I had friends, but not the constant companionship of a best friend. My parents noted, however, that I was very self-contained. I did not require much attention to find ways of spending my time. I practiced the piano, played my record collection for endless hours, and explored the neighborhood.

After she got her driver's permit, my mother faithfully drove me to piano lessons, drum lessons, Cub Scout meetings, and the Arlington County library. Each morning she laid out the clothes I was to wear and sent me off to school with a good breakfast. Eggs and cereal alternated, day by day. It was a comfortable, secure upbringing.

IV

We moved into a spacious new house, a bright rambler with picture windows, when I was thirteen. I soon met a boy in the neighborhood, Craig, who introduced me to the pleasures of the flesh. Our sessions together were in no way passionate or anything other than an exploration of how the equipment between our legs works. At a newsstand in Rehoboth Beach, I discovered a "muscle" magazine, *Tomorrow's Man*, whose pages featured men clad in what I found utterly seductive, posing straps. Craig and I were entranced by these photographs. I even subscribed, looking forward to the monthly deliveries, which arrived in a plain envelope, for the next two years. I also discovered a newsstand in Washington where I was able to purchase similar publications. Some of them included a bit of news on the "homophile" movement which, in those pre-Stonewall years, was still in its infancy. There were, then, flickers of recognition that I was not completely alone in my same-sex attractions.

I took pride in the fact that a subterranean, homosexual culture existed, even though I did not dare to venture into it. In fact, it was, as far as I knew, a world of hustlers and freakish, effeminate men. Jean-Paul Sartre's *Saint Genet*, a panegyric to the work of Jean Genet, instilled the notion that this was a world with heavy, criminal undertones. But from my place of unremitting isolation — intellectual, emotional, and social — I secretly delighted in the knowledge that there were others like myself out there, somewhere, and that they had chosen to act on what I was denying myself. Genet's descriptions of homoerotic attraction were, after all, not foreign. In *The Thief's Journal*, Genet's description of the mesmerizing movement of a leather belt against the back of a young workman resonated. That was the kind of detail I, too, would notice. In a national magazine, I came across a photograph of hustlers perched on a fence and wearing tight jeans and T-shirts, a look of which I will never tire.

There were other signs, however, that spoke of the dangers of being homosexual. With my parents, I saw *Advise and Consent*, a 1962 film based on the novel by Allen Drury. It starred Don Murray as a United States Senator, Brig Anderson, who slits his wrists after being blackmailed on the basis of his homosexual past. The film includes a brief portrayal of homosexual life in New York City. I was much disturbed by the scene where Senator Anderson enters the walkup apartment of an effeminate, fat queen, in an effort to track down his former lover. Later, Don Murray becomes nauseous, after briefly scanning the crowd in a gay bar. The cause of his sudden nausea confused me. Even to my unschooled eyes, the barroom seemed tame and commonplace. Nevertheless, I left the theater with a keener awareness of the shamefulness of my secret longings and the ugliness that clung to those who dared to live such a life. We stopped off for frozen custard, never discussing the film.

In 1964, Walter Jenkins, Special Assistant and close friend of President Johnson, was arrested for soliciting sex at a YMCA near the White House. I followed the sordid news accounts with breathless anxiety. I knew this YMCA. It was an old building. I had gone there as a young boy for swimming lessons, which, for unknown reasons, boys were required to take in the nude. My only proud accomplishment at the Y was to win a contest by giving the best estimate of the number of jellybeans in a jar. Swim class, however, was a disaster. The pool was unpleasant and dark, the water cold. Naked before my peers, I felt more vulnerable than ever. In my childish inexperience, I never saw or thought about anything sexual in that bleak place. Whatever Walter Jenkins was doing there did not seem like something that I would want to do. Still, I was mesmerized by the news stories, because I knew deep down this had something to do with me. If a man of such importance could be destroyed so suddenly by homosexuality, what good could come of it? A gut-wrenching fear of the consequences of exposure compelled me to keep my homosexuality hidden and suppressed. Mentioning it to my parents or Mr. Williams or a teacher at school was completely out of the question.

Although I was ingesting the messages that the heterosexist world wanted me to ingest — to be afraid, to hate myself, to hide my feelings — many were not fooled, especially my peers. My male peers, presumptively heterosexual, also picked up on society's expectations of them and were, as a consequence, eager to demonstrate their fitness to take their places in the world of men. Sexual joking, bragging and sneaking girlie magazines into school were typical and even expected behaviors. So also were the use of sexual language, curse words, and the manifestation of a toughness that appeared ever ready for a fight, even if few fights actually took place. Theirs was a world to which I could never belong. To my world's bullies and self-appointed guardians, ever assessing themselves and others against some implicit scale of masculinity — it is all about "scoring," after all — I simply did not measure up. The result was not so much that I was picked on, beaten up and called "faggot" at every turn, but, rather, that I was made to feel different, deficient, not worthy to be included in the world of guys, a society of sports and girl-chasing and cars. There were moments where the exclusion was explicit. Once, as I was leaving a classroom, I heard a boy make a crack about the way I walked. I do not believe that I was effeminate or that my gait differed significantly from that of any other male, but suddenly I was made to feel that even my bipedal behavior gave me away as a hopeless queer. I was, simply, an excluded person, someone who did not fit into the world of men.

V

I did not retreat completely into the world of religion. I discovered during these years another culture that stands on the margins of society, that of writers and artists. Dostoyevsky's *The Brother's Karamazov* was the first important work of literature that I read. I was impressed by the character of Alyosha and drawn to his decision to be a "monk in the world." I was also strongly drawn to Beat writers such as Allen Ginsberg, Lawrence Ferlinghetti and Jack Kerouac. Kerouac's descriptions of a free-spirited, Bohemian world held a special fascination. George Orwell's *1984* provided literary confirmation of my fears that dangerous forces were afoot to destroy our world by taking away our freedom. Indeed, I held an underlying view, which I seldom expressed, apart from personal journals, that Orwell's work was prophetic and described a horrifying vision of a future that was inevitable. As I looked to Christianity, political conservatism and contemporary literature, my underlying assumption was that I needed to find the resources to face an ugly, technocratic, authoritarian future. As reading took hold, my teachers made encouraging observations about my writing.

It was at this time that I met Amy. Amy picked me. I did not pick her, nor could I have, so intense was my isolation.

"Paul. Pa-ull!"

Exiting the school, I was oblivious to my name being called. It was late, well after the end of the school day. I had remained behind to browse in the school bookstore, a converted custodial closet where wire racks from floor to ceiling were stuffed with paperbacks. The selection was small, but I never tired of perusing its contents.

"Paul Murray, you are going to have to get rid of that inferiority complex!"

That got my attention! I turned. Who was this, I wondered, and how did she know my name?

"Hello. Have we met?"

"Yes, we met before, but just briefly. I'm Amy. Amy DuBois. That's Doo-bwah, if you go by my mother's pronunciation. Dad says it Doo-boyz. But I have decided to be Doo-bwah. Anyway, I have noticed you and want you to know that you are a much smarter and more attractive person than you think."

"Well, thanks."

Amy looked out of place at Yorktown. She had a thirties look, with frizzy brown hair, reddish cheeks and a flower print dress. But it was not a chosen, cultivated look. It was just who she was. Yorktown was too modern for her. She looked as out of place there as I felt.

I wondered why she said I had an "inferiority complex?" I knew I did, but how did she know it? Did she just say that because I failed to respond when she called my name the first time? Was I lost in thought? Or is it that I am just unaccustomed to having someone call out my name?

"Why don't you come over to my house for lunch on Saturday?" Amy suggested.

"Okay, that sounds good."

I accepted my first ever invitation to lunch from a schoolmate.

Amy lived in an old, wooden house surrounded by a huge yard and tall trees. In the backyard was a swing suspended by ropes from a tree limb. We lunched on grilled cheese sandwiches and lemonade.

Her brother, Fletcher, was three years her junior, almost the same age difference as between Reba and myself. Amy and Fletcher, however, were more relaxed in each other's company than my sister and me. In fact, they actually seemed to enjoy being together. Fletcher, who was learning the guitar, serenaded us in the backyard with folk songs. He had a rich, nasal, Dylanesque voice. This type of music did not make sense to me, so I merely listened politely. The DuBois household, Amy explained, was strongly supportive of the civil rights movement.

"Ma picketed the White House, carrying a placard and wearing long white gloves!" Amy burst with explosive laughter.

Amy's mother, Angela, was a glowing woman whose magnetism attracted dozens, indeed, hundreds of people to their home. She came from a Boston family of sufficient prominence for their name to appear in the Social Register. Fletcher and Amy inherited their nasal voices from their mother's side of the family. Angela chain-smoked Camel cigarettes and was never too busy to stop what she was doing, and, after lighting up a cigarette, launch into deep, probing conversation with any and all visitors. She had the talent of making each person feel that they were the center of the universe. Her sight was extremely poor, and the bottle-thick round lenses of her eyeglasses availed but little. To read anything she had to hold it close to her face. Deeply religious, she thoroughly approved my interest in the ministry. But Angela linked religion to justice issues, such as the civil rights movement, in ways that I, as yet, did not.

Dr. DuBois, the father of Amy and Fletcher, a research psychologist, was a friendly, but remote figure, the very opposite of Angela. He was uncomfortable around people and, in fact, conceded that he had little interest in their home's numerous guests. He took his evening cocktail and dinner in seclusion, in the den and bedroom, while the rest of the house bustled and burst at the seams with laughter, strumming guitars and impassioned debates, the scene of a never-ending party.

Angela, Amy and Fletcher were the first people I knew who had some personal involvement in civil rights. Their house generally served as a gathering place for the like-minded, many of them school friends of Amy and Fletcher, members of CORE (the Congress of Racial Equality) and SNCC (the Student Non-Violent Coordinating Committee).

I was uneasy about the civil rights movement, mostly because I feared the disruption that racial integration would bring to my white suburban world. I was, in fact, profoundly ignorant of Black people. I knew that they had problems, but I did not think that bursting into my world was the way to improve anything. My views, however, took shape in a very tiny social environment. By both example and argument, the DuBois family and their friends taught me much about freedom and respect. They appealed to my Christianity, where the arguments against equality and integration are easily exposed as hollow and selfish. I did not join any picket lines or sit-ins, but some stones were knocked away from the wall that isolated me from the larger world.

The DuBois household (dubbed by its extended family the "Iced Tea House of the August Moon") and *Portfolio*, Yorktown's literary magazine, on which I served as co-editor of poetry, became important havens, along with church. My newly developing identity was that of an intellectual and a writer. There was a place for me, after all.

Amy became my girlfriend, by default. One did not have to look closely to see that this was not really a girlfriend/boyfriend relationship. I was not physically affectionate with her and it barely occurred to me that I should be. After I went away to college, she sent me a letter of mild reproach for not having so much as held her hand. I was both embarrassed and pained by this, because I knew she was right. Amy deserved more. Her friendship was a true gift of grace, unmerited, that lifted my self-worth. I cannot imagine what would have become of me without it. But I could not give her what I did not have to give.

Under the influence of the Iced Tea House of the August Moon, I came to identify, in a very limited way, with the growing counter culture of the 1960s, which included remnants of the precursor, beat generation, civil rights activists, whether authentic or self-styled, folk singers and their fans, peace activists, war protesters, poets and intellectuals. Nevertheless, I continued to think of myself as fundamentally conservative and to emphasize church as a major facet of my life.

While my interests in church, writing and the freedom-loving youth culture were real, I had little understanding of the emotional damage I was inflicting on myself by using them to suppress my sexuality. In my junior year of high school I wrote a story, "Arnold Among the Clay," that appeared in *Portfolio*. It drew notice and praise from friends and teachers. The truth is it was a desperate cry for help. Arnold was a young man who saw no reason to live. He lived with painfully acute individuality in a world of "clay," a symbol of the malleability and conformism that I saw in my peers. Arnold devised a plan to kill himself dramatically during lunch in the school cafeteria by ingesting poison. Miss Glynn, the faculty sponsor of Portfolio, toned down the story, by leaving the outcome, the death of another student who unintentionally drinks the poison, to the reader's imagination. I had no conscious thoughts of suicide during my high school years, but my sense of isolation was quite profound. But for Amy and the Iced Tea House of the August Moon, I might well have sunk into a much deeper place.

VI

Sexual feelings dogged me, despite my intellectual, social and religious endeavors. In libraries and bookstores I thumbed through psychology books, often turning immediately to the index and checking every entry under "homosexuality." I was searching for understanding and hope. These books told me, in simplistic reiterations of Freudian doctrine, that I must have a weak or relatively absent father and a domineering mother. I was alternately convinced and unconvinced by this theory. All I knew for sure was that I had had these feelings as long as I could remember.

I once sat in my room and wrote, "I am a homosexual" on a piece of paper, which I then held up to examine. This was an attempt to objectify this part of myself, to make sense of it, perhaps even to find some peace in it. But, of course, the paper had to be torn up at once. I tried to rid myself of sexual feelings. I took my male magazines down to a creek near my home, where I burned them, in a desperate effort to leave behind such carnal desires together with all traces of their existence. My ascetic resolve was, however, short-lived.

The social worlds to which I was drawn, for example, high church Anglicanism, turned out to be homosexual havens. At St. Paul's, for example, there were large numbers of "bachelors." I was invited to a few of their gatherings, where there was nothing very explicit happening; but the sexual undercurrent was unmistakable. A few years later, when I was nineteen, a young man, Bill, put his hand on my leg as we drove back from a party in Mount Vernon and suggested that I spend the night at his house in Washington. We were fortunate to have survived that drive, because Bill was so drunk that he had turned left into the oncoming traffic on the George Washington Parkway. I declined and nervously redirected him to the proper lanes. Later, Bill sloughed off that night as a moment of drunkenness, when I myself attempted, in more sober moments, to get better acquainted. I was attracted to Bill and wanted nothing so much as to have sex with him.

One Sunday Evening, a group of men were gathered at Bill's house, including Father Richard Martin, then a chaplain at George Washington University, when the conversation turned obliquely to Father Roland.

"Did you notice his friends standing in the back of church, after Benediction?" Father Martin queried the group in his refined, lilting voice. Father Martin was a chubby, cheerful man, whose thinning hair appeared always to have just been meticulously combed and lacquered into place.

"They were there," Jack nodded his assent.

"Does he think people don't notice?" Father Martin queried further.

"It's sad to see someone doing this to his career right at the outset," Bill suggested.

"No one forced that collar on him!" Father Martin snorted, his upper lip tightening, as he drew in a deep breath while the group silently pondered what he had just said

I, too, pondered in silence. Breathless silence. The meaning of his words was clear: Father Roland was a homosexual and had homosexual friends! One could only imagine where they went and what they did together! The effect of Father Martin's moral pronouncement on the group was bracing. These were Christian gentlemen, the kind of men who could think of nothing better to do on a Sunday evening than return to church, where they had been to High Mass earlier in the day, for Evensong and Benediction of the Blessed Sacrament. They were, on Sunday evenings, regular attendees in a small congregation that was remarkably devoid of women. Never mind that several of the men in that room were certainly homosexual. Thus, even in the world of religion there was no escape from homosexuality and, of course, its rigorous condemnation. I never heard of the matter going beyond that room. The discussion had been nothing more than a momentary indulgence in voyeurism and the perverse pleasures of moral judgment. It taught me that I dare not relax my guard at *any* moment, anywhere. Thus, the shame soaked in; indeed, I sucked it in as I made choices that fastened my emotional bonds tighter and tighter over the next few years.

Amy and I went together to the Senior Prom and had a pleasant evening, in a friend/friend kind of way. I looked at a male magazine before getting dressed that evening. The inconsistency and hypocrisy, the unfairness to Amy, all bore down on my soul, but I saw no way out. Homosexuality was forbidden and heterosexual dating *de rigueur*. And while I was struggling just to keep up appearances, some of the guys roared with excitement about their plans to take their dates afterwards for a weekend at the beach. Even if they were crude, they impressed me for knowing what they wanted and the camaraderie they obviously enjoyed in that.

VII

The following September I enrolled at Bard College. Bard is a small, progressive, liberal arts college in the Hudson Valley, a bit more than midway north, between New York City and Albany. Founded in 1860 as St. Stephen's, a pre-theologate for aspirants to the Episcopal priesthood, the college metamorphosed during the 1940s and 1950s into a campus known for its connections to literary circles. "Independence, rebelliousness, iconoclasm, and a disregard for the structures of a conventional society were prized at Bard," according to a self-descriptive report prepared by college administrators, "an institution that celebrated individualism and creativity and saw itself as an alternative." I was drawn to Bard precisely because I understood it to be such a place. I needed that kind of freedom not just to grow, but to survive.

The campus occupies a stretch of hilly acreage generously endowed with forsythia, honeysuckle, lilac and trees, lots of glorious trees with heaven-reaching and earth-swooping limbs — hemlocks, maples and oaks. Lining Stone Row (predictably dubbed "Stoned Row"), at the campus's center, ivy took possession of several dormitories, whose gothic touches stoically testified to the college's original mission, amid the latter-day hedonism of long-haired, often-bearded, self-proclaimed "hippies." Speakers placed at open windows opulently poured forth the sounds of Bob Dylan and the Rolling Stones.

I was assigned to Ward Manor, a dormitory at the northern edge of campus, a pretentious, though not especially large mansion built by a couple, who, it was said, failed to gain acceptance in Hudson Valley high society. It had long been shaded by a massive elm tree, which had, by then, begun to yield its vitality to the assault of Dutch elm disease. The house claimed an impressive view of the Catskill Mountains across the Hudson River. The sun setting behind the misty, blue Catskills, as I would come to appreciate in the years that followed, is a captivating, magical sight in which, as Washington Irving notes in "Rip Van Winkle," the summits "glow and light up like a crown of glory."

During my first month at Bard, something magical occurred that forever changed my life. Alex walked into the splendid, mahogany-paneled common room of Ward Manor, where I, sitting on a couch, was making a halfhearted attempt to read Herodotus's *Histories*.

"Hello. What is that book that you are so diligently reading?" Alex was six feet tall. Brown eyes and brown, wavy hair. Thin lips stretched into a mischievous grin. He leaned back against a table.

"Oh, it's just Herodotus. For Toomey's course."

"He's crazy, you know. Toomey takes himself too seriously."

We were speaking of Mr. John Toomey, professor of ancient history, whose introductory course on Greek and Roman history was required of all freshmen. Toomey had achieved a kind of cultic status. Visitors attended the first few of his famously dramatic lectures, each year.

"Well, I am just enjoying the opportunity to get acquainted with these classics," I said. "What's your major?"

"I'm an art student. I paint."

"What kinds of things do you paint?"

"Oh, anything. I'm mostly just into the sensuousness of it. The feel of the paint. The colors. Shapes."

Alex's open, receptive face broke into a gleeful, satisfied smile, as though he had just said something very clever. A train chugged past, down by the river, its horn complementing the valley's tranquility. Alex took out a soft pack of cigarettes and pounded them upside down.

"What's that for?" I asked.

"It keeps the tobacco nice and tight," he explained.

With his long fingers, Alex delicately removed the cellophane end and tore off the foil. Knocking the pack against his index finger, until a few cigarettes poked out, he selected one and removed it. The pack was returned to his shirt pocket. He removed a silver Zippo lighter from his pants pocket, which he flipped open with his thumb and tried to ignite. Nothing. A second time. Nothing. Finally, on the third try, a bluish flame. He lit the cigarette and snapped the lighter shut. Alex sucked smoke into his mouth, which suddenly came back out, in a rush, across his upper lip, disappearing again into his nostrils. I had never seen anyone smoke this way.

I could not keep my eyes off Alex. I was mesmerized by everything about him. His hair, his eyes, his nose, the gum line that showed above his teeth during those mischievous smiles, his red and white athletic jacket, his hands, his cigarette. Did he notice? I was trembling. Nothing like this had ever happened before. The thought then crossed my mind, "Is this how it is going to be for the rest of my life? To feel such attraction and, at the same time, to contain, suppress and forever hide my feelings?" I wondered if, now that I was in college, where the men were more developed, muscular and attractive than in high school, I would be able to sustain the pressure. Or would it destroy me? Acting on it or doing anything positive with those

---

feelings was not an option.

I did not listen to the inner voice asking me if this is "how it is going to be." I chose, instead, to extend and deepen the pattern of life I had chosen in high school, even though the feelings were now more powerful than any I had previously known.

I joined Alex and some of his friends that evening for drinks at Adolph's, the local pub. Alex and I became fast, close and even inseparable friends. Before we became that, however, there was one hurdle that had to be overcome. That was Alex's friendship with Phil Royce. To this day I have feelings of remorse about having somehow contributed to the demise of that friendship. In fact, I had nothing to do with its demise and attempted to continue friendships with both men, but eventually found that impracticable.

A few weeks into the Spring semester, Alex told me he had broken off his friendship with Phil. I asked:

"How did this happen? You were always very close."

"Phil and I had an argument. It was nothing serious, but I wanted to be alone. He left my room and I took a nap. An hour later I woke up and found him curled up at the foot of my bed, asleep."

"Why was he there?" I asked, with anxious, morbid curiosity.

"Who knows? He's a masochist. He said something about coming back to my room to ask my forgiveness. He won't just let things be. I can't have him around me anymore. I can't have anything to do with him. There's something pathetic about him."

"Is there anything I can do? Perhaps I can talk to him. Maybe you can be friends, but just not as close as you were."

VIII

Infatuated as I was with Alex, I was privately relieved to have Phil out of the way. I wanted time alone with him. We took long walks on a neighboring farm, where we explored abandoned buildings. Alex was the bolder, more adventuresome one. Where I was sensible, a bit nervous about walking onto someone else's property or into abandoned buildings on remote, wooded acreage, Alex led the way. He was a warm light that enjoyed and accepted me as I was, but who always insisted on pushing into new frontiers.

Loving Alex, I also loved his art and enjoyed watching him work. We each had friends of our own, but Alex and I were inseparable. When we were separated and, say, he went on a brief excursion with others, I was jealous and counted the minutes until his return. But Alex's bright smile was always there to assure me that "we" were special friends, friends with a bond that went beyond whatever he shared with others. We repeated to each other the words of Cicero, "*Amicus verus est alter idem*" ("A true friend is another self"). These words captured how we felt about each other: I found something of myself in him and he in me.

The question of homosexuality could not but hover around such a relationship. Were we or weren't we? Would we or wouldn't we? There was no question in my mind that I loved this man intensely and wanted him in the totality of his being — mind, spirit and body. I remembered the incident with Phil, however, and knew I had to avoid Phil's mistake of demonstrating desire too openly.

One evening, when Alex had a car on loan from his parents, we went down the road, to Adolph's, for a sandwich and beers. While driving back to Ward Manor, Alex said:

"You know, I could go either way."

"Either way?" I could hardly get the words out: "What ever do you mean?"

"I mean that I could go either way, AC or DC, with men or with women."

I ran my little finger against the inside of the door handle, wondering what to say. Mostly I was concerned about what not to say. I thought this might be a trap, rather than a genuine invitation. I did not want to be shut out of Alex's life suddenly, as Phil had been. I retreated to observational mode, because it seemed safely impersonal:

"I know what you mean, but there's no future in it, that is, in being with men. It is not socially acceptable."

This was formally a lie. I did not pretend that I did not have an interest in the subject. And it was true that homosexuality was not socially acceptable, although, at Bard, that argument had a hollow sound. It was, however, a lie in the truest sense: a use of speech to dissemble. Rather than honestly state my feelings to Alex, I gave what I believed to be a response that he would find acceptable. I wanted to remain close to him, even at the incalculable cost of denying my feelings. To borrow a word from the old *Book of Common Prayer*, this single lie did "inestimable" harm to my person.

The irony is that when I made this choice, both Alex and I knew the truth of the matter. I was passionately in love with Alex. He was, I believe, in love with me, too. The choice, at that moment, was to continue to be with the person I loved, even if it meant doing emotional violence to myself, or not being with the person I loved. We consented to build our friendship on a lie.

IX

The depth of the harm that I was inflicting on myself was underscored the following summer. Alex secured a position as a camp counselor through his friend, Ron Feeney, an Episcopal seminarian. Camp Arrowsmith, in Maine, was a summer camp for the sons of the wealthy. The heirs to major fortunes summered there, as well as the offspring of politically powerful lineages. I do not know whether Camp Arrowsmith had a formal affiliation with the Episcopal Church, but most of the campers attended Ron's Sunday services. Alex invited me to join him in Maine for the summer and, of course, I could hardly imagine declining the opportunity to be with this man, the "*alter idem*" from whom I had become inseparable.

Though Alex brought me along, he did seem quite content to let us be separable. Ron, the son of a wealthy, Connecticut couple, drove up to Camp Arrowsmith in a new convertible. From the start, it was clear that he was Alex's friend, not mine. A car full of counselors, Alex included, drove off with Ron, heading down the nine-mile road to town, leaving me behind and forlorn. Because I was just a "friend" of Alex, I seemed to be in no position to press any claims or object to this behavior. It was left to my imagination to wonder what they might be doing and how they might be enjoying themselves. The ease with which Ron had apparently and intentionally separated me from Alex, and Alex's complicity were hurtful experiences.

In addition, I found myself in the rustic, uncertain terrain of a camp, where daily life was focused on sports and skills in which I was hopelessly inept. As "nature counselor" my job was to instruct campers on local flora and fauna, a task for which I was completely unprepared. The campers' greatest nature interest, of course, was snakes. Captured snakes were placed in the nature hall's "snake pit." Campers loved handling these reptiles for endless hours. One even suffered a snake biting into his ear and hanging on for dear life. Fortunately, I managed to get through the summer without the necessity of handling even a single snake myself.

In the middle of the summer I wanted to quit. I was approaching the point of emotional breakdown. Dick Thornton, the director, met with me at his house. Dick was lean, energetic, a middle-aged man who loved his wife, his steaks, his booze, his tobacco, the camp, the counselors and campers, the forest, the lake, the wildlife. He was a man who had found the spot for which he had been born, and thoroughly relished it. Dick was a good man and I respected him, but his world had little to do with mine. Nevertheless, there we were, director and counselor, attempting to talk through a situation. Dick said:

"Paulus, I know this isn't what you're used to. I could tell that the first night we met, when you didn't even know what a loon was. If you want to go, you can, but I want you to reconsider."

"Dick, I'm the fifth wheel around here. I'm neither needed nor wanted. I don't know how to do any of these things. I don't know how to steer a canoe or shoot arrows. I don't think anyone here really likes me. I just don't have anything to offer in this kind of setting."

"That's where I know you're wrong," Dick's voice dropped a few tones to convey deep conviction. "The guys here do respect you. More than you know. They respect you, because you're different. Because you insist on being yourself. You could open up to people more. You could let them know more about who you are."

"Yes, you're probably right," I found my resolve to leave weakening.

"I can't promise that the rest of the summer will be easy. But I think you should give yourself a chance. These are good guys here. Give yourself a chance to get to know them. I know you will be glad you did."

Somewhat persuaded that I brought a dimension that would otherwise be lacking to life at Camp Arrowsmith, I decided to stick it out. Ron Feeney took an interest in the matter, as well, and took me for a drive to discuss it.

"What's this I hear about you wanting to leave?" Ron asked.

"It's true that I considered it, but now I've decided to remain. This has been a rough summer. I came here because Alex invited me to. But again and again I find him going off with you and others in your car and he tells me that you did not invite me."

"Yes, it's true that I did not invite you. I did this deliberately, for your own good. You see, Paul, I have a personality that strongly affects people. Many have a tendency to become dependent on me. I did not want that to happen to you. You are going into the priesthood. You and I will probably know each other long after we have lost touch with the other people here. I wanted us to get to know each other apart from here."

I was not convinced by this pious self-exculpation. But neither did I have the emotional freedom to tell him that I thought he was threatened by my friendship with Alex. Nor could I have told Dick Thornton the true cause of my turmoil that summer. When one accepts society's stigmatization of one's very self, a great many problems and dilemmas that, in truth, admit of quite simple explanations, are made to seem more complicated and mysterious than they are.

X

As a young man drawn to religion, a "churchy," in Bardian lingo, I found the mystery that surrounds religion attractive. I veiled myself — even from myself — behind the construct of a religious mystique. This served to put beyond question several aspects of my life, such as why I had no girlfriend.

I spent many hours in the school chapel, a little, gothic jewel box, even claiming the basement as my preferred space for study. Bard's chaplain, Father Frederick Q. Shafer, was a warm and wizened man who seemed older than his years, even ageless. I often had lengthy, wide-ranging discussions with him; and he seemed, for his part, to enjoy assisting me in my questions and struggles. While Fritz was open, accepting and non-directive to a fault, preferring instead to let sharp questions or suggested reading do their stuff, he did challenge me about my move toward an increasingly rigid approach to religion. I fancied myself "Anglo-Catholic," no longer simply "Episcopalian." And my taste for high church liturgy opened into increasingly rigid approaches to doctrine and spirituality.

I made my first confession of sins while at Bard. Confession is not a routine practice of Episcopalians, except in the high church. Now, however, I was eager to embrace all things "Catholic," which meant going to confession. On the west bank of the Hudson, to the south of Kingston, is Holy Cross Monastery, where an Anglican community of two or three dozen white-robed men live a semi-contemplative life. I had seen some of their literature, including a booklet by Father Karl Tiedemann on how to make a confession. I confessed to Father Tiedemann himself, following night prayers, in a small, plain room, fragrant from the immaculate, polished woods with which it had been constructed and furnished.

My confession was an earnest affair that was based on the premise that I was, of course, a miserable sinner and that whatever sins I might confess, however numerous and minuscule, I had only a partial understanding of the wrong I had done. Father Tiedemann did not comment at all on my ostensive sins. Instead, he declared this a "happy day," a time for celebration, because of the important step that I had taken in making use of this sacrament. My assigned penance, some simple prayer, seemed absurdly light, in view of all that I had confessed.

I left Holy Cross the next day in a state of ecstasy. The words of the Three Young Men's "Song of Creation" percolated through my mind: "O all ye Works of the Lord, bless ye the Lord: praise him, and magnify him for ever... O ye Sun and Moon, bless ye the Lord: praise him, and magnify him for ever... O ye Showers and Dew, bless ye the Lord: praise him, and magnify him for ever." This Old Testament canticle, which I had sung since childhood, somehow came to life. It described the vivid sense that I had of God's presence permeating the whole world. Some young ruffians threw snowballs against the side of the bus in which I returned to Kingston and I rejoiced. God was in the snow and in the boys. I discovered that when we have eyes to see the world in every detail is radiant with grace.

Evening Prayer with a small group in Bard's Chapel of the Holy Innocents became a daily practice. There were also long periods of prayer alone, whether in the chapel or walking near the river or watching the setting sun transform the Catskills into a cluster of jewels.

My appetite for spiritual experience extended to drugs, especially hallucinogens. I counted several ardent practitioners of the "psychedelic revolution" among my close friends. Their gentle and kindly spirits impressed me. I wondered if, indeed, LSD and other drugs might not be God-given instruments of spiritual growth. The fact that drugs were against the law was quite beside the point. I began to join my friends in sharing joints of grass. While I enjoyed the altered sense of time and space and heightened sensitivity to music that it produced, I did not find the experience remarkable. Wondering if there might be something more to be discovered in this realm, I seriously considered taking a "trip" with acid, but finally ruled it out because of the health risks.

XI

I began to develop into a thoughtful, eager student, although not in a disciplined, systematic way. I chose medieval history as a major, impressed by a demanding, young professor, Julius Kirschner, who said encouraging things about my work. This also enabled me to delve into the history of Catholicism and, of course, the papacy.

The split within Latin Christendom that occurred during the late fourteenth century, when there were simultaneously several claimants to the papacy, fascinated me. That dispute was ultimately resolved by the Council of Constance in 1415. I was impressed by the notion that the Catholic Church needed this central, authoritarian figure to maintain unity and discipline. For the same reason, I was impressed by Pope Innocent III, of the early thirteenth century, the first pope to claim exclusive use of the title, "Vicar of Christ," in an effort to establish forever the supremacy of the papacy over secular rulers. The controversies and battle cries of those centuries resonated with me, because I longed for what I presumed would be the orderliness of an authoritarian society. And what better accoutrement to authoritarianism than the cloak of godliness?

My appetite for authoritarianism was soon to be nurtured by a group within the nation's conservative movement. During the fall of my sophomore year, my father sent me a news clipping about L. Brent Bozell, Jr., editor of a Catholic conservative monthly that was set to begin publication out of Washington. My father noted that much of what Bozell was saying sounded like what I had been saying. Specifically, Bozell claimed that Catholic principles provide the best political and economic foundations upon which to base a society. Influenced by historian Christopher Dawson, who was forever trying to recall and return to Europe's Christian roots, I had, indeed, been thinking in this vein myself. I looked up Bozell, when I was next in Washington, and soon had a standing offer of employment on the editorial staff of *Triumph Magazine*, as the new publication was to be called, whenever I was home.

Triumph represented a small faction that had broken away from William F. Buckley, Jr.'s *National Review*. Through my association with Brent Bozell and the staff of Triumph, I became acquainted with aspects of the "conservative" movement that had little regard for most people who so labeled themselves and what they understood conservatism to be. Bozell had ghostwritten Barry Goldwater's landmark treatise, *Conscience of a Conservative*. But at *Triumph's* editorial meetings the talk was of the power of the Jews, the deficits of democracy, and the need for a more authoritarian government from which truth and order might be imposed on an apparently foundering American society, notions far removed from the aspirations and hopes of Goldwater enthusiasts.

XII

At the age of twenty, I was a Gordian knot of paradoxes, with cords pulling tightly in different directions: Bardian free-spiritedness, political authoritarianism, Anglo-Catholic piety and intellectual ambition. The knot's hidden center was homosexuality, which manifested in me as a tension between self-loathing and overwhelming love for another man.

My next move was not so much a choice as a reflex. The knot of emotions and ideas in my life was not smooth, but coarse, turning abruptly from one level to another. I imagined that I might find something more harmonious and peaceful in life, by adding still another level of complexity and tightness to the knot: Catholicism, *Roman* Catholicism, with a capital "R" and a capital "C."

Intellectually and spiritually I had, I imagined, prepared myself for such a step by years in the Anglo-Catholic tradition, which had even brought me to the point of frequenting a monastery and going to confession. I was studying church history. And from my association with the editorial staff of *Triumph*, I fancied myself something of a critic of contemporary, post-Vatican II trends in Catholicism. Especially in the American church, those trends seemed to represent a foolish and dangerous departure from the clarity and stability of the past.

In a sense, I was pushed into this step; or, perhaps better, I invited a push and someone obliged. He was Michael Lawrence, a young, senior editor of *Triumph*. The occasion was a staff outing in July 1968. We gathered for dinner at A.V. Ristorante Italiano, a cheap, but passable establishment, where we consumed more scotch than pasta. Michael pressed the question:

"Why don't you become a Catholic, Paul? This is where you belong."

"I have always believed that I must be faithful to the church where God has placed me. I'm an Anglican. There are a lot of things about the Episcopal Church that I don't like. I find my church much too wishy-washy on doctrine. But it is a true church, with bishops and priests, Mass and confessions."

"But what about the pope, Paul? You believe in papal authority."

"Yes, and so do many other Anglicans. We are, as the Second Vatican Council put it, 'separated brethren' from you Romans. Even some Anglican bishops regard the pope as an authoritative religious figure, *primus inter pars*, first among equals. But the difference is that for us he is this by custom, while for you, he is this *de iure*, by right."

"Look, that's all very well for those people, but you have changed. You can do a lot more by being in the Catholic Church than by working from outside."

Michael's pitch to my future gave me pause. By remaining Episcopalian, I would forever be part of a minority movement, trying to push the church in directions where most of its members did not want to go. I wanted a church that would be more decisive and clear on doctrine than the Anglican Communion ever would be. I had found a kind of refuge in the high church, but this was a small enclave within a larger structure. Perhaps Michael was right.

In the past, I had discussed "going over to Rome" with Angela DuBois. She also felt the attraction of Rome, but we both shared the belief that the Episcopal Church was where God had planted us and where we should remain. I had, however, begun to doubt the legitimacy of the Anglican Communion in lands outside of Great Britain. Whatever arguments might be advanced for the Church of England, I thought, the Episcopal Church in the United States was surely an historical anomaly that had no theological justification. We should all, I had begun to argue, recognize the primacy of Rome and have done with it.

I took a weekend for reflection at Virginia Beach, where I stayed with Florence Norton, a secretary who had long been part of the *National Review/Triumph* extended family. She was house sitting and offered me a room.

I spent most of my time there walking along the shore, taking in the ocean's vast and deep embrace of the Earth. The sight and sounds of waves gently rolling in momentarily to lick the shore and receding again to the deep were calming. I yearned for a truth as vast and deep and certain as the ocean.

I wrote a poem about ocean, sun, surf, sand and lovers, as a reflection on my conversion. I had written poetry since adolescence, much of it, like this poem, an attempt to capture some momentary observation. My conversion to Roman Catholicism, it turned out, marked the sudden disappearance of poetry — both reading and writing — from my life, although years later, in rare moments, I would occasionally draft a few lines. The exercise of poetic imagination, the process of going inside oneself to perceive the world afresh, which is inherently an act of freedom, lost interest for me, becoming somehow irrelevant, at a time when possession of the "Truth," which is to say, the Catholic hierarchy's imposed version of it, became all important.

Something besides poetry emerged that July weekend, something that was to intertwine with my life in unexpected ways in the years ahead. *Humanae Vitae*, the encyclical by Pope Paul VI on artificial contraception, was released.

I first heard on the radio news that an encyclical was forthcoming. On the return drive, Monday morning, I heard a great deal about it on the radio. I drove directly to *Triumph's* offices on McPherson Square. When I arrived, there was a great hubbub, indeed, a jubilant atmosphere. After all the advances of "liberal" stances that followed the Council, here, finally, was a decidedly traditionalist action taken by the Church's highest authority. At one point we leaned out of Bozell's office windows to pose for a photographer from *The Washington Daily News*. The photograph was not used, but Brent was quoted in an article the next day: "the Pope's courageous reaffirmation of Christian truth in the teeth of the world's scorn is proof that God... is with us. Paul VI has invited the world to return to sanity."

I had my own news to share in the midst of the heady glee and somehow it seemed to confirm that God was indeed in heaven and the world was returning to sanity, which was, of course, to be found at the pope's toe. A call came from the Archbishop of Washington, Cardinal O'Boyle, who had heard that Father Charles Curran and other theologians who dissented from this decision had scheduled a press conference for that evening at Catholic University's Caldwell Auditorium. O'Boyle asked representatives from *Triumph* to attend, ostensibly as members of the press, but also for the purpose of reporting back to him. I tagged along with the staff. The dissenting theologians were, I could see, smart, serious men. But what were they doing to the Roman Catholic Church? I was leaving the Episcopal Church, because I wanted clear, authoritative guidance from the church. I was angered by what I took to be their arrogance. The fact that the domain of their dissent had to do with sex, made it seem tawdry and foolish. Sheltered in Brent Bozell's fold, I knew I was on the right side, certainly the winning side. Church officials would deal with these dissenters I had no doubt.

XIII

I decided to formalize my entry into the Roman Catholic Church under the auspices of my local parish, St. Agnes, in Arlington, Virginia. This decision reflected my intention of doing everything by the book. The Catholic Church has, to be sure, many rules. And I wanted to believe that all of these rules were well founded and represented centuries of accumulated wisdom. The parochial system whereby Catholics worship at the parish within whose boundaries they reside made perfect sense to me. As an Episcopalian, I had been accustomed to people making choices about where to worship based on many factors, including whether they liked the clergy, social ambience, liturgical style, and music. The Roman system's indifference to personal preference seemed to reflect a higher ideal. What matter are the sacraments, not personalities or aesthetics.

I dutifully introduced myself to the pastor of St. Agnes, Monsignor Nott, a large, extraverted man. He placed me in the care of his associate, Father Dinges, a thin, serious man. Monsignor left on vacation and was not to return prior to my return to Bard for the Fall semester. I expected to be received into the Catholic Church quickly and return to Bard a "Roman."

Father Dinges selected as our study guide, *A New Catechism*, the Dutch Catechism, which was, at the time, new and controversial, because it presented Catholic truths in contemporary language. I did not tell him that I had written a critical piece for *Triumph* about this book (without having read it). No, I wanted to be a purist. St. Agnes was the parish in which I resided. The pastor of St. Agnes had placed my reception into the Roman Church into the care of Father Dinges. This must be the will of God. I must comply.

My meetings with Father Dinges, however, quickly became contentious. I was the conservative who was sure I knew it all. Father Dinges proposed the value of other perspectives. It became evident that he had no intention of rushing along my reception into the Catholic Church. Indeed, he suggested, we might only just be getting started on my instruction, which could be continued at a Catholic parish near Bard. A break of sorts came one day, when our discussion turned to birth control and abortion. Father Dinges said:

"As a priest, I find it is not enough simply to tell people the rules. I have to look at what is happening in their lives. For example, a couple has four children and is struggling to make ends meet. How can I tell them not to practice birth control?"

"But Father, the pope has spoken on this. The church's position is clear."

"The church also teaches about conscience. I have an obligation to instruct them in official church teaching, but I cannot tell them, in the final analysis what decision they must make."

"Well, Father, I think there are some absolutes. Take abortion, for instance."

"Even here, we must consider the choices that people face in real life situations. Suppose a widowed mother with three young children learns that her pregnancy endangers her life? What is the right thing for her to do? Can I presume to tell her that she must proceed with the pregnancy?"

I was distressed that my efforts to embrace Roman Catholicism had resulted so quickly in my being placed in the care of one so heedless of church teaching. What I was hearing harked back to the situation ethics that I had learned about from the seminarians at St. George's. With Monsignor Nott away, however, what recourse did I have?

John Wisner, a senior editor of *Triumph*, intervened by putting me in touch with Monsignor Thomas Lyons, the pastor of St. Thomas's parish in Washington. I met with Monsignor Lyons on a Saturday afternoon for two hours. He was a serene, affable, and modest man. To my relief, he quickly concluded that I was sufficiently knowledgeable about Catholicism to enter the church without further ado. We arranged my formal reception into the church for the following Saturday.

At my rite of reception I would make a profession of faith. I would also make again a "first confession," since confessions made to Episcopal priests no longer counted. There would be a Mass and I would receive my "first" holy communion.

I asked about baptism. Monsignor Lyons said that the Catholic Church did, of course, accept the validity of my baptism as an Episcopalian. I pointed out that President Johnson's daughter, Luci Baines, who had been received into the Catholic Church two years before, had been baptized, although she also had been previously baptized Episcopalian. Monsignor Lyons relented and agreed to baptize me conditionally, as part of the ceremony. Conditional baptism means that the rite is performed as usual, and is recorded in the parish's baptismal register, but the priest mentally adds the words, "in case you have not already been baptized" to the baptismal formula: "I baptize you in the name of the Father and of the Son and of the Holy Spirit."

In my heart I knew that this conditional baptism was unnecessary. To friends I gave out the explanation that I wanted my going over to Rome to be definitive, not like the experience of some, who restlessly flit back and forth between the Episcopal and Roman Catholic Churches every few years. In reality, I had another reason in mind. I expected to go into the priesthood and hoped that one day I might even be considered a candidate for the episcopacy. I imagined that my Episcopal baptism might be considered an encumbrance to advancement. A clean break, marked by a Roman Catholic baptism, seemed a very sensible beginning to my new life and career.

A few friends gathered at St. Thomas — associates from *Triumph* and Ann, a high school friend who had also studied for a time at Bard. My parents were also present, a gesture which I appreciated, since I knew that the departure of their son into Roman Catholicism was a difficult moment. I was baptized in the baptistery near the church entrance. Then, kneeling at the altar, I made a profession of faith, reading from a laminated card a list of distinctively Roman Catholic doctrinal assertions: that the Mass is a "true, real and propitiatory sacrifice for the living and the dead," that "in the holy sacrament of the Eucharist the body and blood together with the soul and divinity of our Lord Jesus Christ is really, truly and substantially present," that Purgatory exists, that the church has the "faculty to grant indulgences," *et cetera*. I proudly identified myself with these beliefs, feeling, I recall, a certain thrill at my plunge into an antirational belief system that set me at odds with all that is modern and scientific. Moments later, after entering the confessional, I made a confession of sins no less meticulous than the one I had made two years before to Father Tiedemann. This time, however, I renounced, as well, the "heresy" of Anglicanism to which I had pertinaciously held, I claimed, even after I had come to believe the Roman Church to be the one, *true* church.

During the Mass, my new godfather, John Wisner, prayed the rosary aloud, so loudly, in fact, that it was difficult to follow the Mass. This was intentional. It was John's way of enhancing the gulf between sanctuary and pew, priest and laity. What the priest did in the "sacrifice of the Mass" was, from John's traditionalist perspective, a mystery not to be apprehended directly by the people. This is why many so-called traditionalists were alarmed by the changes in the liturgy that followed the Second Vatican Council. The use of the vernacular tongues, instead of Latin, and the celebration of Mass with the priest facing the congregation, rather than with his back to them, were perceived by traditionalists as developments that drained the rite of mystery. They decried these changes as vain attempts to make the inexplicable mystery of the Mass understandable. John Wisner's answer to the innovations was to pray the rosary with such ostentation that his prayer, in effect, reexpressed a boundary that was being diminished or even eliminated.

During the small gathering that followed my reception ceremonies, Gary Potter, a staff writer and columnist ("Potter's Field") for *Triumph*, noted that this was St. Bartholomew's Day and insisted that Monsignor Lyons's allusions to this fact had been very pointed. St. Bartholomew having been one of the apostles, albeit not one about whom much is known, in my innocence I saw nothing especially noteworthy in the saint's invocation. But Gary did not have St. Bartholomew, the apostle, in mind at all. He was referring gleefully to St. Bartholomew's Day, August 24, 1592, when thousands of Huguenot Protestants were massacred in France by papalists. I knew then that Monsignor Lyons had no such connection in mind in his brief and pious references to the apostle, but I allowed myself to swallow silently a bit of the extremism and intolerance that finds a home in Roman Catholicism.

In the days that followed my reception into the "Roman church," as I continued for many years to call it, I searched for some new feeling in myself, some clue that becoming Catholic had made a personal difference. I imagined, rather vividly, that I was receiving now, for the first time, the "true" body and blood of Christ, rather than the mere symbols of them that were available to Episcopalians who lacked, in my newly formed under-standing, the valid holy orders necessary to confect a valid Eucharist. I imagined, somehow, that I had indeed found a new peace, but this assertion, like the credal assertions that I affirmed at the altar that day, did not ring true at the deeper levels of my being. I was trying to convince myself, by saying the kinds of things one is supposed to say, when newly venturing into a religion. All the same, the fact that I tried to feel something revealed my implicit assumption that the ultimate authentication of belief is to be found at the level of the human spirit. If it does not bring peace, what good is it? The persistent search for spirit is what would carry me forward in the years ahead and ultimately bring me into a critical distancing of self from many aspects of the Roman church.

The personal impact of Roman Catholicism was to make itself felt in the next few years in ways that were unexpected. The sense of mystical connection with the divine, however, remained elusive, though I worked hard at it and was intensely prayerful and pious.

XIV

By changing churches, I became aware of differences between Catholicism and Episcopalianism that were rooted in their respective cultures, rather than in doctrine. The Episcopal Church is often caricatured as the church of the elite. While this is certainly an oversimplification, it is true that I hailed from a tradition of more refined manners and taste than what I found in the Catholic Church. For example, I was accustomed to people dressing nicely for Sunday worship. Without giving it a second thought I had always worn jacket and tie to church. In Catholic parishes, however, I found little regard for appearance. On the other hand, it was clear that the Catholic Church encompassed a greater level of ethnic diversity and drew in larger numbers of blue-collar workers and the poor than I had seen in Episcopal parishes.

The shift from Elizabethan English to contemporary American was especially jarring. It did not help that the new, post-Vatican II translations of liturgical texts seemed almost perversely commonplace and devoid of all sense of the transcendent: "*et cum spiritu tuo*," for example, became, in the new liturgy, "and also with you."

I was accustomed to singing. Hymn singing and chanting are prominent features of Anglican worship, where church pews are equipped with thick hymnals. In the Catholic Church, where congregational participation and singing were more recent and uncertain developments, I quickly distinguished myself from fellow worshipers merely by joining in on the hymns.

A more profound difference, and one based on doctrine as well as culture, came in the confessional. Where confession had been an option that I had employed as an Anglican, a tool, I thought, for spiritual growth, in Roman Catholicism I found it takes on a crucial importance. For Roman

Catholics, the Sacrament of Penance is essential as a means for maintaining or, more properly, *returning* to the "state of grace." Sins, especially "mortal sins," must be confessed to a priest and absolved in order to return to the state of grace necessary to receive holy communion. Church tract racks and Catholic prayer books offered forms for the "Examination of Conscience," checklists of sins for review prior to confession. As a zealous convert, I was anxious to do everything right and soon had gathered a collection of these checklists. I preferred, of course, the more exhaustive ones.

As a young man struggling with the sexual energies of youth, it turned out I had much to confess. In fact, try as I might, it seemed I *always* had something to confess. And, as one struggling with homosexuality, I was at pains to make my confession in a way that was as neutral as possible on the nature of the attractions that I experienced. I bracketed that out as an irrelevant detail. Sin, however, was not irrelevant, especially sins of the flesh. I found myself frequenting this sacrament — once a week, twice a week, three times — as I felt more and more the oppressive weight of "sin."

I know now that I was developing a bad case of scrupulosity. Scrupulosity is a disorder that afflicts Catholics who become obsessively anxious about remaining in a state of grace, making a good and thorough confession, and observing strictly every possible requirement of Catholic teaching and discipline. A heart seeking solace in the absolute will find in the Sacrament of Penance, if it chooses, an absolute taskmaster indeed: did I feel a bit of pride? a touch of vanity? how many times did I have impure thoughts? and was that merely a passing thought or lust that I had intentionally entertained?

Sadly, from the start, I picked up the message that such were the concerns of true Catholics. And such concerns sent me flying into the city, where churches scheduled daily times for confession, or at Bard, to the telephone, where midweek confessions in nearby Red Hook had to be arranged by appointment. I was locked into a system of thought and a set of practices that have nothing to do with growth in holiness. Confession certainly did not bring me any peace of heart; to the contrary, with it, I added to my soul, already burdened with the immovable weight of homosexuality, a new layer of anxieties about being pitched into the pit of hell for the most ludicrous infractions. I was even anxious, on one occasion, about whether I had broken the Eucharistic fast by licking a postage stamp.

To be fair, only a small fraction of Roman Catholics suffer from scrupulosity and it is a problem that wise pastors recognize as such and seek to address. It is, however, a perfectly logical conclusion, if one takes to heart, as did I, all of the checklists and official church pronouncements about what Catholics must and must not do. As I rushed anxiously to the sacrament, after only one day, to confess some bit of "impurity," I do not recall, save once, in those early years, being told to relax or try not to make so much out of ordinary peccadilloes. No, Catholicism was well organized to receive and nurture such obsessive concerns. Indeed, it is arguable that much of the power of Roman Catholicism is rooted in its ability to do so.

I returned to Bard, in September of 1968, an "Anabaptist," as my mentor, Father Shafer, put it, with characteristic irony. I also returned to a Bard that was now devoid of my soul mate, Alex, as well as most of our friends, who had been in Alex's class. One close friend, Robert Stephenson, remained. We rented rooms together in a house off campus. Robert was impressed by my move into Roman Catholicism and, within a year, would take the same step himself. Even with his companionship, however, I felt quite detached from whatever Bard had to offer, both socially and academically. My other interests and connections seemed so much more compelling: Roman Catholicism, *Triumph*, the conservative movement. I wanted to write a book. I was restless. My studies seemed pointless. I therefore dropped out mid-term during my senior year, to return to Washington and work at *Triumph*.

On the return drive, I wrecked my car on the Glen Echo exit from the Washington Beltway. The balding tires of my Peugeot failed to take a sharp curve, causing the car to slam into the abutment of a bridge and be thrown across the road, where it halted against the railing. There was such an air of unreality about the accident that after climbing out I made a point of checking to see whether I was still in the car. No, I was not dead. The radio continued playing, although the car engine had died. Mary Hopkins pertly sang: "Those were the days my friend, we thought they'd never end."

CHAPTER 2

VALUES

I

Steel-gray clouds closed over Washington. McPherson Square, empty minutes before, became the site of a gathering cluster of protesters. The object of their protest was less clear than the fact that they looked the part: young men and women baptized well in the waters of political protest. There were Vietcong flags among them. Ban-the-bomb patches on their denim jackets. Grotesquely ski-slope-nosed Nixon masks. A line of cops came running from Vermont Avenue into the square.

Watching the afternoon spectacle from my office at *Triumph*, I found the sudden escalation of tensions confusing. I could not see that the protesters had done anything illegal. To be sure, they were doing their best to offend. Yet the cops, many of them close in age to the protesters, moved in. From above, it appeared, at first, little more than an overblown game. But as police and protesters faced off in the center of the park, where a Vietcong flag flapped from the base of General McPherson's Statue, the raw emotions sparked.

The protesters' offense was nonspecific, yet, to the cops, a most abhorrent crime. It was the offense of denying America's moral superiority. Their blue helmets fastened into place, I could see by their intrepid faces that the police knew themselves to be defending the honor of their world: America, the middle class, work, religion, decency. Who were these scruffy, pot-smoking, ill-begotten miscreants to thumb their noses at this great land?

A chase began in earnest, as protesters and cops scattered throughout the park, hopping over benches and trampling shrubbery. Billy clubs were raised, but not cracked against any skulls. This was, at bottom, a family quarrel. One group of protesters moved to Vermont Avenue and started running toward the White House, two blocks away; police chased after, in a scene worthy of the Keystone cops.

"Well, Paulus Waulus," John Wisner said, joining me at the window, "the republic is flying apart!"

John spoke approvingly, a touch of merriment in his voice, as he twirled a rosary back and forth around his index finger. He continued:

"Our young men are no longer willing to fight and die for the country, and why should they? Having abandoned Christianity at the Enlightenment, we have said that man could build a nation without God. But without God, there is no moral purpose. The 'truth' we have come up with without God has given us the atom bomb and incredible stinks in the air. Our highest purpose now is money: selling Coca-Cola. The guys harassing the cops down there are right. They should not sacrifice their lives for Coca-Cola. And the cops know it too."

"I know, Uncle John, that's why I've turned to the church. We have a two-thousand-year-old tradition. The Catholic Church is a steady beacon in this darkening world. And as our world gets darker, more and more people will notice that beacon."

"Paulus, the Church has the truth. That's why we have been around as long as we have. We've had degenerate and foolish men running the church, generation after generation, but the truth that we have is great enough to sustain us in spite of that. Empires have come and gone, but Catholicism and the papacy remain. That's because we know how to tell a man, a nation, the world what it means to lead a moral life."

My office felt warm, bright and secure, as I gazed on the dwindling remnants of the fracas below. A tussle engulfed pedestrians on a traffic island on K Street, knocking over the bus stop sign. Not exactly the stuff of revolution, but there was, nonetheless, something profoundly disquieting in the air. A few months before, Washington had been deeply scarred by rioting that followed the assassination of Martin Luther King. Two months later, Robert F. Kennedy was slain. Anxiety hung over the city, intensified by hovering helicopters in search of whoever or whatever looked out of place.

II

After quitting Bard, I returned to my job as an editorial assistant at *Triumph* and to my parental home. My parents were protective of their erratic son. I heard no complaints about my leaving college mid-term, although they took a loss on the tuition. My mother was saddened by my decision to leave the Episcopal Church, but she and my father respected my right to make this choice. And yet, despite this seeming independence, this freedom of thought and movement, I was in many ways still quite dependent on them. Although I had a job and entered, with my parents, into the daily commute into and out of downtown Washington, I had little interest in becoming a part of the world of commerce. I began to wear a plain wooden cross that was suspended from my neck on a thin cord. Wherever I went, whether dressed casually or in suit and tie, this simple cross was there to announce a kind of boundary: "I do not belong to this world."

Monsignor Lyons agreed to serve as my spiritual director. We met in his downtown office, where he worked as director of the Archdiocesan school system. While his office was executively swank, his affable and thoughtful manner made me confident of his abilities as a priest.

The first time we met as spiritual director and counselee, Monsignor Lyons pulled from his desk drawer a thin, violet stole and started to put it on. I said:

"No, Monsignor, I'm not here for confession."

"You're not? He raised his eyebrows, puzzled. But I thought you were here for spiritual direction."

"I am, but to me that's different from confession. I'm here to learn about prayer, meditation, contemplation, the teachings of the church, the saints, all kinds of things that I need to learn about, since I was not raised a Catholic."

"Oh, very well, he said, carefully placing the stole back in the drawer. I am not very experienced in that kind of direction, but if you think I can help, I'll be happy to oblige, he said cheerfully. Where should we begin?"

"I would like to know more about the different kinds of prayer. I've heard of contemplative prayer and mental prayer, but I don't know much about them."

"It's been a while since I've studied those things myself. But I have a book, Tanquery's *Spiritual Life*. To be honest, I haven't looked at it much since seminary days, but why don't you borrow it? If you see anything that you would like to discuss, we can go from there."

I agreed to this plan and picked up the book at St. Thomas's a few days later. Tanquerey offered a boiled down gloss of the Catholic tradition's rich spiritual resources — church fathers, monasticism, asceticism, mysticism, Francis of Assisi, John of the Cross, Teresa of Avila — all tidily defined, categorized and outlined. For the two generations of priests ordained just prior to the Second Vatican Council, Tanquery represented the best that could be known on these subjects. Dry reading though it was, I was deeply grateful to receive this impressive volume.

My thoughts soon turned to the priesthood and, by the end of 1968, within four months of my reception into the Roman Church, I met with Father Bill Curlin, Vocations Director for the Archdiocese of Washington. Monsignor Lyons knew, he said, that I would enjoy meeting Father Curlin, a "friendly, young priest."

Father Curlin, whose hair was graying at the temples, did not seem young to me. There was a slight Irish lilt in his voice. He was very chatty. In the months ahead, I would meet many times with him to hear endless talk, mostly about himself and his own piety. There were stories about his visits as a parish priest to the poor and infirm, about a seminarian who died of cancer, about priests and seminarians who were dangerously liberal. He meant for these narratives to be instructive. They were Father Curlin's way of setting forth the ideals of priestly life. They also conveyed warnings. One day, shortly after arriving for one of our chats, he remarked breezily:

"Oh, this has been a rough day. I just had to dismiss a seminarian for homosexuality. I never suspected a thing, but someone brought it to my attention. I confronted him and he did not deny it."

"Yes, I can imagine how difficult that must have been for you."

"Well, Paul, it is, but when we see this, we must act quickly. This kind of thing can be very disruptive to seminary life."

I spoke disinterestedly, as though the topic were of no greater significance to me than traffic conditions. I tried not to notice the panicked clamping down of my guts. Did Father Curlin suspect me? Why was he disclosing such a weighty decision? I was not asked then, nor at any time prior to ordination, whether I was a homosexual. But occasionally, indirectly, signals were sent out to communicate that "homosexuality" would not be tolerated.

After a few weeks, in early 1969, I was accepted into the priestly formation program of the Archdiocese. Father Curlin made a point of saying that in my case he was making an exception to a rule that required five years to elapse after conversion to Roman Catholicism before entering a formation program. I was grateful to have my entry into seminary expedited. In hindsight, I think some delay would have been wise. The Catholicism that I knew was the version found at *Triumph*: insular, antimodern, proud. Of the realities of a church with a population that had largely shifted to the suburbs during the previous two decades, I was woefully, even willfully, ignorant.

III

At Triumph, my work was focused on writing and editing. I had the privilege of honing my skills under the guidance of polished professionals. Our views may have been outlandishly critical of modern society, but there was nothing amateurish about our product. We were absolutely convinced of our possession of the Truth and our ability to bring that Truth's implications to bear on every current social and ecclesiastical issue: women, birth control, civil unrest, Vietnam, dissident theologians, changes in the liturgy.

My conversion provided a small example of the power of *Triumph's* truth, a truth that, in the end, would Triumph. I was flattered by the interest and support shown me by this group of writers and, most especially, by John Wisner. Uncle John was a man in his mid-fifties, who sported a gentlemanly style proudly out of touch with his own time and culture, a style that harked back to some earlier time in pre-Enlightenment Europe. He drew with ease from his vast reading in history and the classics, to make his arguments. His belly protruded curiously, unapologetically, an anatomical enhancement of his mystique as one who lived in flagrant disregard of conventional, modern proprieties, which, as a "black-hearted reactionary," as he liked to call himself, he thoroughly disdained. Raised in China, John was from an affluent, New York family. He served with distinction as a paratrooper in Europe, during the Second World War. His position as a senior editor at *Triumph* was his first experience of anything that approached the conventional workplace.

John's prose was thick with sweeping generalizations and scathing assessments of technology, "scientific-rationalism," capitalism and democracy. His muscular prose held a fascination for me and I began to fashion my own writing after his example.

I unquestionably overreached in the area of historical generalizations. John did have the stature, in that circle, to opine in his grand style, but for me, it was presumptuous and silly. Brent Bozell cautioned me about this. John, however, took a patronal interest in my life as an aspirant reactionary, and urged me to disregard Bozell's cautions as mere timidity. John's cosmopolitan air and erudition, his convincing contempt for modernity, modeled for me a style, a way of being a man that seemed viable and strong.

There was a consensus on the staff that I was the person best equipped at *Triumph* to handle theologically based articles. I was entrusted, for example, with the arduous task of editing manuscripts submitted by Archbishop Marcel Lefebvre, Superior General of the Holy Ghost Fathers. Archbishop Lefebvre was a reactionary who rejected the legitimacy of the Second Vatican Council, a position that even many conservatives who disliked the results of the council could not accept, since it fundamentally undermines church authority. Eventually, Lefebvre gained international notoriety by separating from Rome and establishing the Society of Saint Pius X as an alternative church with bishops and priests trained in pre-Vatican II models of church belief and practice.

Notwithstanding all the religious discourse, socially, *Triumph* had a frankly secular environment. This tone was set by Bozell himself, who prided himself on being an ardent Catholic. But this was an ideological, doctrinal Catholicism that did not manifest itself in the customary signs of devoutness. Triumph's offices, for example, were devoid of images of the Sacred Heart, crucifixes, and statues of the Blessed Mother. At a time when I was still living in the pious afterglow of conversion, I could not but notice the lack of any common devotional life at *Triumph*. Indeed, some recalled that at *National Review* in New York there were occasional staff outings to Mass. At *Triumph*, our extracurricular outing was a monthly dinner with binge drinking.

To my untrained eye it seemed there was an exceptionally high level of discontent and conflict for an editorial staff of less than ten persons. In a memo to Bozell, I commented on the lack of common Catholic devotion at *Triumph*, an ostensibly and emphatically Catholic periodical. I also alluded to staff tensions and suggested a linkage to the lack of prayer. Bozell took offense:

"An office is not a monastery!" he snapped.

And so, I was fired. Strangely, while removing me from the payroll, Bozell encouraged me to stick around and continue to attend staff meetings. My pride gravely wounded by the dismissal, however, I removed myself from *Triumph*, while maintaining personal ties with some of the staff, especially Uncle John.

IV

Being fired was not a grave concern, since I was now preparing to enter the seminary. Father Curlin discussed various seminary programs with me. He suggested that I consider Christ the King, a seminary run by Franciscans at St. Bonaventure's University in western New York. I arranged a visit, which I combined with a brief stopover at Bard. Thinking it best to look before leaping, I traversed the length of New York state by rail and bus to the remote site of CKS in Olean.

The rector, Father Juvenal, was a pensive, elegant man, whose words conveyed a depth that merited more than the usual level of attention. From the start, I was impressed and captivated by him. We connected on a personal level that transcended the roles of rector and prospective seminarian.

Father Juvenal arranged for me to meet some seminarians, including the men from Washington. He also wanted me to meet one in particular, Michael Perry, from the Diocese of Brooklyn. Michael, a joyful, round-faced man, invited me to tea.

Tea that evening proved to be an awkward experience. Michael prepared a pot of Constant Comment for the group of seven men who gathered for what had become a nocturnal ritual. I said little, as they entered and flavored their tea with their choices of lemon, sugar, and milk. The decor of Michael's room — brilliant icons and the photograph of a medieval sculpture of Mary — bespoke taste, spirituality, and warmth. As they conversed about persons, classes and subjects of which I knew nothing, I said little. Eventually, they directed their attention toward me. After a few nervous words about my background — convert from Episcopalianism, Bard, *Triumph* — I asked, shifting the focus from myself:

"What do they teach you here?"

"To be honest, academics is not CKS's strong point," said Tom Wells, a tall, handsome man with chiseled features. "I found the program here so weak that I have supplemented it by working on a master's in English lit at the university."

"This place can be what you make it," declared Michael, in his unapologetic, Brooklyn accent, spoken in a commanding bass. "The Franks have some good men, even some holy men on the faculty. They are all strong individuals, some of them real characters, and it takes time to know them. There was one," he laughed, "Father Albertus, who died a year ago.

Albertus was a tough guy, but it was all an act. He was a real joy in confession. When he would hear a guy's confession in his office, he would start cursing at the top of lungs, 'God damn it! Shit! What the fuck?' whenever anyone walked near the open window. As a penance, he often ordered guys to sneak into the friary and steal cigars."

I listened politely, but was bewildered. I did not know how to relate to this klatch of lifelong Catholics well on their way to ordination. Michael admitted later that had Juvenal asked him for an assessment, he would have recommended against admitting me to the program. That was not Juvenal's purpose, however. Intuitively his choice was on target, because Michael became a close friend and one of the very few men from Christ the King with whom I would remain in touch many years after ordination. In addition to being a man of gifted insight and aesthetic sensibility, Michael is one of the few priests I have known who is genuinely at home in the world outside the church.

V

During the months that remained before the start of my seminary program at CKS, I acquainted myself with a number of the parishes of the Archdiocese. I went to Mass every Sunday at a different parish. I confined these visits to city parishes. The Archdiocese of Washington includes not only the District of Columbia, but also the five southernmost counties of the State of Maryland. As a priest, I might be sent to a parish in any of those places. It never occurred to me, however, that I might really be assigned to rural Charles County or even the affluent suburbs of Montgomery County. As an intellectual, I instinctively envisioned myself in an urban setting, the world of journalists, activists and artists. Suburbia, in post-war America, rapidly displaced cities as the center of American social, political and economic life. Alienated from the mainstream of American life, I instinctively rebelled against this centrifugal, suburban trend. For me, the attraction of the city was that it endured as the place for writers, would-be writers, thinkers, and free spirits. The city, even smallish Washington, unlike the suburbs, was a place of conversation and the exploration of ideas.

I entered the seminary ignorant of the realities of Catholic parish life and of the manner in which most diocesan priests live and work. Had someone attempted to explain this to me I would have dismissed their concerns as irrelevant. My vision of Catholicism was of a glorious past that had only to be invoked to be reinstated. The mundane realities of how the Catholic Church actually functions today were of little interest.

My parents took me on the long drive, at the end of summer, to Christ the King Seminary. I had purchased the requisite supplies: cassock, surplice, and clergy shirt. I was surprised that I would be wearing a clergy shirt as a "first philosophy" student. We were to wear them for our "apostolates," weekly excursions to sites for ministry (religion classes for hopelessly uninterested public school children and special education programs). My parents paid for these supplies and provided support for basic necessities, books and transportation, throughout my seminary years. There was no such support from the Archdiocese, which covered only tuition, room and board. Later I would learn that the Archdiocese expected to be reimbursed for half of its costs, following ordination. I gave little thought to the financial implications of these arrangements, and none to the compensation package that would be provided to priests after ordination. I was not even aware that my father had extended my health care coverage on the group policy in which I had been included as a minor.

At this point, my needs were simple. I was grateful for my parents' generosity and, during my seminary years, would come to reflect increasingly on it, since they were supporting their son's choice of what must have seemed a strange life in a church that differed in striking ways from their own.

VI

Christ the King Seminary was a comfortable place. The impressive, three-storied, tile-roofed edifice was set well back from the road on a substantial piece of land adjacent to St. Bonaventure's University. Olean is set in a geological basin surrounded by forested hills. On one hill, to the south, there was a sizable clearing in the woods that was known at the university as "Merton's heart." Thomas Merton taught English briefly at St. Bonaventure's, before entering the Trappist monastery at Gethsemani, Kentucky. An agnostic, Merton was a writer and poet with a master's in English from Columbia University. His autobiography, *The Seven Storey Mountain*, a phenomenal best seller, describes his conversion to Catholicism and romantic attraction to monastic life. He was an avid hiker. Whether or not Merton's heart was an actual destination, this distinctive, topological feature evoked the memory of his brief association with St. Bonaventure's, one of the university's few brushes with greatness.

I found the seminary's vast, gleaming corridors and high ceilings reassuring. Within this immaculate and impersonal structure, within institutional Roman Catholicism, I expected to find release from the burdens of my own tormented personhood. I, too, would become impassively clean and polished.

There were about one hundred fifty seminarians in six classes. Most were in the four-year theology program. About two dozen of us were in theology's prerequisite program, two years of philosophy, which were linked to the final two years of college. "Philosophy" meant neo-scholasticism. This program of study was a remnant of the pre-Vatican II era, when theology and philosophy were reasoned and argued in the systematic style of medieval thinkers.

While it has its moments, scholasticism is dry fare. It presents a logically flawless face, but for those with a modern sensibility, it leaves a feeling of emptiness, as though the logical precision has no more meaning than a sleight of hand. The direction and outcome of Catholic scholastic arguments are highly predictable, because they represent conscious attempts to maintain a worldview that finds its completion in Catholic doctrine. For example, André Munier argues defensively in his *Manual of Philosophy* that the "creation of the world is a rational truth, even though it did not come into the history of philosophical thought independently of Judaeo-Christian revelation." In the section of "proofs" that follows, several "false" hypotheses, such as pantheism, are weakly argued, only to be struck down, until, at last, we arrive at that "which alone is possible and which alone is true. The Cause of the world is necessary in its existence, and the world is contingent. The world and its Cause are irreducibly distinct. There is, therefore, nothing of the world which is not caused; the world is caused totally, that is, created."

I recognized these difficulties with the material being presented and found myself variously engrossed in a system of thought that harked back to the Middle Ages and bemused by its detachment from the subjective experience of human life and modern sensibilities, a problem which is ultimately rooted in an unshakable dualism: the "irreducible distinction" scholasticism finds between God and the world. I wanted to believe that the scholastic approach would provide a comprehensive, *absolute* guide to truth. My heart occasionally murmured its discontent, but I tried not to listen to my heart.

VII

A great and terrifying loneliness settled over me during my first year in seminary. It came quite suddenly during Mass, about six weeks into my first semester. Notwithstanding my newfound friends, for the first time I felt completely alone. I wept openly. Whether or not I attracted notice, no one spoke to me about it. But I was troubled. Something was very wrong and I did not understand what it was. All I knew was that a blanket of loneliness had wrapped itself around me. What did this mean?

I consulted Father Juvenal. Juvenal was a remote and exalted figure. As rector, he was not the person to whom one would normally turn for counseling. This loneliness, however, did not strike me as an ordinary experience. It was exceptional and I needed advice from this exceptional man for whom, from the start, I had felt a certain affinity.

Father Juvenal was reassuring. This crisis would pass. But, he said, there were some things to which I should attend. One concerned personal development. He urged me to consider the meaning of personhood and to try to develop as fully as possible as the person that I am. He recommended a book by a Swiss psychiatrist, Paul Tournier, *The Meaning of Persons*. Tournier's book had been widely acclaimed in religious circles, since its publication a decade before, for its attempt to integrate Biblical faith and modern psychology in the project of personal self-discovery. Juvenal's advice was extraordinarily on target, although I did not make much of it at the time. It was a moment, however, that announced what was to be the central theme and core struggle of my life as a priest: claiming the freedom to be a person.

Father Juvenal's second point was more practical and was the one on which I focused afterwards. He said that I intimidate people. As one who had so little sense of my own power, the very notion that I could somehow be intimidating to others was quite bemusing. He said that I, as a serious-minded introvert, did not understand the effect I have on people. He spoke, he said, from experience, as one who faces the same dilemma. People such as us need to find ways to put others at their ease so that they know we are persons with feelings, as well as thoughts.

Juvenal's advice concerning my introversion also announced a major theme that was to unfold in the years ahead, in both the seminary and the priesthood. There was a gap, somehow, somewhere, between others and myself. A gap that was self-imposed, yet invisible to myself. A grave demeanor masked the gentle spirit that yearned for simple companionship.

There were friends. Mike Perry and company. Classmates from towns in New York and Pennsylvania. Fellow Washingtonians. We ate together. Watched films. Traveled. Laughed. Did laundry. Listened to one another's gossip and complaints. CKS was very comfortable. The loneliness, however, remained. It was always there when I returned to my room, however deep the laughter or late the hour.

Bill Olesik became another friend, a kind of teacher. Mike introduced us. Bill was also introverted, although, unlike me, very sure of himself. I might not even have noticed him, without the introduction. Early in our acquaintance, Bill startled me by saying that he felt like punching me in the face. He meant it, I could see, in a friendly way. It was, I suppose, a Zen-type thing to say. Bill practiced Zen meditation. He was trying to tell me about the facade I had erected for myself.

Bill was also one of the few really capable theology students in the house and had a keen appreciation of contemporary theologians, especially Karl Rahner. Rahner was a German Jesuit who undertook the most comprehensive effort of his generation to reexamine and restate Catholic truths in contemporary terms. Bill became an important sounding board for my ideas and, no doubt, he helped to temper some of my rigid and doctrinaire enthusiasms. I was always a bit in awe of him and felt uncertain, when I knocked on his door, whether he could possibly have time for me. As my absolutist version of Catholicism ebbed, the deep, personal insecurities that it had masked slowly emerged. Bill did punch me, not in the face, but in the façade.

VIII

At Christ the King I worked hard at assimilating the beliefs and practices of Roman Catholics. My "going over to Rome" was somehow incomplete. For example, I harbored a Protestant reserve about Roman enthusiasm for Mary and devotion to the saints.

In the chapel, which I found appealing in its simplicity — white walls, rounded apse, a square, marble, freestanding altar behind which a tabernacle was set between columns — I spent long hours in prayer. Prayer before the tabernacle. The tabernacle contains the consecrated hosts, the bread over which the priest at Mass repeats the words of Jesus, "This is my body." I had asserted, in becoming a Roman, that this is "really, truly and substantially" the body of Christ. Roman Catholics pray before the Blessed Sacrament. They know that this means something. As I entered the chapel, I would often find a few seminarians there, each in prayer before the Blessed Sacrament. In the evening the chapel was dark, except for a spotlight on the golden tabernacle. I, too, would take my place to focus on that golden box. Waiting, watching, praying. Surely there was something I was supposed to be experiencing in such moments, yet I was not experiencing it. But I was not willing to concede defeat. I persisted and would persist for years to come. Breakthroughs did come in future years, but none that would have occurred to the pious imagination of my youth.

I also made a serious attempt at praying the rosary. Intellectually, I did not comprehend the relevance of the "Hail Mary" to the "mysteries" which the rosary invites one to consider. When meditating on the agony of Jesus in the garden, for example, the first of the "sorrowful mysteries," I did not understand how repeating the words, "Hail Mary, full of grace, the Lord is with thee," *et cetera*, could in any way enhance my appreciation of it. In fact, the prayers drew my attention away from the subject of meditation. Nevertheless, I tried. I was, after all, a Roman Catholic, and praying the rosary is what one does as a Catholic. For a time, I prayed the rosary after dinner each evening, with a small group that had been pulled together through the unrelenting efforts of an older seminarian, Jack, an engineer who, for some years, had worked as a test pilot. With a brittle personality and rigid literalism, he was socially awkward, although his pious intentions were clear.

It was from reciting the rosary with Jack that I first learned the prayer that many Roman Catholics recite between the mysteries of the rosary: "O my Jesus, forgive us our sins. Save us from the fires of hell. Lead all souls to heaven, especially those most in need of your mercy." Anxious and scrupulous as I was about myself, somehow the personal salvation model on which this prayer is based had never been central to my understanding of Catholicism. As an Episcopalian, the "fires of hell" had never quite sunk in as an object of genuine concern. Now, as I repeated Catholic prayers, I attempted to assimilate an appropriately Roman view of things. Jack obviously believed in this prayer and its efficacy. In fact, however, my vision of Catholicism was much more focused on how its truths could help to set individuals and nations on the right course in this life. I eventually moved on from these postprandial recitations of the rosary for other, more worldly activities, such as watching the CBS Evening News. I was trying to be a good Catholic. That, however, was a problem that did not escape my notice, namely, that I *needed* to try.

IX

Another struggle surfaced at this time, one that was to bedevil me for the next seven years. It was an imaginary problem in the truest sense. As I struggled to insert myself into seminary life, I did my best to ignore the lack of fit. But when one struggles hard, as I did, to deny some existential truth, something deep within the psyche cries out. In my case the imagination cried out by frequently insinuating vile images that featured the organs, functions and products of sexual and excretory activities. The more I applied myself to pious thoughts, the more did these bizarre images with blasphemous implications present themselves. Thus, the bright white chapel became a massive urinal, filling up with piss. The face of the priest presiding at liturgy became a giant penis. And so forth. The images presented themselves in an endless stream. Was I going mad? This was such a cockeyed problem that I did not know what to make of it. I certainly did not want to discuss it, because it caused me shame to think my imagination capable of such blasphemies. Surely, I thought, this bespeaks the demonic. From the lives of the saints, I knew that many had struggled with demons. Saint John Vianney was troubled at night by demonic tormentors. Saint Thérèse of Lisieux believed that she struggled against temptations so terrible that she had never heard of anyone else suffering them. Were her sufferings similar to mine?

Shamed as I felt, I presented this dilemma haltingly, tearfully, to confessors. I was concerned that I might actually have *consented* to these thoughts and thus was guilty of blasphemy. Bill Olesik dismissed it as the product of a fertile imagination. It was, certainly, a sign that I had clamped down my humanity much too tightly. Something within was gasping for air and light. It would be some years, however, before I would make the connection that now seems so obvious between these obsessive thoughts and my repressed sexuality.

As I embarked on my Roman Catholic journey, where I made so many mental leaps and elisions for the sake of what I expected to be the ultimate answer to the questions of life, sexuality was an area that I set aside as irrelevant. I knew I was homosexual and yet, somehow, did not know. Had anyone asked me, "Are you a homosexual?" — and no one ever did — I would have said, in all honesty, but perhaps after a nervous swallow, "No, certainly not!" To the extent that I allowed myself to think about this at all, it was in terms of having "homosexual tendencies." Tendencies, however, do not constitute an identity. A homosexual, I believed, is someone who *acts* on those tendencies. I thought of homosexuals, that is, male homosexuals, as effeminate men, the kind of men who wear mohair sweaters, style their hair and speak "girlishly." Homosexuals were arrogantly disdainful of social proprieties. Their easy divestiture of masculine traits was, to me, quite horrid. *That* was not me.

At the same time, I found myself in an institution that positively rippled with homosexual tension. I recognized that there were fellow seminarians and, probably, also some of the friars, who were actively homosexual. Some of my closest friends in seminary were highly campy in their speech. In the parlance of the day, they were "dropping pins," that is, conversational cues that would be recognized by other homosexuals. Having bracketed out homosexuality I knew all this and yet did not know.

X

As my first year at St. Bonaventure's progressed, I longed for the academic depth and challenges that I had known at Bard College. Although I would receive a Bachelor's degree the following year from St. Bonaventure's, I knew that it would not be representative of my intellectual roots in the way a degree from Bard would be. I therefore arranged to complete my degree at Bard, which only required that I write a "senior project," a thesis, on an approved topic. Because my advisor, Jules Kirschner, left Bard that year, I arranged to write my thesis under the tutelage of my old mentor, Father Shafer. I chose for my topic the concept of the layman in late medieval ecclesiology, a much too ambitious undertaking, as the final paper painfully disclosed. Thus, in my second year, in addition to my regular course work, I pushed along on my thesis for Bard, glad for the occasion, once again, to pore over literature on the medieval period that had drawn me to the Roman church in the first place. But this project also represented an important step, unbeknownst to me at the time. By undertaking it, I was reaching beyond Roman Catholic institutional life. Having jumped in with both feet, I was now regaining my balance, by placing one foot outside, even if I was writing on church history. In so doing, I was establishing a realm of freedom for myself. It was an admission that somehow I could not be contained within the world of Roman Catholicism. I was *in* it, but not fully *of* it. I needed something more than what I found there.

XI

During the summer of 1970, back home in Washington, I became acquainted with a budding spiritual movement, "Catholic Pentecostalism," as it was then called, later to be known as the "Catholic Charismatic Renewal." Intrigued by an announcement posted at Catholic University about prayer meetings in Caldwell Auditorium, I decided to go to one. Notwithstanding my rigid stance on church authority, I was, at heart, a spiritual seeker. I knew, from my first year in the seminary, that whatever the value of daily Mass, the Divine Office, the rosary, prayer before the Blessed Sacrament, prayers to saints and frequent confession, there was something that I lacked. I knew, I felt, I hoped there was something "more."

The first charismatic prayer meeting that I attended was led by a tall, handsome professor named Robert Nicolich. He was nattily dressed in a blue blazer and tan chinos, which contrasted sharply with the ubiquitous jeans in the hall. Robert started us off by calling on the assembly to praise God. We sang songs from mimeographed sheets to the accompaniment of acoustic guitars. After a few songs, all around me people spoke words of praise to God with apparent ease and exuberance. They praised God's goodness, God's love, God's glory and the Spirit's work in the world and in their own lives. I focused especially on the utterances of a young woman seated close to me. After praising God in English, she shifted to non-English syllables, a flow of sounds that also suggested praise, even a touch of ecstasy. This, I learned, was "speaking in tongues," a form of prayer that seems to flow spontaneously from somewhere deep within, without depending on conscious thought. At the same time, the ability to speak in tongues is just that, an ability, a prayer language that remains under the conscious control of the speaker just as much as the ability to remain silent or to speak in one's own language at any given moment.

The hum of gentle praise rose from the gathering of some one hundred fifty persons and seemed to hover over them, not as a discordant cacophony of each doing his or her own thing, but as a profound unity. The hum suddenly turned musical and the assembly, in a harmonious spontaneity, sang praises together, in a mixture of "tongues" and English, and then, as if following some covert cue, stopped. All was still for a few minutes. Then someone read a passage from the scriptures. Another spoke a message as if directly from God, in the first person:

"I have created you and called you to be my people. I love you and I delight in your praise. Know that I will be with you always to guide you, to instruct you, to heal you and to make you my witnesses to all the world."

Praise would then start up again, growing still more exuberant. And then silence quickly returned. After a while, someone stood up to speak to the entire group. Then others spoke. They spoke about the experience of God in their lives, for example, how they had worried needlessly about personal finances and how the experience taught them to place greater faith in God.

I was impressed. Very impressed. The young woman seated close to me continued in her earnest praise of God throughout the meeting. Clearly she and the others present knew something that I did not. They had found a joy and satisfaction in their faith that I had not found.

From the start, I accepted this departure from the solemn religious ceremonies that I had always preferred, as spiritually authentic. I decided, however, to put this form of prayer to a test. A time came for prayer requests. I sat in a circle with persons who had special requests, while others from the group stood just behind us, placing their hands on our heads and shoulders. I prayed for a friend, Mike, who, I said, had been behaving irresponsibly and was failing to face the reality of his own life. Mike was out of town, when I offered that prayer. A few days later, he stopped by my home and, as we sat on the porch, explained that he had come to some realizations while he was away. He saw that he had been behaving irresponsibly and that he needed to change the direction of his life. I had not said these things to Mike, and yet I found my words being repeated back almost verbatim. Had something really happened here? Had my prayer actually worked? I was brushing against mystery, I sensed, the real mystery, the truth that lies behind the appearances and forms of religion.

After this, I knew I had to be a part of these Pentecostal gatherings. I had to have what these people had. I started to attend the weekly meetings and, afterwards, attended a series of instructional sessions for newcomers who sought prayer for an experience called the "baptism of the Holy Spirit." After a few weeks, I was deemed ready. A small group that included Robert Nicolich gathered around as I knelt in Caldwell Chapel. Placing their hands on me, they prayed for the outpouring of the Holy Spirit. I wondered what, if anything, would happen? Would I feel something new? Would I speak in tongues?

As I left Caldwell Hall, I did feel ebullient and peaceful. But was I noticing anything different? I was not sure. I got into my car and started driving home. As I drove I began to sing: "We are one in the Spirit, we are one in the Lord... and they'll know we are Christians by our love." This was a song that, only a few weeks before, I had found particularly irksome. We sang it in the seminary. As a conservative, I did not much care for guitars at Mass and this was one of the guitar songs that I found especially annoying. Its lyrics are dull, the melody pedestrian. But there were many such songs in Catholic worship. What I really detested about this one was its phony sentimentality: "we are one." We certainly were not one. We were divided: conservative against liberal, liberal against conservative. There were rifts between individuals and cliques. Often the tensions ran high. Trying to cover everything over with a happy guitar song seemed a stupid denial.

This night, however, the night of my "baptism in the Holy Spirit," brought a new insight. As I sang, "we are one the Spirit," for first time I felt the words to be true. Somehow I had been touched by the Spirit. Something *was* different! I was being healed! The rigid, ideologically bound self was giving way to something new. Who that new self was I did not yet know. But it seemed a happier, more peaceful self. A self that was ready to look differently at faith and the church. A self that would, above all, push forward for truth, real truth, truth that resonates in the heart, and never again be satisfied with formalisms, the insistence on the external forms of speaking in particular words, or worshipping in particular ways, or thinking particular thoughts. My Catholic trip to this point had been largely that, an exercise in formalism. That, I knew, would no longer do. I sought now an approach to religion that would be *personally* satisfying. The Catholic charismatic renewal appeared to offer that. It promised and, I found, delivered an experience of God. As for Catholic traditionalism: while I continued to find much that was attractive in that arena, the effort to turn back the clock to the pre-Vatican II era lost its hold on my imagination.

XII

By the summer of 1970, Father Curlin decided that I would study theology in Rome. "Baptized in the Spirit" though I may have been, Rome had a big hold on my imagination. There I would be at the epicenter of Roman Catholicism. I would see the pope — not once, but often. Perhaps I would even meet him. I would also meet people who worked in the Vatican on important business that affected the life of the church throughout the world. There would be abundant opportunities to shape and advance my ecclesiastical career. I tried not to have a fat head about it, but found it hard to resist a sense of pride about having been selected to study there.

As I prepared to leave Christ the King, a classmate, Jerry, stopped by my room, where I was packing. He said:

"Good luck in Rome, Paul. You must be looking forward to it."

"Thanks, Jerry. Yes, I am. It's a big challenge. I don't know a word of Italian, you know, but I understand that doesn't matter. We'll pick it up there."

"Well, we'll miss you here, but we'll try to stay in touch. Listen, Paul, I've been thinking and there's something I have to tell you."

"What is it, Jerry?" I was apprehensive, because his tone was serious.

"You didn't really let us get to know you here."

"I didn't?"

"No, Paul, you didn't. But it's not just that. You took the easy way out. You hung out with people you felt comfortable with. They didn't challenge you at all. You didn't do anything to extend yourself to others. And I can tell you that other people would have liked a chance to get to know you."

"Well, Jerry, I think I understand what you mean. I'll think about what you said."

"Please do, because you have something to offer, but you just have to learn how to reach out to more people."

I recognized the truth of Jerry's observation immediately, although I had not given the matter much thought before that. I had settled into a comfortable routine, especially during my second year, and failed to get close to any additional people. Partly this was due to shyness. I was also busy with my senior thesis for Bard. But these were excuses. Just as a sense of loneliness had engulfed me shortly after my beginning at Christ the

King, so now my tendency to wall others out — or myself in — had to be acknowledged. Bill Olesik should have punched me in the face.

When the academic year ended, I graduated simultaneously from St. Bonaventure's and Bard. I attended commencement exercises only at Bard, where I felt personally connected. The lack of connection that I felt to St. Bonaventure's should have been a kind of warning to me about my relation to Catholic institutions generally. The graduation at Bard, to which I wore a clergy shirt, was a characteristically casual affair, a parody of the gravity with which such ceremonies are conducted elsewhere. Even in my clerical duds, I did not especially stand out from the rest of this motley class of individualists, clad in denim, psychedelic colors, jackets, ties, whatever. Bard was my true alma mater.

XIII

The North American College was housed in a massive, post-Fascist edifice that overlooks the Vatican from the Janiculum hill. Its six stories rise around a courtyard, complete with fountain and orange trees. NAC offered a safe haven of Americana. Exotic foodstuffs, such as peanut butter and corn flakes, were imported to accommodate our need to reassure ourselves, from time to time, with familiar tastes. We wore street clothes most of the time, even in chapel and at class.

NACers enrolled in the theology programs offered by either the Gregorian University or the Angelicum. Father Richard Foley, NAC's Academic Dean, explained to me the difference between the two:

"At the Greg, courses are taught in Italian. This is difficult, if you don't know the language, but our students work together to produce notes and generally manage to get through it. The Angelicum is just beginning to offer a program of instruction in English. They are having difficulty attracting good faculty. The college is just beginning to offer the Angelicum as an alternative to the Greg for our students."

The Greg's stellar reputation made the choice easy for me. A 1969 *Life* magazine article described the Greg as the "Church's Sorbonne, Oxbridge and Yale/Harvard all combined." Six of the last eight popes had studied there, as had slightly more than one-third of the current members of the College of Cardinals.

"Father, I choose the Greg. It seems by far to be the more interesting program."

"No, your place of study is not yours to choose."

I was embarrassed by this trivial reminder of my subordinate status, but maintained my composure:

"Very well, then, Father, may I have your permission to go to the Greg?"

"Yes, you may," Father Foley announced with a subtle, self-satisfied grin.

The New Man Show, an in-house variety show staged annually to welcome the first-year students included, that year, a parody of Father Foley's interviews with first-year men. My dialogue with him was presented almost verbatim. Apparently I was not the only one to have felt the sting of the dean's imperious behavior. But Father Foley was no buffoon. His words were an intentional reminder of a fundamental of Roman Catholic clerical culture: there is no place for personal choice, except, of course, within the higher strata of the hierarchy.

The Gregorian turned out to be a drab and confusing affair. My Italian was weak, though I am doubtful sharpened language skills would have done much to improve the experience. The pedagogical method was foreign to Americans. It emphasized lectures, note-taking, memorization and, at examination time, regurgitation of whatever had been imparted in the lectures. There was, in this approach, little place for research or independent thinking. Several weeks prior to examinations, which, by choice, could be taken either orally or in writing, a booklet of theses was published for each class to guide students' exam preparation.

I considered myself a decent student, but nothing in my background prepared me for the ordeal of the rote memorization of massive amounts of material required for these exams. In some cases, for example, Father Rasco's course on the synoptic gospels, the theses bore little resemblance to the material presented in class. I managed to get through Rasco's exam by studying publications that alluded to at least some of the points mentioned in his theses. Several of my classmates failed, however, which meant they had to retake the exam in the fall, during a special exam period. Often, course material would begin to make sense and become interesting only during exam time, which struck me as unfortunate and wasteful of the weeks spent in lecture.

I once complained to Bishop Hickey, the rector, that I was not learning enough theology. He looked at my marks and concluded that I was wrong.

Of course I was learning theology. My grades proved it!

The Greg did not represent a particular school of thought. No single, coherent methodology or way of doing theology was presented. There were, rather, recurring themes. The overall approach was what contemporary theologians call "anthropological," that is, human experience, both at the societal and individual levels, was taken seriously as the site of God's self-disclosure. God's word, the truth, is not imposed from above in some changeless form. The individual person's pursuit of integrity and meaning is critically important and must not be suffocated by immutable creeds and formulas (the kind of things I recited on becoming a Catholic). This focus corresponds to the dictum of Jesus, "the Sabbath is made for humankind, and not humankind for the Sabbath." Static ideas of God and the world, the hallmark of pre-Vatican II Catholicism, were giving way to dynamic ones. The consequences of this change are most obvious in moral theology, where we were taught by Josef Fuchs, one of the preeminent moral theologians of the time, that moral judgments must be linked to cultural contexts: lying does not mean the same to an Italian that it does to a Scot, for example. And also this: homosexual behavior does not have the same moral significance for an individual within New York theater society, where it is accepted, that it does in societies that condemn it! The overarching theme that came through in every course was that church teachings on doctrine and morals must be critically reexamined in terms of their biblical and historical foundations, in order to be reinterpreted for the modern world.

This was, in short, a program of theology that had been radically restructured in the light of Vatican II. Several of my professors had been theological consultants to the Council. The influence of Karl Rahner, the Catholic theologian most associated with a radical, historical-critical reevaluation of doctrine, was evident throughout the program at the Greg, although his works were not heavily cited and he himself visited the university only sporadically.

Although I found the Greg pedagogically dull, my understandings of Catholicism were crumbling under hammer blows from its faculty. Without fully realizing it, my understanding of truth was radically reshaped by the Greg's focus on each person's life as a sacred mystery. A brief conversation with Father Giles Dimock, an acquaintance from the prayer group, underscored my transformation. We were seated outside a cafe on the Piazza Venezia, enjoying the afternoon sun. As I stirred sugar into my cappuccino,

I said:

"Giles, I am beginning to understand better what the bishops said at Vatican II about how God's spirit is at work in all kinds of ways in the world, even in other religions."

"What do you mean, Paul?"

"Well, I've been reading Rahner's paper on the 'anonymous Christian' and I find it fascinating to consider that at some deeply personal level people can accept Christ and open their lives to the spirit, even though they know nothing about Christianity. In fact, organized Christianity might get in the way, depending on their culture. What matters is that they are making a choice for truth and personal integrity, which means that, in their own way, they are opening their lives to Christ, or what we mean by Christ."

"Don Paolo," Giles said in a barely audible voice, "*quest'é eresia.*"

"Heresy, Giles? Are you saying Karl Rahner is a heretic?"

"I'm saying that you need to be very cautious about this kind of theology, because it contradicts church tradition."

I was bemused by Giles's concern that I had brushed up against heresy. "Heresy." The word seemed so antiquated. The church had embarked on a new course, I could see, one that was profoundly respectful of persons and cultures. Accusations of heresy belonged to the bad old days, not to this new age.

In truth, theology was marginal to the concerns of most of the men at the North American College. Only a few made the effort to be serious, methodical students. Father Foley, who taught a church history course for first-year students, remarked that the church does not reward intellectuals. He may have been reflecting on his own experience. Holding a Ph.D. in history from Harvard, where he had also taught, Foley was the best-educated man on the faculty, yet his career as an ecclesiastic had gone nowhere. Eventually, he would be forced off the college's faculty for being openly critical of the rector.

XIV

A kind of learning that has little to do with theology mattered more to most students at the college. The North American was, as we put it, a college for "baby bishops." Many American bishops are selected from the ranks of the college's alumni. Indeed, when the college was founded, in 1859, the training of future bishops was mentioned in official correspondence as part of the rationale. Thus, many of the students were men who had begun to play the political game even before arriving in Rome. They were personally familiar with their diocesan bishop, had come from wealthy backgrounds or were otherwise well connected.

At the college, socializing among students was more purposeful and less recreational than what I had found at Christ the King. Many of the students were men who, with an eye to career, positioned themselves to befriend others, both students and faculty, who might be useful. One clique, for example, hosted a large party each year to which those deemed upwardly mobile were invited. I made it to the list of invitees by my final year. In such an ambience, there was little use for either academic prowess or devotional fervor. What mattered was the *bella figura*, the ability to socialize well, to make in some fashion an impressive and elegant presentation of self. In the case of the students of the college this included dining at fine restaurants and cultivating connections with notables, especially Vatican curialists.

Notwithstanding the importance placed on social skills, every year, without fail, the college would be plagued by some controversy that polarized much of its population, both faculty and students. During my first year, the crisis had to do with holding ordinations in December. Since its inception, the custom of the North American College had been to ordain men to the priesthood on its patronal feast, December 8th, the feast of the Immaculate Conception, during the fourth year of theology. This was a half-year ahead of schedule for most American seminarians, but was a cherished custom that set the college apart from its States-side counterparts. The rationale given by loyalists of the tradition was that ordination in December afforded the men an opportunity to celebrate Mass at various revered sites before completing their studies. The preferred sites included the major basilicas, especially St. Peter's, St. Paul's Outside the Walls, and the catacombs.

Bishop Hickey, however, opposed the custom. He argued the need to bring the college into line with contemporary practice. It was believed by many students, however, that he had other, hidden motives for advocating a change. Hickey assumed his duties as rector at a time when students were becoming more independent, even rebellious. This was, after all, the era of student protest in many parts of the world, as well as a period of comprehensive reform within the church. The times were, as Bob Dylan

declaimed, "a-changin'," even in seminaries. Hickey's immediate predecessor, Bishop Reh, had resigned in disgust at student demands, after a
brief tenure.

Hickey's style was more subtle. He worked meticulously behind the
scenes to exert control. And in this he was highly successful. He emphasized compliance with what had become the norm of serving a full year in
the diaconate prior to ordination to the priesthood. These were years when
many were leaving the priesthood and attention was focused, in formation
programs, on educating seminarians to the permanency of the priestly
commitment. Ordination was often likened to marriage. The priesthood
was not just a job, but a total commitment of the person to God and the
people of God. The diaconate year was regarded as a kind of test that would
result in a better-informed, more mature decision, at the time of ordination
to the priesthood. In most cases, the diaconate year was spent largely in the
fourth year of theology study and included only a brief, summer exposure
to parish ministry.

On the face of it, Hickey had a point. But the suspicion was that his
unspoken purpose was to bring the fourth-year men into line. Delaying
ordination until the end of the academic year enabled the faculty to hold
over their heads the final recommendation for ordination. In a public
conference, Hickey denied that discipline had anything to do with the
change. This was flatly contradicted, however, by minutes of a Board of
Governors meeting, which were copied and slipped anonymously under the
door of every student. Hickey was caught in a lie.

The Vice Rector, Monsignor Larry Breslin, responded by calling a
house meeting, where he shrilly denounced the revelation as an act of
treachery. He said that all a man has in the priesthood, at bottom, is his
character and when that is taken away, nothing is left. His anger rising to
the point of shaking, Larry declared, "Bishop Hickey is a *bishop* and that's
more than any of you will ever be!" and then stormed out of the auditorium.

It was an uncomfortable moment. I was bewildered. I felt a bit of an
outsider in this debacle. I had been inclined to credit Hickey's side; but the
disclosed minutes and the unfortunate spectacle staged by his deputy gave
me pause. The episode, in which, of course, Hickey ultimately prevailed,
served as an important introduction for me to clerical culture or, more
precisely, to clerical culture's executive branch, the hierarchy. The lesson
here was that appearances are everything. Lying, if it can be accomplished

plausibly and elegantly, is permissible, even necessary, at times. Clearly, I was in an environment that was far removed from Christ the King Seminary. I was in a place of intrigue, ambition and, to my mind, not much spirituality.

XV

For spirituality I had the charismatic prayer group. Meetings took place on Sunday afternoon in the Gregorian's Frascara, a Renaissance palazzo where one enters through an imposing, dark portal to discover a bright, modernized interior. The college and the Greg became, for me, necessary evils, trials to be endured as the cost of living in Rome and progressing toward ordination. The charismatic renewal was where the action was, that is, the action of the Holy Spirit. Here a spiritual awakening was taking place that, I believed, would profoundly reshape the church in years to come. For my part, I sought to reshape my own life through the renewal's resources. In prayer, I was constantly asking God to reveal His will for my life and to transform my mind and heart. As I had once sought to lose myself in the sterile rigidities of institutional Catholicism, I now sought to lose myself in spiritual fervor.

The prayer group, which eventually came to be called, "Lumen Christi" (Light of Christ), grew to draw about one hundred persons on a typical Sunday, during the academic year. Soon there were offshoots from the English-language group that gathered for prayer in Italian, Spanish and French.

In 1972 two of the movement's prominent leaders, Ralph Martin and Father Edward O'Connor, visited our group, which, simply because of its location, could play a crucial part in the charismatic renewal's development. As the renewal took root in many countries, Lumen Christi, nestled safely at the Greg, in the crossroads of Rome, served as a showcase to curious bishops, priests, theologians, nuns, monks and assorted seekers, who wanted the opportunity to examine a prayer meeting firsthand, in the anonymity of a foreign city. We joked about being a spiritual peep show.

Ralph was a founder and leader of The Word of God, a covenant community in Ann Arbor, Michigan. Many of the members of The Word of God, including Ralph and his wife, Anne, lived together in group households. Ralph was a powerful speaker, "charismatic" in the fullest sense, despite his disarmingly slight build. His light green eyes drank in every detail of person and place, while suggesting that somewhere behind them, unseen by mere mortals, was the real Ralph Martin, in communion with God.

Father O'Connor was part of the community at the University of Notre Dame and author of a book, *The Pentecostal Movement in the Catholic Church*, that introduced tens of thousands to the renewal and provided some theological context for understanding it during its early years.

The visit of these leaders of what was rapidly becoming an international movement helped to solidify the identity of Lumen Christi with the charismatic renewal as it was developing in the United States. Within a few years, Father O'Connor would withdraw from the movement, because, as he disclosed in a statement that he sent to the American bishops, he found that its self-appointed leaders were becoming convinced of their own indispensability and, indeed, infallibility.

I had no such misgivings. I managed to visit Ann Arbor during the summers of 1973 and 1974. This vibrant and growing community of hundreds of people shaped my understanding not only of the renewal, but of prayer and the church. In the households, where a few dozen members committed themselves to lives of shared simplicity, I found a warmth and level of caring that were exemplary of Christian community.

I stayed several times in the household of "the brotherhood," a group of young men who had committed themselves to living "single for the Lord." They modeled themselves after the primitive community of St. Francis of Assisi. They did indeed live in a simplicity that rivaled that of contemporary monasticism: sleeping on the floor, sharing clothes and eating very plain fare.

In the morning, after breakfasting together, the brothers gathered in the "prayer room," a bedroom that had been designated for the purpose. Except for carpeting, a Bible on a crate and a chair or two, the room was unfurnished and unadorned. The next hour or so was spent in prayer, though not as a group. Each man prayed on his own, whether standing, kneeling, prostrate, in silence or aloud, in English or in tongues. Sometimes the room was full of sound and sometimes, especially toward the end of the hour, still, with a rich silence. No prayer meeting that I had attended came close to this level of energy. Prayer time was followed by scripture study. Eventually, the men showered, dressed and headed off to work. A few worked for the Word of God itself, which published books, tapes and a monthly magazine, *New Covenant*.

Apart from reading everything about the renewal I could get my hands on and listening to tapes, I spent much of my time in Ann Arbor studying theology texts, which, away from there, seemed bland. At the Word of God, where there was a vital and convincing faith life, not just in individuals, but in the community itself, the reasoning and language of these texts somehow became more convincing. While I respected my professors for their scholarly depth, there was no question in my mind but that The Word of God outweighed the Gregorian as a place to seek wisdom and understanding of how God works in our world and in the church.

The Word of God placed a strong emphasis on leadership (or "headship") and obedience. The Lord entrusted some individuals with overall responsibility for the community. These individuals had to be men (yes, *men*) of prayer who would listen carefully to the Spirit's guidance, which meant knowing how to listen to their hearts.

In addition, each household had a head and, within the brotherhood, which attempted to live this ideal to the full, each man had a "head" with whom he consulted at least once each day. All of this attention to structure and authority I found very compelling. The notion of clear authority had attracted me to Roman Catholicism. In the charismatic renewal, I found what I took to be a fresh, more authentically spiritual form of authority. Once again, I was drawn in by a kind of absolutism. And I was a quick pupil. I absorbed and made my own the prayer styles, theories, texts and discourse of the charismatic renewal, as found in Ann Arbor.

In hindsight, it is obvious that a subliminal homoeroticism was at work in my attraction to this community. At the brotherhood, I resided in a household of a dozen men, most of them in their early twenties. At breakfast and dinner we sat in close proximity around the dining room table and, at meal's end, hugged one another. At night, the entire household gathered to hear each man talk about his day. Sometimes the details and admissions of wrongdoing were quite intimate. The honesty, vulnerability and trust demonstrated in these meetings were, I knew, well beyond anything approximated by official religious orders and may, indeed, have reflected in spirit something akin to the life of the early Franciscans. The care shown by the heads was impressive. I recall one instance, when a head and his charge stayed up into the early morning to discuss a problem.

For a man with secret and unfulfilled homosexual longings, this was a highly charged setting. I was not especially feeling lust, though I recognized, now and again, attractions that I did not consider appropriate. But the embrace and acceptance of this deeply spiritual brotherhood brought me a wondrous sense of fulfillment.

XVI

The North American College was, to my mind, a sorry contrast to the hopefulness and spiritual vitality of the renewal. The college was plainly an environment of ambition and its twin, contention. I had friends at the college and enjoyed its frequent banquets and comfortable ambience as much as anyone. But it was not a place where we did much listening to the Spirit, let alone one another.

During my third year I attempted to do something about the college's contentious atmosphere. Together with some fellow seminarians and faculty, I proposed the establishment of a "Roman Forum." The idea was to promote a sense of community through the sharing of views and information. Previous efforts at student government had collided with the seminary's administration and collapsed. The Forum would avoid this pitfall, I thought, since it would not be a decision-making structure. The idea arose from my experience of the charismatic renewal, where I had seen feelings and thoughts candidly expressed in a supportive environment. I thought the same might be possible at the college. To get started, I established a committee with two students from each class and one faculty member. This group would simply select topics for discussion and make the necessary logistical arrangements for community discussions.

While there were several successful meetings of the Forum, the effort met with opposition and suspicion from both faculty and students. Some suggested that the organizers all had "something in common." What that was supposed to be, other than the desire to promote social harmony, I never knew. But it carried a sinister implication.

One topic that interested me concerned the decision to hold the college's retreat at a site other than the college, a move that set that enclosed environment abuzz with discord and rumor. I met with Father William Ward, the college's Spiritual Director, to discuss the possibility of holding a Forum meeting, so that the community could come to an appreciation of how he had arrived at this particular decision. Somehow there were crossed signals between us, because when the topic and date for a

Forum discussion were announced, Father Ward shouted at me from ten feet behind in the corridor, on the way to Mass:

"You are devious! Devious!"

I heard the shouting, but did not comprehend, at first, that it was directed at me. I glanced behind to see what was happening. There was Father Ward — Willie Wonka, as we called him — vigorously marching his short, plump body along the corridor. His soft, round face was harmless. He continued:

"You heard me, Murray. Yeah, you!"

I turned and stared in amazement. Why was this benign man so unaccountably angry with me? He continued:

"We had an understanding. And yet you have gone ahead and scheduled this Forum thing about the retreat."

"Yes, Father, I wanted to bring you in on the discussion. I offered you the opportunity to participate by setting up the discussion for us."

"That's not what I recall. I recall saying that I did not want any such discussion to take place."

"Well, excuse me, Father, but that is not your choice to make. This discussion will give anyone in the house who cares about this issue a chance to express his feelings. It also, if you choose, will give you an opportunity to explain why you have decided that the retreat take place outside of the house. I'm sure you must have your reasons. We would just like to hear them."

"I have written a letter about you," he snorted, "and it is going to be a permanent part of your file."

Father Ward snapped his head back and continued his progress toward the chapel.

The broadside left me momentarily bewildered, though unconcerned. Students at the college regarded the opinions of individual faculty members as bearing only slightly, if at all, on their futures. The administration was thought to be concerned not to offend the bishops back home, who had gone to the trouble of selecting for study in Rome men whom they regarded as some of their finest candidates. I knew that a single letter from one man on the faculty would be seen for what it was, an outburst of personal pique. The bellicosity of Father Ward's opposition to community discussion did, however, underscore my unease about the values and structures that pervaded life at the college. I was not asking that we put the matter to a vote, simply that we have a chance to understand it better. As an American, I could not but believe a good town meeting would be beneficial. But I was not in America. This was Rome.

XVII

The North American College was a privileged setting, and I was not averse to basking in its ambience of privilege myself. Bishops, cardinals, theologians and acclaimed scholars were frequent guests and speakers. In 1973, when four American bishops were elevated to the College of Cardinals, NAC hosted a great banquet. In the corridors, television cameras focused on the new cardinals as they greeted well-wishers and dignitaries. I watched a bright smile fade from the face of Boston's Cardinal Medeiros just as the klieg lights were cut. Here were some of the most accomplished practitioners of ecclesiastical *bella figura*.

Cardinal Wright, who as prefect of the Congregation for the Clergy was the highest-ranking American prelate, was in rare form. His jowled face was a collage of angry red lines and patches. A red sash proudly accented his potbelly. This was a man who knew power and enjoyed it. With grand arrogance, he defied the Italian government's Sunday ban on automobile driving, during the Arab oil embargo, on the basis of his immunity as a Vatican official, while most other curialists meekly observed it. Arriving at the college, where he was greeted by a nimble, fawning Bishop Hickey, Wright grabbed him by the shoulders and, shaking him back and forth, bellowed:

"And how is our dear, beloved rector today?"

Wright belonged in the sixteenth century, where his antics would have been unremarkable. During the banquet, which was served as a buffet, he approached one of my classmates, "Mark," who, with his pastor from the States, was searching for a table. Mark's plate was loaded with cannelloni, meat-filled tubes of pasta, covered with sauce. The powerful cardinal approached the pair and said:

"And what have we here?"

With his bare hand, Wright scooped up some of the cannelloni from Mark's plate and shoved the saucy pasta into his ample mouth. This story was told and retold later, to endless amusement. But our laughter was tinged with unease. This, after all, had not been *bella figura*.

On the numerous occasions when I heard similar tales about the lives of our superiors, I did so with detachment and humor. The church, greater than any individual, had seen worse before, many times. I saw no sense in being so stiff and proper as to divorce myself from the church over such matters. I was, in fact, as vulnerable as any other seminarian to ambition. At the same time, I lacked any genuine connection to ecclesiastical power. I had no patron, no influential priest or bishop to watch out for me. I had no meaningful personal acquaintance even with my own bishop.

More than that, however, I had no patience for the conformity that careerism of any kind requires. I was too much the Bardian free spirit to be truly useful in the church's bureaucratic settings. Through the charismatic movement's vision of church, I had become much more interested in shaping the future of the Catholic Church than in allowing its deadening structures to shape me.

Nevertheless, I felt a strong, kindred spirit with what we at the college affectionately called "Romanitas." *Romanitas* is the mythic spirit of Rome. This means ecclesiastical Rome, of course, but always with an eye toward the broader social environment in which it is set. Romanitas is an ambiguous term that nevertheless encompasses a number of easily identifiable attitudes. It means, for example, having a special reverence for the Holy Father and keeping abreast of the themes that are currently being emphasized in papal allocutions and Vatican documents. But Romanitas also means not taking any of this *too* seriously and recognizing that church laws can be set aside for compassionate, "pastoral" reasons. An education in Rome is valuable, in the eyes of many students and alumni of the college, not so much on account of the specific information one learns, as for the general outlook that one acquires. Charismatic speaker-in-tongues though I may have been, I also acquired, during these years, a profound love for Rome and respect for the papal ministry.

XVIII

I was ordained a deacon by Bishop Hickey on May 9, 1974. I returned to Washington for the requisite deacon summer, a brief internship in a parish. Sacred Heart Parish, in Bowie, Maryland, a blue-collar community in Prince Georges County, was selected for my assignment. In fact, I was picked for Sacred Heart by one of its associate pastors, Father Tom Wells, a friend from Christ the King Seminary. Tom, a friendly, ever-laughing extravert, remembered the good times we had enjoyed in seminary, as well as my strident conservatism, an outlook which he and the pastor of Sacred Heart, Father John Hogan, shared. My views had seasoned considerably, but I was still able to make appropriately conservative noises, from time to time, decrying simplistic, "kicky-relevant" Catholic periodicals, the alleged consecration of a jelly roll as Eucharist at a midwestern seminary, and appalling "folk music" at Mass, to their endless delight.

Sacred Heart should have been a breeze, given these circumstances. My summer there, however, followed by a stay in Ann Arbor, convinced me I should not continue on to the priesthood. It was not that anything went terribly wrong in Bowie. I preached at Sunday Masses somewhat successfully, though certainly too long, a typical beginner's mistake, took communion to the sick and joined in a parish festival. The problem was that this was not me.

Sacred Heart was my first meaningful exposure to Catholic parish life. Instead of the exuberance I had found in the charismatic renewal, I found a consensus, shared by clergy and laity alike, that worship should be brief and to the point so that everyone might get on with the real stuff of life — barbecues, televised sports and trips to the beach. Instead of a hunger for the scriptures and the guidance of the Spirit, I found contented minds tightly shut in the certainty that they — or their leaders, anyway — already had the truth. There, I was a "penguin in the tropics," I explained a few weeks later to Washington's new Archbishop, William Baum.

In early October, I wrote a letter to Archbishop Baum in which I stated that I wished to remain a deacon, but not to continue on to the priesthood. I did, indeed, believe that I had a vocation to serve the church, but I felt that my form of service had to be somehow unconventional and outside of the usual framework of parochial ministry. By remaining a deacon, I would have the grace of holy orders and an official status that would enable me to *collaborate* with the Archdiocese. I was thinking in terms that are quite foreign to modern Catholicism. I wanted to function as a free agent within the church. Since the center of gravity in my life, at this time, was the charismatic renewal, I believed that my calling had something to do with integrating the insights of charismatic spirituality into mainstream Catholicism.

Weeks passed, however, with no response from the Archdiocese. During this time I prayed and studied. I imagined what my life would be in Washington. Would I be able to earn enough money to support myself in ministry? I felt a certain satisfaction that by refusing priestly ordination I was showing a kind of solidarity with women, especially women religious, who could not be ordained. I do not know how that thought came to mind, because I had not yet developed much of a sensitivity to questions regarding the status of women in the church. In Lumen Christi, however, I had come to know several women well, both secular and religious, and came to accept the need for the church to welcome fully women's gifts and insights.

As my wait for some word from Washington — from Father Curlin — stretched on, I watched as classmates enrolled in the various universities and started into a new semester. I had time on my hands and took long walks in the city. One of the places I visited was the Vatican's Gallery of Modern Religious Art, which Pope Paul VI established in a newly renovated section of the Apostolic Palace. It being late October, there were few tourists and I had this lovely museum almost to myself. Pope Paul had long cultivated a personal interest in modern art. What impressed me as I went from room to room was how radically these works of art and the freedom of spirit and individuality they express contrast with the life, decor, costumes and styles of the Vatican, which generally hark back to the Renaissance.

Pope Paul had essentially spent his life in the service of the Vatican. He had been present in 1929 as a young priest for the signing of the Lateran Pact with Mussolini. I wondered what his predecessors, Pius XI and stern Pius XII, would have thought of his fondness for modernity. In any event, his interest had finally blossomed into a worthy addition to the Vatican Museums. For me, the gallery signified hope. If a career curialist such as Paul VI can also have a side that is this open to the world, I reasoned, then there must be many seeds of change in the church, even where they are least expected. Because of this, I rethought my decision to refuse priestly ordination and decided to remain and complete the fourth year of theology. I telephoned Curlin to inform him that I would remain. He said I might not be ordained at the usual time, but that would be the Archbishop's decision.

XIX

It happened that 1975 was to be a "Holy Year." Holy Years are normally designated every twenty-five years in the Catholic Church. They are supposed to be times of increased devotion and pilgrimage, especially to

Rome. Two events in the upcoming Holy Year would intimately involve me. The first was an international conference of the Catholic charismatic renewal. The second was an ordination to the priesthood of candidates from the various colleges in Rome, as well as others who journeyed to Rome for the occasion.

The Vatican itself took an interest and even a supportive role in enabling the charismatic conference to take place. There was some confusion and bickering that had caused initial plans to break down. Yes, even the charismatic renewal, I learned, was subject to human failings. A call came to the college from a "very high source" in the Vatican, I was told, with instructions that John Smith, David Carey, someone outside of the college and myself were to be the core of a new organizing committee. I was told that our names had somehow "surfaced" on a pad on Archbishop Giovanni Bennelli's desk. Bennelli was widely thought to be the most influential man in the Vatican, outside of the Holy Father himself. He was mentioned often as one who was papabile, a likely candidate for the papacy, although not as successor to Pope Paul himself. My involvement in the charismatic renewal suddenly gained a respectability for the college's faculty that it had not previously enjoyed. The faculty had declined in the past to accept this activity even as an "apostolate," that is, as pastoral work that qualified as part of my training. Their wariness stemmed, no doubt, from its novelty. It did not fit within conventional categories. Their reservations were swiftly set aside after the phone call from the Vatican. Indeed, the Vice Rector, Charlie Kelly, graciously made his own suite available for our meeting with Father Kilian McDonald, the point man from the United States.

The conference, attended by some ten thousand persons, took place on the grounds of the Catacombs of Saint Callixtus on the outskirts of Rome's historic center. The culmination of the weekend was a Mass at the high altar of St. Peter's Basilica on Pentecost Sunday, followed by an audience with Pope Paul VI. It was, in every sense, a charismatic Mass, complete with prophecies, singing in tongues and spontaneous dancing "in the spirit." Yet it was also taking place at the epicenter of Roman Catholicism. It seemed a dream come true! Reform was possible! In his remarks, Pope Paul declared that faith is not only in a teaching received, but is also a lived experience. His words confirmed what, for me, had been the renewal's attraction, its insistence on faith's experiential dimension. The church, at its highest, hierarchical level acknowledged the need for the reform that the charismatic renewal promised.

I had seen a lot since my arrival at St. Peter's nearly four years before. When I first arrived, there had been only a tiny prayer group that had little contact with the charismatic renewal in the United States. Now, four years later, St. Peter's Basilica was ours, for the moment. Cardinal Suenens, the Archbishop of Malines-Brussels, and a staunch supporter of the renewal, joined Pope Paul at the altar in a mutual embrace, a gesture that ended a public rift of several years' duration. It seemed that reform and healing were taking place before our eyes. It seemed that the seeds of change were sprouting. It seemed that the two great loves of my life, Rome and the charismatic renewal, had embraced and kissed under the blue sky of an Italian summer day.

The second great event of the Holy Year, for me, was my ordination to the priesthood. Archbishop Baum and the college faculty had somehow set aside whatever reservations my attempted departure the previous fall might have generated.

The ceremony took place at the end of June on the Solemnity of Saint Peter and Saint Paul. This happens to be the patronal feast of Rome, where both of these men were martyred. It was also the twelfth anniversary of the installation of Paul VI as pope. The celebration was held on the steps of St. Peter's Basilica, under a deep blue evening sky. Not even the slightest puff of cloud drifted past to offset that demanding infinity of darkening blue. Three hundred fifty-nine white-robed men from around the world were ordained together. St. Peter's Square was packed. As with the charismatic conference, there was a sense of fulfillment. I was ordained by a man I had admired for years. His example had inspired me to go forward even when I faltered. I was very much at home in St. Peter's. What better, more auspicious circumstance could I have found in which to be ordained?

I celebrated my first Mass, the following day, at the ancient church of San Giorgio in Velabro. I was drawn to its stark, irregular stone walls and thirteenth century, canopied, stone altar. San Giorgio was the titular church of Cardinal Newman. Its patron, St. George, recalled the Episcopal church in which I had been raised. I was unquestionably Roman, but the Anglican roots were still vital. Generous clouds of incense enfolded the joyful worship of the small gathering of friends, professors and my parents.

CHAPTER 3

IDENTITIES

I

"Paul, how very good to see you!" Cardinal Baum, extending his thin, elegant hand, greeted me in a soft, tranquil voice.

It felt good to be there. I had enjoyed the brief meetings I had had with Baum since his appointment as Washington's archbishop, two years before. He is a slight man. The brightness of his eyes is magnified by the sharp angularity of his bald head. His manner is pensive, faintly hesitant. On sojourns to Rome, his companion, Monsignor Jim Gillen, provided a counterpoint of boisterous extraversion that bordered on comic relief. Although Baum was unquestionably in charge, Jim did the talking.

I sensed in Baum a kindred spirit. We shared, for one thing, a similar sense of humor, picking up on life's incongruities, the subtle disparities between appearance and reality. Several chancery officials remarked that Baum and I had the same laugh, the same tendency to chuckle quietly at observations that we kept to ourselves. Beyond that, Baum spoke passionately of his commitment to church renewal at every level. He appeared open to radical change, even hungry for it, but intelligent change, change grounded in a deep, purposeful vision of the church. He was well known for his work in ecumenism, which interested me, because I sought to maintain some connection to the Anglican church.

"Thank you, Archbishop, it is good to be home," I said, gently clasping his hand.

I sat on the deeply cushioned couch to which he gestured, while he sank into a commodious chair. The desk had been placed before a large, arched window that looked out onto Rhode Island Avenue. Very little noise filtered through and the view was partially screened by a blind and heavy drapes. It was hard to imagine that practical concerns, details about the running of a medium-sized diocese, ever intruded on this room's regal peace.

"Are you ready to get to work?" Baum asked cheerfully.

"I have been looking forward to this for many years. I can hardly believe I have reached this point. Yes, your Eminence, I am more than ready."

"Good. Before I give you your assignment though, I want to tell you one thing, Paul. I always say this to newly ordained men. You will always be a good priest, if you pray. And you will never be a good priest, if you do not."

"Yes, I know that to be true. As you know, Archbishop, I have been deeply involved for some years in the charismatic renewal. I have learned much from it, especially a love for prayer. I also enjoy the Divine Office and praying the psalms, throughout the day. As my confessor in Rome used to say, the psalms are a 'window on God.'"

"Yes, I like that image," Baum said. "I know you are here for your assignment, so I will give it to you now."

The Cardinal got up from his chair, dialed the intercom, and spoke briefly to someone on the other end of the line. After a moment, he hung up the phone and sat down. We continued to chat. The phone rang. Baum got up again, turning toward the window, and spoke into the receiver. He hung up the phone and sat back down.

"Paul, I'm sorry. We do not, as yet, have an assignment for you. I will call you in a few days."

The announcement of a priest's first assignment is a defining moment. It is one of the rites of passage in clerical life about which stories are told and repeated. Many times, in seminary, I had heard about bishops who insisted on giving the newly ordained word of their first assignment themselves, sometimes immediately after, never *before*, the ordination ceremony. The giving of the first assignment expresses the complete dependence of the priest on his bishop and the idea that ordination subjects a man to the possibility of being given *any* assignment the bishop chooses.

For my bishop not to have an assignment ready for me a week after ordination left me bewildered and a bit empty. Surely they knew I was coming home. Yet somehow, once again, I had been overlooked, much as I had been when Bill Curlin failed to answer my letter declining priestly ordination. I was experiencing something about the Archdiocese that transcended the quirks of Curlin's personality. A continuity, a pattern of sorts was becoming evident, although even then, as I waited some three weeks for word of my assignment, I failed to admit this to myself. The reluctance to admit that something-is-wrong-with-this-picture would, however, vanish, a few months into my first assignment as an assistant pastor at St. Jane Frances de Chantal Parish in Bethesda, Maryland.

The pastor of de Chantal was Monsignor Martin Christopher. Marty was a stern, remote man in his fifties. His gentle side, well hidden, was reserved for children. He enjoyed visiting classes in the parish school and making the children laugh. Otherwise, he was reclusive and unemotional. His secretary, Ela, a Cuban refugee, had worked for him when he was Vocations Director of the Archdiocese and, in an unusual display of loyalty (or mutual support), moved with him to his successive assignments.

Ela more than made up for any deficits in Marty's emotional qualities. She was easily excitable, especially concerning anything that might intrude on the serene life that they enjoyed together. She was his instrument for dealing with the outside world, which made it possible for him to disappear for much of the day into his modest, second floor suite.

Within a month of my arrival at de Chantal, I had a confrontation with Ela that told me in no uncertain terms that in the pecking order of that household I was her inferior. On Wednesdays, the cook's day off, Ela prepared gourmet feasts of expensive meats and seafood that the cook, Hedwig, would never have been permitted to touch. I had happily partici-pated in a couple of these grand feasts. Then, one Wednesday morning, Ela stopped me as I was heading upstairs:

"Father, what are your plans for dinner?"

"I have no particular plans," I said, puzzled. "I will eat dinner here."

"Will you then be joining Monsignor and me for dinner?"

"Yes, I will," I said, my confusion increasing.

"I ask that, Father, because I prepare these dinners on Wednesday evenings for Monsignor. It is something that I do for him. It is not part of my job. I wanted you to understand that."

"Yes, Ela, I see. Very well, I will not be joining you and Monsignor at your table. Count me out. I will make other plans."

I angrily returned to my room. On Wednesdays, it seemed, the dinner table was *their* table. I was damned if I would consent to being treated as a guest in my own house. Or was that not the point? This was not in any sense my house. I had no house. This was Marty Christopher's house. And the pastor's ownership was not communicated to me directly, but indirectly, through Ela. Gradually it became clear to me that the relationship between pastor and secretary had a personal dimension that was analogous to marriage. I drew from this no inference that their relationship was sexual. It was, however, an exclusive relationship that contributed to the distancing of Marty from his associates. I was an outsider.

On one occasion I saw Marty leave the rectory with luggage, which he placed in his car. As he drove off, I asked where he was going and Ela remarked that he had just left for a vacation in Mexico. That was the first I had heard of it. On another occasion, workmen arrived in the morning and ripped out all the carpeting on the first floor, causing a significant disruption to life and work. New carpeting had been ordered. Ela knew all about it. I, of course, had not been informed.

The other assistant, Donald Brice, was not reclusive, but almost totally absent from the rectory. Donald was an outstanding priest, who was much loved and even adored, by parishioners. He served as chaplain of Suburban Hospital, where he spent at least part of every day. Because he was close to many of the families, he had the lion's share of weddings and funerals. Donald was someone with whom I could speak with a good measure of openness, although the opportunities for doing so were few. He was gone throughout the day and dined with us, at most, once a week, on Saturday evenings.

There was also a retired priest, Eddie, who maintained a residence at de Chantal, but was there no more than one or two nights a week. Eddie was a kind man who was one of the few priests in the Archdiocese to hold a doctorate in a non-theological field. His was in education. On a few occasions, he fell in his rooms, while drinking. He called for me to help him up — no easy task, as Eddie was a big man and, having suffered a stroke, his weight was largely dead weight.

Such was the social environment in which I now began to understand and establish myself as a priest. The rectory was a large, gray stone house set well back from the road, on an ample, arboreous piece of land. Behind the rectory, an elderly Polish couple that had been displaced during the Second World War lived in a small house. They had found refuge and work at de Chantal: the wife as cook, the husband as groundskeeper.

By eastern U.S. standards, de Chantal was a typical, suburban parish. Its complex included an elementary school run by the Sisters of Charity of Greensburg. Their order was founded in the early nineteenth century by St. Elizabeth Ann Seton, a convert from the Episcopal Church. The order's numbers had declined to the point where, by the mid-1970s, the school was staffed by no more than a half-dozen sisters. These lived in a convent, a bare, functional building at the rear of the parish complex.

The church itself had been erected as a transitional structure: the cinder block building was to serve eventually as the school gymnasium, when the parish could afford to erect a "real" church. Stained glass was added during my first year, a sign that economic realities had rendered the original plans obsolete.

This was my first extensive exposure to Catholic parochial life. I soon realized that I was still a product of attitudes inculcated during childhood about "church." My expectations were contradicted in several ways. De Chantal was busy in a way that the church of my youth, St. George's, had never been. For two of the Sunday Mass times, Masses were offered simultaneously in the main church and downstairs, in the basement, where a makeshift altar and folding chairs were set up for the purpose.

Many parishioners arrived late for Mass, during the readings. The Mass consists of two main parts: the Liturgy of the Word, which generally includes scripture readings from the Old Testament, the Epistles and the Gospels, and the homily, comments and teachings based on the readings; and the Liturgy of the Eucharist, in which bread and wine are consecrated to become the body and blood of Christ and distributed as communion to the people. That a few persons might have difficulties leaving home on time, especially where children are involved, is understandable. What I found, however, was that consistently as much as twenty to twenty-five percent of the congregation arrived during the scripture readings and homily, often with children trailing behind, and, to find seating, many were compelled to walk to the front pews. All of this tended to put us in an atmosphere of ongoing distraction that said, in effect, that expectations that the scripture readings and homily might somehow actually matter were low indeed.

The challenge of proclaiming God's Word in this setting was compounded by a problem that I have found in every parish where I have served: the sound system was poor. When, to the general distraction created by latecomers, one adds the noise of crying babies and restless toddlers, communication from the sanctuary to the congregation is heavily burdened. The poor sound system, the late arrivals and the noisy toddler whose running back and forth in the aisle seems not even to be noticed by the parents, are not accidental occurrences. They are part of the warp and woof of Catholic parochial life, especially in the suburbs, where the didactic and intellectual aspects of church life are not accorded much importance. The real focus of Mass participation is on the Eucharist, especially the reception of holy communion. Nearly everyone receives communion, and congregants' demeanors during the prayer of consecration are more serious than during the Liturgy of the Word. But the reception of communion is not followed, as might be expected (and as the *Sacramentary* recommends), by silent reflection. Many communicants leave immediately, to head for their cars, without waiting for the final blessing. It is clear that receiving communion matters to them. Suburban Catholics want some contact with God, but preferably in a convenient, brief and well-circumscribed moment that does not otherwise interfere with the active pace of their lives.

At de Chantal I learned that the parish priest is valued, above all, for his sacramental power to confect the Eucharist. I was disappointed that Catholicism's rich spiritual and intellectual heritage, which was crucial to my attraction to the Roman church, held little interest there. Moreover, as a charismatic, I was eager to communicate to Catholics the transformation of their lives and of the church that would be possible by opening themselves to the experience of the Holy Spirit. A few welcomed my efforts enthusiastically, but the overall environment was discouraging.

I did take steps to liven things up at one of the drab, basement Masses. My purpose was to build community and, of course, I had the vivid example of The Word of God of Ann Arbor in mind. I knew I could not simply launch a charismatic Mass at de Chantal, complete with prophecy and tongues. The pastor would not have consented to that. Instead, I pulled together a core of parishioners who did want more out of church. This group took a degree of ownership over what we dubbed, "The Rejoice! Mass," which featured guitar-based music. The Rejoice! Mass offered refreshments afterwards — coffee, tea, punch and cookies — to encourage parishioners to linger and get acquainted.

To his credit, Marty Christopher gave permission for all of this, although it was completely foreign to his experience. In the Episcopal Church, I had known coffee hour after the Sunday service as a familiar, indeed, ubiquitous feature of parish life. Several months into this new effort, Marty suggested that the real reason people remained after The Rejoice! Mass was to get free refreshments. I said nothing, but considered the remark emblematic of the differing perspectives we held about the church and the meaning of pastoral work. I wanted to build a community of persons who would take responsibility for the parish and care about each other. Marty wanted a sacrament dispensary where the priest was unambiguously in charge.

II

Six months after my arrival at de Chantal I was depressed. I continued to perform my duties adequately, but I was troubled that I had somehow gotten into the wrong place — a "penguin in the tropics." I wrote of this period's wastefulness to a friend: "hours of drift, hours of despair, hours of sleeping in the daytime, hours of idle, TV viewing, even in the afternoon, hours of smoking, drinking coffee, snacking on milk, cheese and crackers, cookies, hours of worrying about my weight, hours of feeling unable to fight my way out of a paper bag, hours of looking at the walls of my room as simply preliminary to the walls of my coffin."

I was unable to envisage an alternative future for myself. My monthly salary of $250 (plus $90 car allowance) was not enough even to begin to look at tuition, should I want to go back to school. I felt powerless and alone.

It occurred to me that a sexual liaison might help. A dutiful Catholic, I considered all genital activity outside of marriage to be gravely sinful. Sin, however, could always be forgiven. What I was experiencing at de Chantal, especially the chronic loneliness, was hell.

I knew that there was a "homosexual subculture" somewhere in metropolitan Washington, but I had little idea where to find it or what it would be like. I decided to go back to my last point of contact, a newsstand on Fifteenth Street, across from the Treasury building, where, as a teenager, I had once fled a man in hot pursuit. Perhaps now, I thought, I would not flee. I drove downtown and parked several blocks away, so as not to be too close to the newsstand, in case I should be followed again. Full of anxieties and misery, I entered the narrow store. The male magazines were still there, but nothing that would connect me to the local community. I tried another store, where I found a rough, newsprint publication that looked promising. I bought it and took it back to my car. As I sat in my Chevy Nova, I removed the publication from the brown paper bag and glanced through it. It had some pictures of fully naked men, unlike the male magazines I had seen ten years before, where the models were clad in posing straps. I was very excited and, as I drove back to the rectory, glanced down at the paper every chance I had. From that publication I learned of "Lambda Rising," a gay bookstore on Nineteenth Street in northwest Washington.

Once again, I journeyed into Washington. I found the address, but wondered if I would have the courage to climb the steps and enter. I watched as two young men left, one of them having purchased a magazine. They were attractive and appeared happy and very normal. I felt that if those were the type of people who go to Lambda Rising it would be okay for me, as well. I entered the tiny shop, where I found a small selection of magazines and books. A pleasant aroma of incense wafted in from a tobacco and pipe shop across the hall, imparting a touch of 1960s counter culture to the place that I found reassuring. I purchased a publication, *Just Us*, about Washington's gay community. As I left, a panhandler scornfully remarked that I had just wasted whatever money I spent in there. My heart knew differently. I had just taken a significant few steps toward my true self.

The first gay club I entered was GT's, in Washington's Cleveland Park neighborhood. I circled the block several times, before finding the courage to park my car and get past the front door. Beyond the front door there was a set of swinging doors. I pushed past these and entered. As the doors swung shut behind me, I surveyed the bar and tables where some thirty men variously sipped their drinks, chatted and gazed about. I felt an immediate and unfamiliar calm. I knew I was with my own. A lifelong habit of repressing my gaze, of trying not to notice attractive men, of hiding suddenly became unnecessary.

Years later a friend called this moment an "epiphany," as I related the story. "Epiphany" sounds right, because it was indeed a manifestation to me of a truth about myself that I had never seen in that light. Before, I had known myself to have homosexual "tendencies." I felt very much alone in that, although I knew others had such tendencies as well. Now I began to see myself for the first time as "gay," part of a community of persons, *persons like myself!* I was not alone! Walking inside GT's did not miraculously release me from years of internalized homophobia and self-hatred, but it was a beginning.

I knew very little about how to interact in this new world. My first night at GT's, where I went only a few times, was a bit awkward. I sat alone at a table, rather than at the bar. A man approached. He had the look of one who had spent far too many nights in such places. He was middle-aged. His face was etched with a look of sexual hunger. I desperately hoped he would not try to speak to me. He did:

"You're new here."

"Yes."

"Hi, my name's Sam."

"I'm Paul," I shook his extended hand.

"Good to meet you, Paul. May I sit down?"

"Sure, go ahead."

"So what are you up to tonight?"

"Nothing much. I just found the address of this bar and decided to come in here."

"Where else have you been?"

"Nowhere. This is my first time inside a gay bar."

"Can I get you a drink?"

"No, thanks anyway. I'm just wondering how people meet."

"Well, I have found that a twenty year old guy gets a twenty year old guy. A thirty-year-old guy gets a thirty-year-old guy. And a forty year old guy gets a forty year old guy."

"I see. And how old do you think I am?"

"I'd say about forty."

Forty! Ouch! A look of anger crossed his face. He knew that I was not interested in him. He knew that age was a factor. That was my first lesson in the sexual combat zone. My interlocutor was a bitter man. Would I be like him some day? I belonged in GT's. I had no doubt about that. But I had much to learn about this world and its ways.

A few weeks later I made my way to St. Mary's Chapel at Georgetown University's School of Nursing, where a Mass for gay Catholics was to take place. It was sponsored by Dignity/Washington, the local chapter of a national organization of gay and lesbian Catholics. In the foyer I met a man who spoke and gestured so much like myself that I began to wonder whether he might be mimicking me. I soon realized, however, that this was a foolish bit of self-preoccupation. Research shows that gay men form a linguistic community that shares many communicational techniques and styles, as well as jargon. Since I was a novice to "queens' English," it is hard to see how I could have learned these patterns, but such experiences confirmed my sense that I was, at long last, among my own.

Dignity drew many Catholics who were exceptionally well informed about their faith. To face squarely the contradiction between official church teaching and the reality of one's own life as being both gay and spiritual, without giving up on either sexuality or religion, requires inner strength. Bucky, for example, an articulate, well-read man in his twenties was a member of an interfaith community of peace activists who also provided food, housing and medical care for the poor. Bucky showed me his personal prayer room where he retreated each day, on the top floor of a dilapidated town house from which used clothing was distributed. The room was dark, except for one votive candle that illuminated an icon of the blessed mother holding the infant Jesus in her arms. Bucky was, at the same time, a very sexual man who spoke with ease and tenderness of his relationships. He described with reverence experiences of even one-time sexual encounters with pick-ups from the Eagle, a nearby leather bar.

My explorations of Washington's gay community included all of its clubs, the principal sites of gay male socialization. My favorite was a disco and restaurant, "The Court Jester," a few blocks north of Georgetown on Wisconsin Avenue. I took to disco music right away, with its roots in rhythm and blues. Although shy and unsure of myself in the disco, I soon made friends and found myself out on the dance floor frequently.

My first sexual encounters as an adult were with men I met at the Court Jester. The first was a slim, Vietnamese man. He took me to his room in a nearby group house, where he turned on the radio for some background music to accompany our erotic endeavors. Midway through the news came on and I started laughing. My companion was bewildered, but I found myself caught up in the irony of the newscaster's grave announcements providing counterpoint to our activities in bed. This lovely man was very kind and patient about my inexperience.

I also had sex with John, an educator employed by the Department of Health, Education and Welfare. John wanted to be rough, but was respectful of my limits. He and his circle of friends became, for a time, my friends, as well. I was open to them about being a priest. This never seemed to shock anyone. Many gay men, I learned, have known priests, either as lovers or close friends.

III

His name was Larry. He was twenty-one, had a broad, captivating smile, curly blonde hair and a gorgeous, swimmer's build. The first moment I saw him was when he entered the Court Jester with a group that included, I was later to learn, his mother, Ingrid. Larry wore a white, loose-fitting silk shirt that was unbuttoned most of the way down his hairless chest. I was dazzled.

Larry spent most of his time on the dance floor — with or without a partner. He was clearly the master of that world. He moved his hips and spun and gyrated about with an unfailing sense of rhythm and balance. At times, other dancers stood aside to admire the performance. Off the dance floor, he moved easily through the crowd, striking up conversations instantly with whomever he approached.

I wanted desperately to meet him. But how could I ever hope to cross the divide between us? Larry was wild and accepting of his sexuality in a way that I could hardly imagine. His friends — the group with which he entered the Court Jester, the night when I first saw him – were strangely aloof. Who were they? Who were they to him? What kind of life did he lead? My heart was beating rapidly and would again, in future weeks, whenever I saw him. As I gazed on him, the distance between us seemed ever more impassable. Our worlds were so different. Even if I somehow found the courage to approach this Adonis, what could I possibly offer that would be of interest?

Not knowing his name, I mentally dubbed him "Angelique." Each time I went to the Court Jester, I hoped I would see him. Months passed. I noticed that I usually saw him on nights when there was a crescent moon. Or was I imagining this? On those all too infrequent occasions when he did show up, my heart would hammer away and I would never cease to absorb, at a distance, as much detail as possible.

Eventually, I worked up the nerve to pray to meet him. Soon after, the opportunity presented itself, when I was driving from Georgetown to the Court Jester. I spotted Angelique hitchhiking up Wisconsin Avenue. He was wearing a white, hooded sweatshirt and looked as wild/angelic as ever. I stopped the car and let him in. He introduced himself:

"Hi, I'm Larry."

"Good to meet you, I'm Paul."

"Could you drop me off a few blocks up the hill, near Good Guys?"

Good Guys was a straight bar next to the Court Jester.

"I'll be happy to let you off at the Court Jester, Larry. That's where I'm headed."

"Oh, you know me," he laughed.

"Well, we haven't met before, but I've seen you there. You are an incredible dancer."

"That's what I do for a living. I dance at Chesapeake House."

"Well, you must work very hard at it."

"Oh, yes!" he gushed, delighted by my interest. "I have dance records at home and practice all day."

"And that's all you do? You don't work during the day?"

"Well, I've thought about other things. Like hair styling. But that takes training and I don't have the money for it."

I pulled up in front of the Court Jester's canopied entrance. After getting out, Larry turned and leaned inside the car.

"Thanks for the ride, Paul. You coming in?"

"Yes."

"Then I'll see you inside," he declared brightly

I drove on, in search of a parking space.

To my disappointment, we did not reconnect, once I entered the club. Larry was absorbed by his usual activities: dancing and working the crowd. Later, after leaving, I found him trying, once again, to hitch a ride. I offered to drive him home, which, I gathered from his vague and intoxicated speech, was somewhere north, in the general direction in which I was heading. Once inside my car, he laid his head on my lap and went to sleep. This was, to say the least, a distraction from driving. I loved the intimate contact, the touch of the soft, blond hair that I had long admired from a distance, his head nestled against my abdomen. I was concerned for his safety. A sudden stop would have slammed his head against the steering wheel. Obviously this was not the kind of consideration to which Larry was likely to give much weight. I left it alone, in any case, because he was somehow in charge. He knew what he wanted to do. I patted his head as we drove along, never having imagined I would actually have the opportunity to examine those golden locks so closely.

As we entered Bethesda, I tried to rouse Larry in order to get specific directions, but was able to elicit only inarticulate grunts. As I tried to rouse him to the point of making sense, I remembered having prayed to meet him. I did not regret meeting this person for whom my heart had hammered away, but I did consider that when we ask God for something, we had better mean it. I stopped to buy coffee and doughnuts. When I returned to the car, Larry sat up. Handing him a cup of coffee, I said:

"Here, Larry, this should wake you up. Be careful, it's hot."

We sat in silence for a few minutes, sipping coffee and enjoying glazed doughnuts. The simple intimacy of sharing food with someone in a car late at night was something I had not experienced in many years, not since being with Alex at Bard. It felt good. But what next? I said:

"Larry, where am I taking you?"

"Let's go to your house."

"No, we can't do that. I live with people."

"Are you married?"

"No, I'm not married, but I live with people who wouldn't understand, if I brought you in to stay with me."

At that, Larry sat erect and became alert. Had the sleepiness been a ploy? Gesturing with his hand the direction in which we needed to go, he said:

"I live in Silver Spring, near Georgia Avenue. Can you take me that far?"

"That's not far. It's only ten minutes from here. Of course, I'll take you home."

As I drove, Larry pointed to a small cross that I had mounted on the dashboard. He asked:

"How long have you been with the church of Christ?"

"All my life. In fact, Larry, I'm a Catholic priest. That's why I can't take you home. I live with other priests."

"I go to church sometimes, but when I go it's to an Episcopal church."

"I was raised Episcopalian, so I know that church very well."

"You turn here."

He directed me to a house on a dead-end block near train tracks.

Larry invited me in. I was nervous, but not about to refuse. I followed him up the driveway to the back of the house, where we went down a few steps that were cluttered with toys, a scooter topped by a Donald Duck face, and other, nondescript debris. We entered the main room of the basement apartment.

"Hi, Mom!" Larry greeted the woman I had seen with him at the Court Jester. "You'd be real proud of me. I didn't get syphilis or gonorrhea this evening!"

She was not fazed by his remark. A beautiful, middle-aged redhead, she eyed me carefully. The second person in the room was a burly young man of angry mien whom I had also seen at the club. He usually danced with his shirt off, sweating profusely.

Larry introduced me to his mother and roommate and explained that I was a priest. I felt uncomfortable and decided on a quick exit. I was pleased, however, that Larry had allowed me this glimpse into his personal life — his extraordinary openness with his mother, the poverty in which they lived, the presence of this roommate. How did such grace and beauty emerge from squalor? On the other hand, Larry's mother was herself a beautiful woman who appeared too sophisticated for such mean circumstances. An immigrant from Lithuania, she worked for a human rights organization. She did not speak of the past and, I sensed, had intentionally separated herself from it.

Larry and I became better acquainted over the next few months. He explained that the Chesapeake House, where he danced, featured nude male dancers at night. I never did see him perform, because that was work and he preferred to keep his friendships and personal life separate from it.

Larry admitted that he was a hustler and that he sometimes even rolled guys who picked him up for their wallet. He wanted to get his life on a more positive track. He had already begun to feel the shock of aging, he said, when, the year before, he reached the ripe age of twenty!

Our relationship was not sexual. Once, when I was driving him home, Larry said that when it came to sex, he was too shy to initiate anything. I also was shy. The reason that I did not pick up on his implicit invitation, however, probably had more to do with fear. In part, it was the fear of contracting some sexually transmitted disease, given Larry's means of livelihood. The deeper fear, I suspect, was of sexual intimacy. Could I open up to someone I cared about deeply and have a sexual relationship? One-night stands were less demanding.

Any concerns about the sinfulness of an active sex life that lingered were on the level of psychological restraint, rather than intellectual conviction. My theological training provided me with sufficient analytical tools to see that the church's condemnation of homosexual behavior was founded on faulty assumptions and an inadequate, impersonal understanding of human sexuality. I had, however, so interiorized a sense of sex — heterosexual or homosexual — outside of marriage as wrong that many obstacles remained to be overcome, if I was ever to enter a satisfying, sexual relationship.

Part of what held me back, as well, was my sense of responsibility for Larry, both personally and pastorally. He revealed that his mother practiced witchcraft. She was, he claimed, a priestess in the Church of Wicca. He thought she was imperiling her soul. This was what had crossed his mind, when he pointed out the cross on my dashboard.

My concern, however, was for Larry himself. I wanted him to get out of hustling. Eventually he met an older man with money, who agreed to pay for his training as a hair stylist. I was envious of the older man, Larry's "sugar daddy," but pleased that Larry was beginning to do something productive. He called me the "rock" in his life. I was proud to be that for him. He said that he prayed for me and I had little doubt that Christ was especially close to his heart and was delighted by his prayers. For his part, Larry introduced me to neglected parts of my own humanity. He taught me to dance and I found him an inspired teacher. We even developed a kind of routine and, unlike most other disco dancers, held hands most of the time, much to my delight. His hands were firm and sweaty. They were hands that I trusted.

During this time, parishioners at de Chantal noticed changes in me. I was more relaxed. Happier. More human. My sermons improved. I could hardly disclose the reasons for these changes, but took the encouraging remarks as a sign that I was on the right track.

Self-acceptance as a sexual being naturally entailed a corresponding intellectual adjustment. Knowing that the church had married priests throughout its first millennium and that mandatory celibacy had been imposed, in the face of much opposition and open defiance, beginning in the eleventh century, it was easy to see that nothing doctrinal was at stake. Of course, as a gay man, marriage was not at issue, since it was not even an option. But six years of seminary training and life, now, in the shadow of an emotionally withered pastor who had long lived in some kind of personal symbiosis with his secretary, inspired no confidence that a sexually ascetic life would prove spiritually fruitful.

IV

I found myself, therefore, negotiating life between two worlds: institutional Catholicism and the gay community. While I sealed out the gay world from my life in the parish, the fact that I was a priest followed me into the gay community. I became more involved in Dignity, periodically presiding at Mass. The gay movement impressed me as a morally courageous effort and I was pleased by the opportunity to support it through my religious role. Lambda Rising, relocated by this time to a larger site on S Street, expanded its selection of books to reflect the burgeoning selection of literature generated by the gay liberation movement, including theological and spiritual writings. I decided to attend Dignity/USA's 1977 convention in Chicago.

I wanted to come out to my family. I wanted to share with them the enthusiasm I felt about my newfound self-acceptance and the gay movement. But how to make this disclosure? Several times I had intended to say something, but could not find the words. I even considered making the announcement during a family gathering in a restaurant. Somehow I held back, intuitively understanding better than I understood rationally, just how difficult this would be. To my chagrin, Reba expressed admiration for Anita Bryant's campaign to repeal Dade County's gay rights ordinance. Her brief remark carried far more significance for me than she could have realized. As a result, I decided not to come out to her at that time.

I made the disclosure to my parents over dinner at home, after rehearsing my remarks during the drive there. As we were finishing up the main course, I said:

"During my vacation this summer, I will fly to Chicago, because there is a convention there that I want to attend. It is the national convention of Dignity, an organization of gay Catholics."

"Why would you want to go to that?" my mother inquired, her voice quivering slightly.

"Because I have come to accept that I am gay and it is good for me to be with other gay persons."

"Oh, Paul Edward!" she moaned. "Why didn't you tell us this before? You're a grown man and now nothing can be done."

My father remained silent, which I found more disconcerting than my mother's vocalized distress. He got up from the dining room table and went into the kitchen to heat water, as usual, for tea and coffee.

"Mother, there's nothing that could have been done or should have been done, in the sense that you mean. I am happy to be who I am and the wonderful thing is that I have now come to accept it after many years."

"You weren't born gay," my mother insisted. "What did we do wrong?"

"He's saying that there's nothing wrong with it," my father explained. "That it's not something we did or didn't do."

Coffee and tea were served. We moved on to other topics, trying to ignore the elephant that had just poked its head into the room. As planned, we went that evening to a movie. *Murder by Death*, a spoof based on Agatha Christie's *And Then There Were None*. An extravagantly queeny Truman Capote appears at the end as the wealthy, manipulative host. Hollywood afforded us no escape.

It was several days before I saw my parents again. They were having a difficult time. They had gone out of town on a brief trip to nowhere in particular to think things over. I tried to think of what might help them in their distress. I brought them a copy of Don Clark's *Loving Someone Gay*, a book that had been written to help non-gay persons with the coming out process of a relative or friend.

We sat in the living room, where a large picture window looks out onto a cluster of tall oaks. They sat together on the couch, facing me solemnly. My father said:

"We have been talking this over and we want you to know that you are our son, we love you and we will not disown you."

"Not disown" me? My feet went cold. I had not even considered it a remote possibility that my parents might *disown* me. My father continued:

"I would have preferred that you have some terrible, disfiguring disease."

"We have never known anyone gay," my mother continued. "There was a man in the neighborhood that we wondered about, when I was growing up. But it is not anything that we're used to. One time, on a trip to Florida, we accidentally entered that kind of nightclub. There were men dressed as women there, and we actually felt sickened by seeing them."

"There's so much that I would like to tell you. It's not the way you think."

"Would you like me to leave the room so you can talk about it to your father?" my mother asked.

"No! You don't understand at all. For me, being gay has nothing to do with wanting to dress up like a woman. I am a man. I am happy to be a man. And I am drawn to men who look like men."

"I thought maybe I was to blame, my mother said, because when you were little I once dressed you up for Halloween as a girl."

"No, it has nothing whatever to do with any of that."

"I thought," my father said slowly, "that when you became a priest that was the end of any kind of sexual thoughts."

"Well, we continue to be human beings. But what I'm trying to tell you is about my sexuality, my sexual orientation. This is a separate issue from anything having to do with sexual activity. I do go out to gay clubs and I have gay friends. But what's most important is that I feel much better about myself for accepting my sexuality."

We left the matter there, that evening. They agreed to take a look at Don Clark's book. We sang a few religious songs, as I strummed the guitar, which I hoped would calm the waters and remind them that I was still the Christian, spiritual person they had thought me to be.

This discussion distressed me deeply. I loved my parents, but I had become a cause of pain by simply being myself. The gulf between their world and the new one that I now claimed was not as easily bridged as I had expected.

Although the home front was worrying, I continued to be pleased with the personal breakthrough I had made in accepting my sexuality. The fear and self-loathing of a lifetime were losing their grip on me. The bothersome images that had tormented me during prayer ceased altogether, a sign that they had originated in my body's protest at its heavy suppression by the intellect.

My parents, however, were not able to understand why any of this mattered to me. So far as they were concerned, my life had suddenly veered badly off course. My father made inquiries through church connections about possible sources of help. He learned of an "ex-gay" man named Guy Charles, who had a local ministry of "healing" homosexuals. My parents gave me the tape of a talk he had given and asked me to meet with him. I was very reluctant to meet with anyone about getting a healing I knew I did not need. My father, however, pleaded with me. He asked that I just meet Charles. How could I refuse?

Guy lived in an apartment with several men, all much younger than himself. I joined them for dinner one evening. It was a charismatic household. All shared the conviction that they had been "cured" of homosexuality. Guy spoke of the woman he had been dating and now planned to marry, although not in a way that gave me much of a picture of who she was. The younger men apparently were not, as yet, so advanced in their cures. In terms of social ambience, this felt like being with any other group of gay men.

Guy and I were not able to agree on the definition of sexuality, let alone homosexuality. He based his argument for healing homosexuality on St. Paul's words about becoming a "new creation" in Christ (II Corinthians 5). For him, to be "saved" meant that one had become new and was already healed of every illness, including homosexuality (i.e., active, genital, homosexual relations). One only needed sufficient help to realize all this and stop the behavior. I held fast that I was not in need of healing, at least, none that had to do with denying my sexuality, which, for me, meant not only genital activity, but my emotional life, affectivity and capacity for love. We were simply talking about different things.

As I left, one of the young men said that if I ever needed their help to come back, because they did not have a "straight" perspective and would understand, a revealing slip. The "ministry" was short-lived.

My parents professed to be glad that I had told them, but the evidence was all to the contrary. They continued to fret about having done something wrong in my upbringing. My mother, following the script she had somehow gleaned from psychoanalytic theory, wondered if she had been too domineering. In no way were they able to accept what I had shared for what I felt it to be: a difficult and courageous step toward personal wholeness. The bottom line for them was that no one must know. They were certain that news of this, were it to get out, would cause longtime friends to shun them.

My coming out process was set back by their response or, rather, my reaction to their response. From the intensity of their reaction, I realized that I had greatly overestimated the capacity of nongay persons to understand what being gay means. I convinced myself that since I did not have a lover, there was no need to call attention to my sexuality. Moreover, as a parish priest, albeit not a particularly happy one, coming out in a public way would be destructive of my career. I would follow the way of prudence.

V

In the autumn I spent a few days at the Trappist monastery, Holy Cross, in Berryville, Virginia. I did not take to the liturgical style of the Trappists, who kept the venetian blinds in their chapel drawn throughout the day. I wondered why trees, birds, and sunshine needed to be screened out from worship.

I reflected and prayed exhaustively on my life in two worlds. It seemed obvious that I did not belong in parish ministry. I had concluded that months before. But where did I belong? Because of my relationship with Larry, I thought the book of the prophet Hosea would be a good place to turn. Hosea married a prostitute as a witness to God's undying commitment to the people. It is wonderful that the prophets, so profoundly radical, are an indelible part of the record of God's self-communication. It seemed to me that my calling was to a ministry "in the world," outside of conventional church structures. Not knowing where to turn with that notion, I drew no conclusions and left feeling that I had not found the guidance I sought.

The night of my return from the monastery, I stopped by the Court Jester. My intention was not to stay long, but to have a drink, see who was there, and leave. Leaning against the wall, I watched the folks on the dance floor for a few minutes. I put my glass down, and was about to leave when I was "told" that I was to go nowhere, but remain where I stood. I did not hear an audible voice, but something spoke or, rather, commanded in a way that was clearer than any spoken voice. I was surrounded by light. A shaft of light came from somewhere above my head and filled me. It came suddenly, as though a window had just opened, allowing brilliant light to pour through. The light was not visible, but was intensely bright. My chest was filled with a sensation of love. It was the keenest, most powerful feeling that I have ever known. I understood myself to be in the presence of God. The words, "you are going nowhere," riveted my feet to the floor. I stood still, looking in wonder at every person. Some were gathered at the bar and at tables, several were dancing. I felt, I *knew*, in the totality of my being, body and mind, heart and soul, that God lives in and is exquisite, intense love for each person there. Tears inched down my cheeks, but I did not move or attempt to brush them away.

What I was feeling I knew to be not of myself. This was love that loved everybody, whether I knew them and liked them myself or not. I was not in control of it. I was somehow being allowed to know it. I wondered how long I would be able to bear this wonderful, yet uncomfortably intense feeling. I thought of what it is for God to have this love, to be this love, for every person in the world, regardless of who and what they are. The love continued to course through me for several minutes, perhaps for a quarter of an hour. A voice told me that it was good for me to be there, that I belonged in this place with these people. Then I saw the room being approached on the perimeter, beyond the walls, by dim, shadowy lions, baring their fierce teeth. I was told that danger was approaching, but I would be protected from it. Then the vision of lions stopped. The feeling of love and the light were cut off quite suddenly. I was free to move, once again, and promptly left the club to return home.

I did not attempt much in the way of interpretation of the illumination at the Court Jester. I took it as a gift, a moment, an insight. I did not attempt to reach theological conclusions or to undertake some special mission because of it. I kept it to myself. Whatever it was, the experience excavated a sacred space within where, from time to time, I remember the feeling of that unlimited love and know that it is the foundation and destiny of the whole world.

There are several reductionistic avenues available to explain such an experience. Psychologically, I was attempting to resolve a classic case of cognitive dissonance — my liking for things that are supposed to be opposed (Catholicism and homosexuality). In sociological terms, this may have been my way of joining my peers in reformulating what A.F.C. Wallace calls the "mazeway" of beliefs and practices provided by society, because I was experiencing too much stress and finding them no longer personally satisfying. In other words, I had reached a point of crisis, where I was beginning to construct a new system, so that I could give myself permission to be a gay man. These perspectives may be useful, but they do not account for the extravagant magnificence that touched me. The scriptures themselves provide the best guidance: "Ask, and it will be given you; search, and you will find; knock, and the door will be opened for you." (Matthew 7:7)

The illumination did help me to accept that it is "good" for me to be with the gay community. In later years I would come to understand that in a very general way as a vocation to serve and love gay and lesbian persons, regardless of religion or any other factor. Before arriving at this understanding, however, I needed a lot of healing.

VI

I yearned for freedom and wholeness, but was not ready to let go of the closet's comforts. I felt challenged by the courageous example of Father Bob Hummel. A priest of the Diocese of Richmond, he came out publicly in 1978. A handsome, thirty-three year old graduate student at Georgetown University, Bob was suspended from the priesthood the following year, two days after the publication of an article about him in *The Washington Star*. A parishioner at de Chantal, Jane, declared over dinner how very sorry she felt for Father Hummel — sorry, that is, that he was gay. Ironically, she was unknowingly entertaining two closeted gay men that evening. Jane, like my parents, was full of stereotypes and misinformation about the meaning of being gay.

So was Bob's bishop. Bishop Sullivan asked Bob to state whether he was remaining faithful to his pledge of celibacy. Bob replied that he would answer that question only if it were also put to every presumptively heterosexual priest in the diocese. He was right. Ultimately, however, Bob left the priesthood. Much as I admired him, his experience reinforced my retreat to the closet. I continued to socialize with gay men and go out to clubs, but I maintained a rigid segregation of this domain from my life as a priest and as a member of my family. I knew several priests of the Archdiocese who did the same thing. Some were pastors, members of an older generation of gay men who took the closet for granted. I regarded my own retreat as temporary, never accepting it as a healthy situation.

At the same time, my understanding of how Catholics should relate to their church was changing, as I faced questions about sexuality, church authority and personal freedom. I read numerous books and articles that address theological and scriptural issues surrounding homosexuality. I learned that the scriptural foundations of the church's opposition to homosexuality were flimsy. The story of the destruction of Sodom and Gomorrah was a story about the sin of inhospitality and the threat of homosexual *rape*, not homosexual love. Cultic practices involving prostitution most likely inspired the prohibition in Leviticus against "man lying with man" as *toevah* (abomination). The few references in St. Paul's letters are probably mistranslations, except for Romans 1, where the central argument concerns the Greco-Roman world's rejection of monotheism. St. Paul uses homosexuality there as an analogy. His argument works only if we understand that the homosexual acts to which he refers are committed by heterosexual persons. Neither this nor any other passage in the Bible concerns the behavior of homosexual persons as such.

The more profound issue for me was the acknowledgment that same-sex *love* is part of the human condition and, as such, is good. I found theological support in the work of John McNeill, a Jesuit, whose book, *The Church and the Homosexual*, was first published in 1976. McNeill constructed his argument for the goodness of homosexual relations on a personalist foundation, an approach that was familiar from my studies at the Gregorian. In a newspaper interview, he was quoted as saying that while many persons may have homosexual attractions at one time or another, such attractions do not make a person gay. You know that you are gay, he said, when you fall in love with a person of the same sex. That experience I had definitely had.

I struggled and prayed over these issues for years, but a crucial moment in self-acceptance came one day, when I was meditating on the gospel story in John 21, where Jesus asks Peter three times, "Do you love me?" I felt that God was asking me this very question, and when I responded with Peter, "Yes, Lord, I love you," tears came to my eyes as I realized that Jesus cared about my response. Jesus wanted my love. I, too, a gay man, could love God. This realization came as a balm that helped to heal the pervasive sense of unworthiness that had vitiated my sense of self. By coming, at long last, to accept myself and to cease being at war with my own feelings, I was free to get my mind off myself.

During this period, two longtime friends, Robert Nicolich, from Catholic University's prayer group, and Bill Hood, my friend from the prayer group in Rome, came out to me. Bill's self-disclosure was halting and painful, because it was made in the context of explaining a recent relationship difficulty. He spoke, at first, of the person in gender-neutral terms. I interrupted Bill, when it was clear what was coming next, to tell him that I was gay. With Robert, the disclosure stemmed from finding ourselves together in the same club. Both friendships grew immeasurably in depth and importance for me. From such disclosures I came to see that my world had always included gay persons, though I had not recognized it.

My pastoral work, especially in the areas of preaching and counseling, continued to be strengthened, by my healing process. I know, however, that I deprived the people of de Chantal of the ministry they should have had, because I still was not able to speak fully from my own experience. No doubt it would have caused an uproar and landed me on the street to speak the simple truth of my life to those good people. There is a timing to such disclosures. Even Jesus told his disciples at the Last Supper that he had "more" to reveal to them, but they were not yet ready for it (John 16). I suggest here only that the accommodation that homosexuals have long made to *keep silent* prevents many good and talented persons from giving all that they might give, because they do not find themselves free to be themselves. I know that when I eventually began to preside at Eucharist for Dignity's Sunday night Mass, I spoke and prayed as never before, because, for the first time, the words flowed from my heart. What came out was an identification with the gay community combined with a passionate anger at the church's hierarchy.

VII

I moved to the Cathedral of St. Matthew, Apostle, a spacious, impressive, domed, red brick edifice in central Washington, in June of 1979. I was looking for a change from the suburbs and this was it! I exchanged the lovely, carpeted suite of rooms with private bath that I enjoyed at de Chantal for one room on the top floor of a house that had been built during the 1890s. The furnishings were beyond decrepit. The dirty windows looked out to the alley and a restaurant's dumpster from which a stench wafted up to my room on hot summer days. These externals mattered little, however, compared to the sense of *life* that I found in the city.

John Gigrich arrived as a new associate at St. Matthew's the same day I did. We met briefly with the pastor, Monsignor W. Louis Quinn, in his study, a formal room of sumptuous seats and heavy drapes designed to impress rather than comfort. Lou addressed us, I noticed, as "Father," establishing from the start an air of formality and personal distance. Lou's style harked back to the glory days of American Catholicism, the 1940s and 1950s, when everyone knew their place. He was steeped in an Irish Catholicism that emphasized personal subordination to structure. Church and priesthood were about grim determination, rather than joyful mystery.

Lou welcomed John and me to the Cathedral by announcing that we would be doing the day-to-day pastoral work. He himself rarely heard confessions and was on the Mass schedule only two or three days a week. It was, for me, an awkward meeting, because whenever I started to speak, John would cut me off. My ostensive confrere, John, a man in his mid-fifties, spoke too elegantly by far in a *basso profondo* that was more self-absorbed than commanding. I had, in John, a man who was too anxious to please the boss. I regretted that we had arrived together, because from the start I found myself paired with this constitutionally competitive individual. In hindsight, I realize that John's presence made no difference whatever to my destiny there. Even if I had had Lou to myself at that first meeting, he would not have heard me. Lou is the kind of man who assumes that he already knows all that is worth knowing. In the world of Catholic bureaucrats that is precisely the attitude to have. In the years to come, there would be many occasions when I would speak out and even cry out to Lou, to no effect.

St. Matthew's is two and a half blocks south of Dupont Circle, the epicenter of gay life in Washington. I was now within walking distance of Lambda Rising, as well as several gay restaurants and clubs. One favorite spot was the Fraternity House, a converted carriage house with a disco on the ground floor and upstairs restaurant with a decor of equestrian prints and horseshoes. The Frat House had a good sound system and excellent DJs, so it held a strong attraction for me. I like music of all kinds — classical, jazz, folk and rock. R&B's sumptuous celebration of everyday life — "I heard it through the grapevine," "Don't leave me this way" — enchants. Coupled with the disco sound – emphatic rhythms, elegant instrumentation, and, above all, compelling vocalization – it generates a space both externally and internally that I find restful and, at times, inspirational. The nightly gathering in disco clubs, during the late seventies and early eighties, provided a generation of gay men a setting where they could celebrate their sexuality openly. The eventual, exaggerated revulsion against the disco era was undoubtedly a homophobic reaction to disco's gay associations.

A few months after my arrival at St. Matthew's, Pope John Paul II came to the United States for his first visit as pope. His stop in Washington included a Mass at St. Matthew's. There was, therefore, during my first summer at the Cathedral, a major stir about the place concerning the impending visit. Since the pope was scheduled to have lunch at the rectory, Lou took the occasion to have his rooms completely refurbished at a cost, it was rumored, in excess of one hundred thousand dollars. I was beginning to get a taste of the man's selfishness. He also planned for his sister to serve the pope's lunch, thus depriving our Sardinian housekeeper, Mrs. Dessi, of what should have been one of the major events of her life. Mrs. Dessi, never known for timidity, was not reluctant to express her views on these matters, including the deplorable sterility of the remodeled rooms, to all who would lend an ear.

As it turned out, the pope was behind schedule when he got to St. Matthew's. There was a further delay, when, upon his arrival, he asked to use the bathroom. It seems that in the hubbub of the helicopter's arrival at the reflecting pool and the drive to St. Matthew's, where he was expected to vest for Mass in the tiny St. Francis Chapel, just inside the entrance, no one had factored in such a basic, human need. The trip to the bathroom (overseen by a monsignor) required some last minute logistical scrambling. There was, in any event, little time after Mass for lunch. Mrs. Dessi did find a way to meet the pope. I also met him, with the other priests of the house, as we stood at the foot of the stairs, when he came down from the rector's suite. Archbishop Paul Marcinkus, his deputy on this trip, later indicted in a bank scandal, tried to shoo us away, but we held our ground. The others kissed his hand, but I, ever the egalitarian, simply shook it. I also had the job of announcing to the American bishops in his entourage, who were lunching elsewhere in the rectory, that they should return to their cars. There was, among bishops and priests, a giddy excitement about the whole event that I knew I could never share. I respect this great office, but am distrustful of modern Catholicism's cult of the papacy.

The next day I left for Mount Saviour, a Benedictine monastery near Elmira, New York. As I drove out of the city, the pope was celebrating Mass for a sea of people on the mall. In Rome I had often seen and been a part of such crowds. Vast throngs of "pilgrims" from around the globe gathering to see the pope, to receive his blessing in St. Peter's Square, has become a standard feature of modern Catholic piety, especially since the time of Pius XII. Such a preoccupation with the man robed in white, strikes me as misguided. Its basis is neither the scriptures nor Catholic tradition. It is a novelty of the modern church that borders on idolatry. Driving away from Washington at precisely that moment focused my attention on how much my perspective on what matters in church life was changing. It seemed fitting that I was heading toward a monastery. Monasticism is, among many other things, the Catholic tradition's ancient, institutionalized locus for nonconformists.

VIII

In the fall of 1979 I fell in love with John Owen. I first noticed John at the end of a Dignity Mass in St. William's Chapel, at Georgetown University. He stood to make an announcement from a pew several rows ahead of me. Even before he turned so that I was able to see his face, I felt some extraordinary connection to him. He spoke to announce an upcoming retreat. His rich, baritone voice made the retreat sound positively irresistible. The thought came to mind that I had known this person in a previous life. Since I had no particular beliefs about reincarnation or special interest in the subject, I cannot account for such a notion coming to mind. Intuitively, in any event, I sensed the existence of a bond between us.

John was twenty-nine. He was muscular, handsome and suave. His welcoming face was adorned with a cautious, half-smile and dark eyes that focused in a steady gaze. We did not meet at Dignity, but at the Frat House, where, following a post-Dignity repast in the restaurant, he followed me downstairs to the disco. After a brief, shy moment, he introduced himself.

Even though he had made the initial move, John seemed reluctant to let me into his life. After several phone calls back and forth, he invited me to a picnic lunch at Meridien Hill Park. Afterwards, he made some excuse about the mess in his nearby apartment, to explain why he was not inviting me up. He wanted me, however, to listen to "Octave," a Moody Blues album. I waited outside, while he ran into the building to fetch it. As soon as I returned home, I played it and felt at once that the gentle rock music and mellow lyrics were speaking to me the spiritual hopes and expressions of intimacy that John could not bring himself to say. "Don't leave me driftwood on the shore" described the sense of abandonment he had alluded to at lunch. Was this song, this album, a plea for help? At that moment I knew I was falling in love. And as these feelings surged through me, I was reluctant to accept them. The notion of "falling" in love became palpable. I was falling from a reasonably well-ordered life into something unknown, some place beyond my control. Having begun the fall, I seemed to have no choice but to let it take me where it would. And with John, it took me into some very strange places indeed.

John began to share his writings with me. Mostly they were spiritual "reflections," written in a spare, confident meditative style. It was clear from the outset that John had a first-rate mind. His I.Q. was in the genius range, he claimed, and I had no doubt of it. At the same time, it was also clear that this was a man who was hampered psychologically. Only later, after I had been drawn deeply into his life, did I realize how profound the problems were. I learned that he was manic, alternating between wonderful, ecstatic highs and lows that were very somber and dark.

The first few weeks were a honeymoon. We spent countless hours together, disclosing ourselves to one another. John brought me, at last, to his apartment, a tiny, roach-infested place on the second floor of a former boarding house, a vaguely odoriferous building, with creaky floorboards and low ceilings. We spoke long into the night. I said:

"John, I feel deeply connected to you. I believe that we have been brought together, because we can help each other. You have wonderful, rich theological insights, but you are isolated, cut off from the world in a way that prevents you from communicating with others. This has something to do with the intensity of your nature. You live and love and feel so intensely that it is difficult for you to modulate what you have to offer so that it gets through to people."

"I do live intensely and love intensely, because that's what it means to live in the Spirit. Do you think Mary was intense?"

"I don't know, I've never thought about it."

"'My being proclaims the greatness of the Lord, my spirit rejoices in God my savior.' Yes, she lived with that focus on God."

"Well, John, that may be true, but we also have to do something about living in the real world. You are barely surviving here. What I'm saying is that you need to think about the future. You have a lot to tell people that's worthwhile. Maybe I can help you with that. Perhaps you could start working on a book."

"You mean *selling* the work of the Spirit?"

"Well, John, that puts it rather negatively. But, yes, the workman is worthy of his pay. You are a good man with some extraordinary gifts. I don't want to see them go to waste. That's all I'm saying."

A former Jesuit seminarian, John had some exposure to academic theology. His value as a thinker, however, had less to do with formal training than with his originality. He was adept at probing church doctrine for psychological content and finding in the experience of interpersonal love the ultimate meaning of Advent, Christmas, the Holy Trinity, the Incarnation. If his handicap — he spoke of "electrical storms" in his head — somehow prevented him from effectively communicating his ideas, I thought I might be of some help.

During these months, John was receiving unemployment compensation. I somehow never thought to ask what job he was unemployed from. I wondered what would happen when that ran out. He had broken off all communication with his parents and had no siblings or other close relatives. So complete was his break with his parents that he had chosen to be called "John," rather than "Eddie," as they had always called him. I became their sole link to their son. It was an awkward position, since I felt very limited in what I could tell them. John would always interrogate me after a phone conversation with them. This role, while difficult, proved, I thought, our closeness.

My first taste of trouble came one night with a phone call. It was 2 A.M. John called on my private line.

"I'm sick of your paganism!" he shouted in a slurry voice that cracked with emotion.

"Paganism?"

"You know what I'm talking about," he said, and hung up.

Paganism? The charge, his voice, the hour, all made this moment so ludicrous that I wanted to laugh. But John was in no mood for laughter. I had confided in him about my own spiritual journey, which included explorations of nonwestern religions, dream analysis, meditation and psychic phenomena. I never had considered these explorations as a turning to "paganism," nor did John explain what he meant. Could he be referring to my attachment to Larry, whose mother was a priestess? I was left to wonder for the remainder of that restless night.

John's phone call exposed my vulnerability. The man I intensely loved was inexplicably, in this moment, a mad man. And I was vulnerable to him, because I had disclosed my life to such an extent that he might select any piece of it to make trouble. As a young priest whose education in Rome and assignment to the Cathedral suggested a promising future, I believed I had a career to keep in mind. These elements combined to make me pathetically vulnerable to John's manipulations and pathologic mood swings. When we next saw each other, John canceled out the paganism accusation with his gentle smile and some word of explanation that suggested it had nothing at all to do with me. This, I later saw, was part of a strategy: to deny me the *terra firma* of the seemingly obvious meaning of his words.

My relationship with John was not genital. I write, "not genital," rather than "not sexual," because here the commonly overlooked distinction between these terms is pertinent. John and I did have an intensely sexual relationship. It was a relationship whose tension, fraught with themes of affection, seduction, attraction, domination and nurturance, was profoundly sexual. I yearned for sex with John. He yearned for total acceptance from me. Neither yearning would be satisfied.

One evening I expected our relationship to take a turn toward physicality. We were in my study. John was wearing snug, white jeans. I placed a record — John Cougar Mellencamp — on the stereo. He sat down on the couch, while I uncorked a bottle of wine. He said:

"Every priest of the Archdiocese should have the kind of intimacy that we have."

At that moment, priests in the Archdiocese were not what I wanted to think about. John, however, was quite adept at using the fact that I was a priest *both* to draw me in and push me away. For example, he addressed mail to me: "The Church at Washington / c/o Fr. Paul Murray." This unique form of address was his way of subordinating my personal identity to my role in the church. A more striking illustration occurred during a period when I briefly assumed payment of his rent, after John moved into the basement apartment of a boarding house. He told the landlady that the "church" was paying for it. And, of course, it was impossible to correct him on such matters. I was the church's representative, wasn't I? Perhaps he should take up the matter with "Jim" (his way of referring to James Hickey, who became Archbishop of Washington a few months after we met). Thus he drew me in as an intimate, a special, "committed friend," for himself, while painstakingly denying to me any reciprocal rights to intimacy and trust.

I lived in constant fear that my identity as a gay man would be exposed. Indeed, a few months after meeting John, I refrained from further involvement with Dignity, out of concern for my career. This fear, I know now, was not simply the rational fear one might have about the impact of the public disclosure of details about one's private life. It was a bad case of internalized homophobia. I had not advanced very far along the path of self-acceptance. Thus, when John pulled this particular chain — and he knew well how to pull it — I felt a wrenching in my guts that was terrifying. It was a peculiarly cruel and ironic bind: the man I loved and to whom I had naturally disclosed the secrets of my heart and my struggles to grow toward personal wholeness, both systematically denied my personhood and threatened to disclose personal information about me.

The nightmare began to unfold that night, when I uncorked the wine and poured out two glasses. John chose that moment to say:

"You know, my sexual attraction to you is about zero."

I was too embarrassed to respond. Sex? Who was talking about sex? I put up a brave front. Fortunately, I had to that point neither said nor done anything overtly sexual. But, of course, John knew from the first moment he sought me out with those penetrating, hungry eyes, that our friendship was enveloped in homoerotic attraction. It served his interests to use my anxieties and inadequacies in this area as a control mechanism. After driving him home, I wept profusely. Devastated to the core, I was up all night weeping. Thoughts of suicide surfaced. *Zero* attraction! How was that possible? The experience confirmed my poor self-image. Who could be attracted to me? Of course, he could not be attracted to me. I was undeserving. And so forth. Some months later, John admitted that what he said that night was not quite true. By that time, however, I had a better idea of what did attract him – tentative, young men, about twenty years of age — as well as why, given John's particular demons, it was by far better not to be an object of his sexual interest.

IX

After a year at St. Matthew's, I still found myself chronically underemployed. My work consisted largely of daily Mass and confessions. On duty days, life was punctuated by "parlor calls" to meet with whomever came to the rectory asking to see a priest. Often they were quite bizarre. Callers included Beatrice, Queen of the World, who stopped by to declare that she was not happy with St. Matthew's. Another was a young man wearing a Harley-Davison T-shirt who claimed that a witch in California was controlling his heartbeat. When, after checking, I declared that I could feel his pulse he said that only proved how clever she is.

Lou Quinn left these sublime encounters to his associates. What disturbed me much more was that he did not consult with us in any meaningful way about the parish. Under these circumstances, it was impossible to develop a sense of working with my presumptive colleagues to build, strengthen or shape the parish community. What help could persons living in mental and spiritual chaos find in a parish that was itself steeped in grandiose illusions and self-deceptions?

In 1980, James Aloysius Hickey succeeded Cardinal Baum as Archbishop of Washington. Baum was to take up a position in the Roman curia as prefect of the Sacred Congregation for Catholic Education. It was suggested by my colleagues at St. Matthew's that I would become his secretary. I probably would have been delighted by the opportunity, but I knew Hickey well enough to know that he would have considered me too independent for the job. He chose, in fact, Morty Fox, Communications Director for the Archdiocese and one of my colleagues at St. Matthew's.

I began to consider academic programs. Studies, at least, would divert attention from the mindlessness that I found in parish ministry. It was John Owen who suggested anthropology. At first, the notion of me in anthropology seemed too improbable. What does one do with anthropology? After reading Ruth Benedict's *Patterns of Culture*, however, I was hooked. The analytical power of the culture concept came as a revelation.

I needed Hickey's permission to embark on studies. I expected resistance. After all, I was not choosing church history, canon law or theology, but a secular subject, a move that might provide a viable out from the priesthood. Theology was already becoming a danger zone for Catholics with progressive views. Since the 1978 election of John Paul II as pope, a chill had quickly settled over theological inquiry. Hans Küng, an ecclesiologist who played a prominent role at Vatican II was among the first of many theologians to be disciplined. In Washington, the long-simmering case against Charlie Curran, a renowned moral theologian with moderately liberal views on sexuality, was pushed with new vigor by Hickey. As chancellor of the university, Hickey eventually terminated Curran's contract, after the Vatican denied him the right to teach as a Catholic theologian. I did not want to commit myself to the field of theology only to be "silenced." By choosing a secular discipline, I naively reasoned, I would be free to study whatever I chose and to speak publicly about it, because I would be doing it in the name of "science."

To my surprise, Hickey readily consented, giving permission for me to enter the Master's program at Catholic University. It annoyed me that he did not permit me to choose from other local universities, but, as it happened, the department at Catholic was the best choice.

The study of other cultures, I soon learned, entails letting go of the familiar ways and understandings of one's own social world. Bob Sholte calls this "alienation from ordinary self-understanding." As I read about the lives of peasants in the Andes, the economic activities of tribal groups in New Guinea, and the social structure of gangs in the United States, I felt very privileged. It seemed a great luxury to have the time and resources to delve into studies that took me far from my own social world. Anthropology expanded my sense both of the world and of myself. I came to see that I was already well along the path of alienation from what my world considered ordinary. I came to think of myself as one of those marginal persons who stand apart just enough to serve as useful guides for outsiders, including anthropologists, to the mores of their own society.

X

John Owen left Washington and, for all practical purposes, my life in 1983. By this time he had moved to the Mount Pleasant neighborhood, where he rented a basement apartment. John developed an obsession with a neighbor, Hardee. His obsession was frightening, because its turbulence suggested that a capacity for violence lurked not far beneath the surface. On one occasion, at John's place, Hardee and I found his behavior so angry and erratic that we decided to leave. As I left, John slammed the door behind me so that Hardee was trapped just inside. For several minutes, Hardee and I called back and forth to each other anxiously through the door, until John finally let him go.

John developed bizarre notions that the companions in the group house where Hardee lived were somehow controlling and corrupting him. He attempted to take on the role of heroic defender and, as a result began to frighten Hardee's housemates, as well. In the climactic episode, he assaulted them with a canoe paddle. Fortunately, they held their ground and were not injured. After that, he fled Washington, presumably to avoid arrest.

Somehow, even through the distorted instrumentality of his tormented personality, John had been a friend. He loved me and did the only thing he knew how to do when he found love — manipulate, control and push away. There were wonderfully intense, intimate and bright moments one day followed by bleak, dark episodes the next. The dark episodes were like prison bars that interposed an impassable boundary between us. But, from time to time, we reached between those bars and found joy and peace in each other.

When John left, I felt both relief and loss. Hardee and I became friends and, for some months, I had a crush on him. Hardee was already in a relationship, albeit a very tenuous one, and was quite adept at being friendly with me, while maintaining distance.

My emotional life was an unsettling flow of attachments and turmoil. Infatuation with a hustler, passionate love for a manic-depressive. I was pushing beyond the boundaries of reason and propriety. Without losing sight of those boundaries, I have found the discoveries to be made there compelling.

Again and again I returned from bizarre encounters with John, from wrestling with demons, to the decorous dinner table of St. Matthew's rectory. One moment I found myself trying to extricate Hardee from John's clutches, in the next I was chatting about the Archbishop's upcoming Sunday Mass. This required a good measure of self-control. I had acquired the skill of compartmentalization early in life. Nevertheless, I yearned for wholeness, a life where sexuality and affectivity are not perceived as being in contradiction to propriety, religion and professional demeanor.

XI

Much of my time and energy at St. Matthew's were expended trying to comprehend and cope with Lou Quinn, the pastor. Lou was an olive-skinned Irish-American who was often mistaken for an Italian. From the way he brushed back his wavy, gray hair, he bore a striking resemblance to Shah Pahlavi. As a young curate, he had worked at St. Matthew's, until he was sent to suburban Maryland to found a Parish. He went from there to be pastor of Blessed Sacrament Parish, in tony Chevy Chase, and, finally, to St. Matthew's, where he remained until retirement. Lou was an administrator and builder. His connections with the rich were perhaps his greatest asset for the Archdiocese.

Lou's pastoral skills were another matter. His principal objective when celebrating Mass was to get it over with as quickly as possible. Even the Sunday Latin Mass, complete with choral music, he was able to finish in just under forty-five minutes, about a quarter-hour ahead of the rest of us. He was famous for visiting the hospitals in Montgomery County; that is, he made himself famous for it by frequently commenting on it. These were, reportedly, masterfully quick stops at the beds of the generally well-heeled, most of them parishioners from his years in Kensington and Chevy Chase.

His hospital visits were well integrated into trips to and from various Montgomery County country clubs, where he was something of a fixture.

At one time upwardly mobile, Lou was still adjusting to the reality of having reached the high point of his career. He was not bitter, I think, but he escaped into a stance of aloofness from both colleagues and parishioners. As long as the talk at table — the dining room was our principal point of contact — remained on the superficial, upbeat level of country club banter, Lou was even fun to be with.

The chasm between Lou and myself had to do with his extraordinary adeptness at avoiding candid conversation. I was deeply angered by his handling or, more often, non-handling of parish and rectory matters. I tried every avenue to engage him in discussion, while Lou masterfully deflected the issues. His preference for superficial talk at meals, his general absence from daily life at St. Matthew's, his refusal to reply to memoranda and to hold regular staff meetings were all pieces of a consistent avoidance of substantive discussion of any kind. He also was very poor at sharing information with his associates that might bear on their life and ministry, for example, that three cardinals were to join us at lunch on Saturday or that he had decided to discontinue the parish's distribution of McDonald's gift certificates to the homeless, which meant that those of us who actually had to respond to parlor calls were left with nothing to offer them.

I was being treated contemptibly, both as a priest and as a human being. I was not alone. The other priests felt the same. When leaving on a trip, Lou would sometimes announce unpleasant news by way of a memo. This was to let us absorb the news without any immediate opportunity to discuss it with him. We all recognized this as a recurring, predictable pattern. Another was that upon returning from trips he would often give one of the employees, especially Joe, the poor and elderly sacristan, a good dressing down about some ostensive deficiency in his work. One colleague suggested that Lou did this because vacations made him feel guilty.

There is no question that more than a decade of being under Lou's thumb had a significant effect. His behavior caused me to reflect extensively on the exercise of power in the church, the workplace, and everyday life. In the gospel readings at daily Mass, I increasingly noticed that while Jesus was understanding of human weakness, he was highly intolerant of the self-aggrandizing use of power by the religious leaders of his own day. I came to see in this material, which is quite pervasive in the gospels, a warning to the church in every generation to avoid such tendencies. In fact, the church should be modeling for the world what it means to be a generous, caring society.

I continued to hold to the model of the church that I had learned from the charismatics. I believed that to develop a parish ministry that was vital and truly responsive to the needs of parishioners and the neighborhood required regular meetings of staff and parishioners for discussion, prayer and heartfelt sharing. With Lou at the helm, I came to see, few meetings of any kind would ever take place. Without regular staff meetings, without a continuous, deeply prayerful and honest discussion of parish needs and directions, I became convinced, true ministry was simply not possible.

For more than four hundred years, since the Council of Trent, Roman Catholics have defined priesthood narrowly, in terms of sacramental functions: the power to confect the Eucharist at Mass and the power to absolve from sin. A more contemporary understanding of priesthood, however, and one that is better grounded in the New Testament, is based on its role of "headship" within a community. A priest (or, in New Testament terms, "presbyter," literally, "elder") serves as the head of a community, with the principal responsibility of seeing that the gospel is proclaimed and taught in its fullness. The gospel is what enables a community to develop as the body of Christ, to employ St. Paul's familiar analogy. As the community grows, so that the gifts and ministries of all the members flourish, it becomes an expression of the resurrection of Christ. As St. Paul wrote: "to each (member) is given some manifestation of the Spirit for the common good." The presbyter stands at the head of this process, to recognize, identify, affirm and encourage the development of all the members' gifts. The sacramental ministries of the presbyter are, then, ritual expressions of this role, not magical abilities conferred by ordination. The priest presiding at Mass to consecrate bread and wine by repeating the words and gestures of Jesus at the Last Supper — "this is my body" and "this is the cup of my blood" — is a ritualized representation of the priest's role of building up the community as the body of Christ. This means that the job of a priest is to study, to know the scriptures, to know the tradition of the church, church teachings and history, and, at the same time, to have the wisdom and discernment to be familiar with what is happening in the lives of people in the community.

To turn to the realities of priestly life and ministry in contemporary

America is not only to awaken from such theological reflections as from a dream, it is to realize that contemporary practices actually frustrate and defeat the purpose of this sacred office on many levels. In Lou Quinn's domain, I was a magical functionary, not a participant in the building and direction of a community. I functioned well at St. Matthew's, as I had at St. Jane de Chantal, in the sense of performing magic on schedule. But there was something missing. I was in St. Matthew's, in the Archdiocese of Washington, in the Roman Catholic priesthood, but somehow not of it. I dined with my fellow priests and enjoyed the conversation, much of it gossip about the Archdiocese, parishioners, and street persons who frequented the Cathedral. After meals, I returned to my studies.

CHAPTER 4

CONCLUSIONS

I

Though our faces were fading from view in the dusk, neither the Archbishop nor I moved to turn on the light. We sat facing one another in the small room he kept for his use on the top floor of the Cathedral rectory. The week before, I had written to suggest that as I continued to find no prospect for meaningful connection with the Archdiocese, it would be best for me to take a leave.

"Paul, when will you finish your master's program?"

"I should be able to finish it by December."

"Then why don't you wait at least until then? Then you will have a credential that will help in finding a job. We don't want to see you in line at the Calvert Shelter," Hickey chuckled.

The Calvert Shelter was an Archdiocesan shelter for homeless men that had recently been opened a few doors away from the Cathedral. It was not run by the parish, but I had assisted periodically with crises involving men who stayed there. I found the reference ominous. It was a reminder that if I left, I would be on my own immediately. The Archdiocese would give me one month's salary and extend health benefits for a few months. I would not need the Calvert Shelter, but financially I was but a step or two away from homelessness.

Obviously Hickey's advice made good practical sense, but loneliness, my sense of disconnection from the church's leadership, and disgust with Lou Quinn generated a sense of urgency.

Hickey and I established in this conversation, once again, that I enjoyed the basics of priestly ministry: preaching, celebrating Mass, hearing confessions, counseling, and teaching. What I did not enjoy were life in the rectory and a lack of direction in my career. Hickey played on my vulnerabilities: financial insecurity and love of the priesthood. My resolve weakened in the twilight. I allowed Hickey to reel me back in, as he uttered patent nonsense:

"If a man loves to celebrate Mass, to preach and hear confessions, then

I don't see how a leave of absence can help him at all. After you complete this degree, then you might want to try another assignment. Or, who knows, you might even go for a doctorate? Have you thought about that?"

"Yes, Archbishop, I have thought about a doctoral program. It would be difficult to finance without the help I receive from the Archdiocese, even though I get tuition remission by being a teaching assistant. There is a lot of expense involved in a graduate program."

"Well, you think about it and then let me know if you want to continue on. I think you would be a great teacher."

"Thank you, Archbishop, I will let you know."

I was not as weak and indecisive as I allowed myself to appear. Since mailing the letter announcing my departure, I had learned that I had contracted Hepatitis B. Hepatitis B is an inflammation of the liver that is caused by a virus. It is a serious and potentially fatal disease. Unlike those of Hepatitis A, its victims are usually asymptomatic. Most people who have the disease are unaware of it and recover fully. I had been generally asymptomatic, although, on learning that I had it, recalled noticing that my eyes had been sore and slightly jaundiced a few weeks earlier.

The discovery that I was sick came as a complete surprise. I suspected that I had been exposed in 1983, during a one-night stand after which I decided one-night stands were a waste of my time. It seemed cruelly ironic that what now held me back from extricating myself from a life of presumed celibacy was an unfortunate, brief encounter, albeit a search, like all such encounters, for true relationship. In any event, not knowing what my medical condition — and expenses — might be in the months ahead, this was clearly not an opportune moment to make a transition into a new career and way of life.

The discovery that I had a serious illness was emotionally devastating. The fact that I had most likely contracted this disease sexually added to my distress and resurrected the lurking demons of homophobic self-hatred. I felt contaminated. I looked back, and back again, at the single event, a moment of male-to-male sexual contact, that I assumed had precipitated the illness. Moreover, with the onset of the AIDS epidemic, I had good reason to fear exposure to another, yet deadlier and more devastating illness. Thoughts of an early death plagued me. I was not ready for death, I thought, because I had not experienced a satisfying, personal relationship. I had always been alone, it seemed. And now my loneliness closed in with demonic force.

Among the principal victims of AIDS, during its advent in the United States, were gay men in their thirties. I was a gay man in my thirties, and I had already contracted Hepatitis B. As news of AIDS spread, I found myself panicking every few weeks out of fear that I was experiencing the onset of this dreadful and *fatal* disease. A raised, reddish spot on the leg or a sore in the mouth would have me rushing off to my physician, to the dermatologist or, for a really quick opinion, to the rooms of John Gigrich, who had already met a number of persons with AIDS. Even though the results of my queries consistently turned up no sign of AIDS, I suspected that something was seriously wrong with my health, something *beyond* hepatitis.

I fortunately had the good sense to seek help. I began a period of intensive soul-searching, which included consultations with a Jesuit priest at Georgetown, who served as my spiritual director, and a clinical psychologist, himself a former priest.

I also did something that, for me, was very different. I telephoned a radio call-in show hosted by Sallee Rigler. In popular parlance, Sallee is a "psychic," a term she herself spurns. Sallee tells people about themselves. I had listened to her for a few years and been won over by her compassion and wisdom. What I found in listening to Sallee was that she used her skills not simply to answer the questions that people thought they wanted answered about love, money and health, but to help them understand the deeper issues. "Will I get a promotion next month?" "Will I start a new relationship soon?" To such questions Sallee often gave specific "yes" and "no" responses. But she also helped the promotion-seeker to accept that he was not happy with this particular type of work and needed to change to another field. Or she pointed out to someone hoping for a relationship that she had chosen poorly in the past and needed to learn how to make a positive choice.

My question for Sallee concerned my sense of being "stuck" in life. How could I realize some changes? Sallee said that I had approached life with a "self-destructive, no, a self-defeating" (she corrected herself) attitude. She said that I had a problem with deserving and somehow I never felt that I deserved anything. She promised that I would move onto a more productive course and suggested I could speed up the process by consulting a transpersonal psychologist. Without my asking, she added that I had a health problem, which had begun thirteen months before, but that it was now over. It had, in fact, been exactly thirteen months since my diagnosis of hepatitis.

I did not know what transpersonal psychology was, but if it could help, I was interested. I attended a transpersonal workshop that was conducted by a former Catholic seminarian, Michael Brown. Michael led the participants through a few hours of guided meditation, with breaks for journaling and drawing. These techniques were new to me and I found the results impressive. For our meditation, we were to focus on some relationship, where we wanted to gain more understanding. I chose to examine my relationship with John Owen. I was able to visualize myself conversing with John in detail. Stopping to record the dialogue and draw (inside a large circle) intensified the mental image, when we resumed meditation. The climactic moment entailed imagining what it would be like to be that person, to be John, to stand inside his skin and see the world with his eyes. When I attempted this, I was impressed that the experience felt authentic. Glimpsing the world — and myself — through John's eyes, I had a better understanding of his fears and vulnerabilities than I had consciously realized. The technique, I knew, was not some kind of magic. It was a way of intuitively accessing the vast reservoir of data that we hold, mostly unconsciously, about people we know. I was sufficiently impressed to enter therapy with Michael for several months.

A year later, I did indeed find myself in a stronger, happier place. Objectively, there was no reason for this. I was still at St. Matthew's. Still lonely. The changes were interior and subtle.

Progress on my anthropology program perhaps contributed to my brightened mood. Under the guidance of my dissertation director, my work in anthropology focused on the interpretive processes that guide people's behavior. This study, "cultural analysis," looks at how people construct their world through interpretive (cultural) acts that are based on understandings that they draw from their social environment.

It was at the Frat House that I came up with the idea for my doctoral dissertation. I would extend cultural analysis to an international secretariat, possibly the Food and Agriculture Organization of the United Nations (FAO) that was headquartered in Rome. I had first been drawn to anthropology, because I thought it might hold some clues about enabling people from differing backgrounds to live and work together. International secretariats, I reasoned, have been intentionally practicing multiculturalism for decades. What had their experience been? The moment this project took shape in my mind, I was immediately committed to it.

II

A rare convocation of the priests of the Archdiocese of Washington took place on February 6, 1986, in Riverdale Maryland. A recent acceleration in the exodus of priests from active ministry compelled Archdiocesan officials to recognize that they had a problem. The convocation was supposed to be a step in formulating a response. It was, by far, the most complete gathering of Archdiocesan priests that I had seen. What immediately struck me was that it was largely a gathering of old men. I had previously heard the statistic bandied about that the median age of our priests was sixty-two. From the gray heads in St. Bernard's parish hall, however, what that meant became evident as never before.

At priest gatherings my sense of alienation from the Roman church seems always to be enhanced, and the 1986 convocation was no exception. On arriving, I found myself chatting with colleagues, many of them conspicuously overweight, between sips of weak coffee and chomps of doughnut, refreshments thoughtfully provided by Father Gatta, the day's rotund and amiable host. Somehow we expect to find common interests. After all, we speak of one another as "brother priests." We presumably share a common commitment to Jesus Christ and to pastoral ministry. Surely we have much to talk about. I believe the common ground is, in reality, there, but at some cognitive level covered over by years of hurt and mistrust, shattered dreams, abandoned ideals and loneliness. A kind of awkward, masculine chumminess prevails. We do not speak to each other from the heart, but out of learned habits of discourse. The discourse of cynical jocularity: "Do you know what this day is supposed to be all about? The men have three squares and a bed, what more do they want?" The discourse of institutionally correct piety: "I think our focus should be on serving the people, rather than on us."

Apart from a small number of priests that I know from seminary days and assignment together, it is seldom that I find a kindred spirit at such gatherings. My colleagues are fundamentally conservative, not ideologically, but in the sense of being preoccupied with the maintenance of parish and Archdiocesan institutions. Maintaining the parish, with its prosaic routine of Masses, confessions and occasional social events. Maintaining the parish school, often with difficulty, as the population of a given parish ages. Maintaining the authority and privileged status of clerics in the face of the demands of parishioners, especially women, for more say. Those who work in the administrative offices of the Archdiocese comment obliquely on their work and cheerfully reference whatever "the boss," i.e., Cardinal Hickey, is doing. Despite their friendliness and, in many cases, sincere dedication to work, I have found it difficult to go sufficiently deep with these men to form significant bonds with more than a few. Where I have formed friendships beyond those with men I know from seminary days, it has either been because of a shared gay identity or a shared sense of alienation from the Archdiocese and the restorationist Catholicism of John Paul II.

By the conclusion of the convocation, I was satisfied that much had been said that needed to be said. The Archbishop had taken copious notes — too copious, I thought, since what mattered most was that he *listen*. In the end, despite the adoption of a policy statement that mandated staff meetings and the crafting of job descriptions for all priestly assignments, nothing came of it. The institutions and institutionalized relationships of priests, I eventually came to see, are profoundly resistant to change. They are expressions of a culture. If I had not bonded with many priests at a deep level, it was because I had never bonded with the Archdiocese itself, that is, I had never embraced its perspectives and modes of operation. I found it pathetic.

III

If ever there was a place impervious to change it was St. Matthew's. I was able to minister happily there, once I learned to accept it for what it is. It is a shrine at the edge of Washington's principal commercial district. In no sense is it a community, despite the existence of a core of steady and longtime parishioners, who give the Cathedral some semblance of parish life. The bulk of worshipers on weekends are tourists, conventioneers and business people. On weekdays, especially at the noon Mass, the majority are employees from Washington's corporate and federal offices, law firms and national associations. They come to church, each to claim his or her customary pew, others to pray before various altars and statues. They come for refuge, peace, guidance and some contact with the sacred in the midst of the workaday world.

St. Matthew's was built on a grand scale. Its broad dome, colorful marbles and glistening mosaics effectively transport those who cross its threshold from the sights and sounds of the modern world to a different space and time. It is a restful space. Many non-Catholics stop by, as well. Where else would they go? Most churches keep their doors locked, apart from services. Just to be there, a shrine on Rhode Island Avenue, is the mission.

After a few years of working in that setting, I absorbed something of the place into my own outlook or, rather, was absorbed, as St. Matthew's shaped me into an instrument of itself. I became one of the priests who periodically emerged from the sacristy to celebrate Mass, recite prayers and proclaim the gospel from the main altar, overlooked by a thirty-five foot mosaic of St. Matthew. Marble walls and arches took possession of my voice to surround my words with a mystic areola that mocked my efforts at merely rational discourse. Sometimes the building would take my soft voice and playfully dash the words into a jumbled echo that defied the attempts of even the most ardent listeners to hear what I had to say. At other times, it would take my words and accentuate them with a resonant authority that I did not yet find in myself. The wonder of this place, which I came to appreciate as a truly sacred space, however ludicrous the goings-on behind the scenes, opened to me as I learned to relax the rigidity of cherished notions about liturgy and community. Not that those beliefs are mistaken. But in the center-city shrine, they seem oddly beside the point. St. Matthew's manages on its own terms to be an expression of the transcendence and mystery of God in the midst of a world that has hemmed itself in with plasticity and gloss.

The building's acoustical challenges compelled me to slow my delivery and project my voice. At first, this felt cumbersome and unnatural, but with time, it became an opportunity to immerse myself in the words. I found myself pausing not for the sake of audibility, but to savor particular words and turns of phrase, in both the Roman Missal and the sacred scriptures.

As a celebrant, I am decidedly solemn, but my solemnity, I hope, is not stuffy and is offset by a touch of the casualness that should be part of any meal. At Mass I want to focus on the experience of the sacred — in the words that are spoken and in the people who gather. The Mass is a time to still mind and heart so as to rest momentarily in a greater reality, a truth deeper than any known to everyday consciousness. I remain close to the text. The words of the liturgy, I find, are more than sufficient. I am very restrained when it comes to injecting my own remarks, apart from the sermon itself. Some celebrants introduce each Mass with comments, sometimes to the point of chattiness. I have misgivings about proffering explanations and interpretations for all that takes place. I prefer to let people see and experience for themselves.

The massive altar at St. Matthew's, paneled with ornate, inlaid marble, also taught me, slowing and shaping my movements as I consecrated bread and wine there. The model of church as community calls for an altar that is scaled down, a simple table. While I find value in both styles, my time at St. Matthew's was about learning to yield to something much larger than myself.

The congregation for Mass, especially on weekdays, was barely congregated. Scattered throughout the church, many worshipers only loosely attended to what was taking place at the altar. Some lit votive lights, allowing the church to resound with the sound of their coins dropping into metal offering boxes. Others recited the rosary. A homeless man petitioned worshipers for money. Those who paid attention to the Mass did so in attitudes ranging from near rapture to outright boredom.

Administration of the Sacrament of Reconciliation, "confession," in conventional parlance, was one of the principal ministries at St. Matthew's. The penitents were mostly noontime worshipers, who stopped in during lunch breaks. Lines were long and people's time limited, so the challenge was to listen well and to learn to make the best of a moment that might last no more than a minute or two. Of course, if circumstances warranted, I thought nothing of taking much longer. One thoughtful observer recommended that we establish an "Express Line" for five sins or less.

Those hundreds of hours in confession reshaped me as much as they did any penitent. I learned to listen to people — not only to their words, but to their tone of voice. I learned to pick up intuitively on what they wanted to say and not to say. I learned how to reflect back what I was hearing by suggesting, especially with questions, alternative ways of looking at their issues. Sallee Rigler's call-in program often came to mind, because people's questions are much the same, whether talking to a confessor or a psychic. Like Sallee, I directed people's attention to the deeper issues, the questions they were not asking.

More important still, this sacrament taught me compassion. I was often impressed and moved by the honest efforts of people to try to understand the meaning of the gospel to their lives as employees, supervisors, fathers, mothers, friends and lovers. It was a great privilege to be invited into their inner dialogue with God.

I took to the Sacrament of Penance while at the same time diverging from official explanations about its function and necessity. I find it to be a sacred moment when persons gain new light on their experiences and difficulties. The sacrament presents an opportunity to step briefly from the flow of everyday life to reflect on choices and directions and ask, in essence, "What kind of person am I becoming? What use am I making of my talents and resources, of life itself?"

To understand this sacrament as a tool of personal reflection and growth does, however, represent a maturity about religion that many Catholics, of whatever age, do not permit themselves to develop. Many were raised with a checklist approach from which they learned to impersonally rattle off their few sins: "I missed morning and evening prayer five times. I told five lies. I masturbated twice." The checklist confession is truly superficial. It does not get to the heart of anything. Checklists, in fact, are quite seductive, because their legalistic approach to self-examination promises to cover everything of importance, while failing to prompt much soul searching about the qualities of one's personal behavior, for example, indifference to a spouse or callous disregard for the needs of subordinates.

For those who make this type of confession, there is little I can do. They do not invite the confessor into their life's journey. What they want from me I readily give, namely, ritual purification. I usually assign a penance and dispatch them quickly so that they do not take up the time needed by earnest seekers. This is a judgment, but not, I think, a harsh one. I try to accept people as they are.

Unfortunately, the official line on confession actually fosters a childish and mechanistic use of the sacrament. There are still many Catholics — and not all of them elderly — who rush to confession, as I once did, out of the fear that they have committed mortal sin by watching a television program with erotic content or missing Sunday Mass.

I long ago decided that I do not believe many of the specific sins, especially sexual ones, that the church officially regards as gravely serious or "mortal," are. That is not to say that there is not a profoundly moral dimension to one's use of sexuality. Unfortunately, the genitally obsessed approach to human sexuality fostered by the hierarchy means that many people think they are in serious sin almost as soon as they are conscious of some sexual thought or feeling.

It became common among priests of the Archdiocese to assert, beginning in the mid-1980s, that they were finding the consciences of Catholics, especially among young adults, to be "malformed." This, the party line, reflected locally the influence of the restorationist pontificate of John Paul II. The idea was that post-Vatican II attempts at reform had led to a loosening of the standards of religious education to the point where a generation had emerged that really did not know what it means to be Catholic, especially with respect to morals. The "malformed" line cropped up in discussions, especially those that took place in the presence of a bishop, who would nod knowingly in response.

From my vantage point, however, as one on the front lines hearing the confessions of a great many young adults, I knew that something had gone very right in their upbringing, including their religious education. True, most had abandoned the checklist and were not greatly preoccupied with the sinfulness of sexual thoughts and actions. On the other hand, they were much more likely to be doing some soul-searching, for example, about whether they were being selfish in a relationship. They asked excellent questions. Occasionally I disputed the party line with colleagues. But the discourse of "malformed consciences" was not about objective observation. It was about obeisance to the shifting tides of ecclesiastical fashion. My occasional assertions of contrary opinions were probably perceived, correctly, as signals that I am not a company man.

Despite the tedium of hearing many formulaic confessions, this is a ministry that I came to enjoy deeply. There is something sacred, something awesome, something much beyond the sum of the parts that occurs when this sacrament really "works." I know that I was given the right words, at times, to cut through fear, anxiety and self-loathing so that people were able to get some glimmer of light and taste of hope, to rediscover joy. There were moments, sometimes very brief, sometimes rather extended, when I knew that to be there, taking on the Creator's care for my fellow human being, was a very good place in which to be.

Such experiences confirmed my sense of priestliness. Celebrating Mass, preaching and hearing confessions came to be fundamental to how I thought of myself. These were joyful, peaceful, sublime and life-affirming experiences. De Chantal had been the dress rehearsal. St. Matthew's made me a priest to the core.

IV

St. Matthew's was also where I became thoroughly disenchanted with the Catholic Church or, to be precise, with the clerical culture that dominates it. The Roman collar is that culture's emblem. The collar is useful in the performance of ministerial duties, such as hospital visitation, where it immediately identifies a person as a member of the clergy. What I chafe against is clerical separatism, the use of the clerical state to separate priests from other human beings. Clerical separatism was once the centerpiece of the American hierarchy's strategy to establish the church as a separate entity, a "state-within-a-state," as Charles Morris puts it in his history, *American Catholic*. Catholic life was organized on the basis of a separatist mentality and institution building until the 1960's. Catholic schools, colleges, universities, social clubs, such as the Knights of Columbus, and even Catholic labor unions were all pieces of the strategy. In part, this separatism was a response to the anti-Catholic bigotry of the dominant, Protestant culture. In part, it was driven by a desire to keep Catholics free of the secular society's contaminating influences, especially democratic values. By the time I entered the Catholic church, when Catholic separatism had begun to break apart, many of its institutions and values looked foolish and nostalgic, like the stiffly proper, faded elegance of aged rectory "parlors," where priests receive callers. What it means for a university to claim a Catholic identity, for example, became a subject of intense debate. Parochial school systems, it was noticed, had failed to turn out graduates with values and beliefs markedly different from those of public school graduates. Few Catholics looked to the church for their social life, as they became better educated and began to participate with greater acceptance in all aspects of American life, following the election of John F. Kennedy as president.

During the 1960s, Catholic clergy suddenly found themselves in a crisis of identity and purpose. Clergy had been the exemplars of the old order, where they enjoyed a prestige based on their role of governance, rather than a presumed wisdom or spiritual depth. They were men of the system before they were men of God.

Lou Quinn was unapologetically a priest of the old order. A colleague described him as "the best that the old school has to offer." But like other remnants of the old order, his formalism seemed merely stiffly awkward and foolish, now that it was loosed from its cultural moorings in a changing church. Lou's insistence on clerical attire at meals and addressing associates as "Father" were part of it. Such practices served not so much to express a deep reverence for the priesthood as to establish and maintain, even in non-ministerial activities, the boundaries and perquisites associated with the rectory's pecking order. The one priest in the house who was of equal stature, Monsignor Gerhardt, officialis of the Archdiocese, Lou addressed by his first name.

I found the requirement of clerical attire at meals ludicrous, as did my colleagues, but complied, rather than cause a ruckus. Doing so was inconvenient, because it meant that when I returned to the rectory from some errand or class, I often had to rush to my rooms and change before appearing in the dining room, since I chose not to dress clerically for everyday tasks. Even at that, I usually removed my collar at table, as a subtle protest.

I saw no need to dress clerically to walk to the post office or drug store; and, in fact, most of my colleagues did not wear "clericals" when out and about either. But beyond that, I became philosophically averse to the collar, because of the version of church it came to represent. I sometimes reminded my colleagues that the use of clerical attire by diocesan clergy was a practice that emerged in the United States only a century before, due to Irish influence. Moreover, a third century pope, Sylvester I, actually forbade the public use of any distinctive garb by the church's priests, since this was a common practice among pagan priests. But such observations seemed only arcane and impractical. Clerical life being in a crisis, most active priests found solace and reassurance in the familiar, if tattered remnants of what once marked their profession's prestige.

Clothing choices of any kind do, admittedly, establish boundaries and nurture identities. By not dressing clerically, I was intentionally assuming other identities. My Lacoste T-shirts, Levi's and sneakers provided visual cues of my gayness that were recognizable to Dupont Circle denizens. Sometimes, as I passed parishioners, especially elderly women, on the street, I detected puzzlement in their eyes, as they scanned me up and down, taking in the tight jeans and thick leather belt with dangling keys attached. They were not necessarily disapproving, and we often stopped to chat, but my appearance in secular clothing seemed somehow always unexpected.

The contrast between Catholics' ideals and expectations of priests and the reality of our lives is a needless byproduct of the clerical culture. The juxtaposition of sacred and mundane not only does not undermine the priestly identity but actually enhances and strengthens it. Christianity celebrates that juxtaposition, the conjoining of heaven and earth, divinity and humanity, sacred and mundane. The Eucharist, in which elements common to everyday life, bread and wine, are consecrated so that they become, in the Catholic view, the body and blood of Christ, is based on this idea. The power of what is communicated in the Eucharist is lost in excessive ritual that loses contact with the sacrament's humble, earthly basis.

This was the problem with the pre-Vatican II liturgy that church officials and theologians sought to correct in the reforms of the late 1960s. It is telling that so-called "conservatives," who reject much that has come out of the Council, seek to nullify precisely the introduction of the mundane into the liturgy. They object to lectors being attired in street clothes, rather than robes, to read the scriptures. They disdain the use of contemporary music. And they strenuously object to the use of bread, whether home-baked or otherwise produced, that looks too much like, well, *bread*, preferring instead the traditional tissue-thin wafers that look and taste like plastic. The display of a Eucharistic "host," i.e., a piece of conse-crated bread, in a bejeweled monstrance crafted of precious metal, for adoration and benediction, is a ritual favored by traditionalists precisely because it is a mystification that removes the Eucharistic bread from its humble origins several steps farther than does the Mass itself.

The real mystery, the wonder, the very point of the Eucharist is that God dwells among us. While I have a penchant for liturgical solemnity, I disagree with permitting it to overshadow the celebration's human dimen-sions. The symbolic power of the Eucharist is not enhanced, but dimin-ished, by turning from what it is: a meal. Similarly, the priesthood is not protected and honored by the accoutrements of special garb, titles and the symbolic removal of priests from "the world," by the imposition of celibacy and residence in church-controlled rectories. On the contrary, such measures mystify "Father" (and "Monsignor") and obscure the wonder of the priesthood that is that a human being somehow becomes a vehicle of God's grace for the Christian community.

To be in the secular world as a full participant neither contradicts nor invalidates the priestly ministry. I am very much aware of being a priest and find myself accepted as a priest however "secular" the setting. Life in Christ does not remove us from the secular world. It propels us into it. Yes, many of us need our shrines and sacred spaces, such as St. Matthew's; but we do not need to live in them to lead holy lives.

Lou Quinn, I know, cringed a bit to see how I went about. One evening, it happened that we both were expecting rides. I went outside, in my customary jeans, to wait in front of the rectory, and it happened that Lou was there, as well. He was dressed in black clericals, complete with gold cuff links. He smiled nervously, but edged away, so that it would not appear to passersby that we had anything to do with one another. This was an amusing, but bothersome experience, because it is never pleasant to be shunned.

As I began to understand how unlikely it was that I ever would have a real place at the table within the church, I increasingly restricted my ministry to the essentials — celebrating Mass, preaching, hearing confessions, counseling, performing weddings and funerals. I was a functionary, useful to the church for my ordained power to turn bread and wine into the body and blood of Christ. Clearly Lou Quinn had no desire for services from me beyond the sacramental. If my superiors did not want my real work, the creative work of my mind and heart, I would apply it elsewhere, in my doctoral program.

V

I planned to return to Rome for my field research, an investigation of the social and cultural environments of UN bureaucracies. For a student of anthropology, a discipline whose fieldwork traditions developed around the model of holistic studies of the villages of indigenous peoples, this was, at the time, an unusual project.

Field research, based on anthropology's localized, village-based studies, traditionally entailed the collection of data about many domains: political structures and practices, economic arrangements, religion, warfare, marriage, kinship, law, sanctions, diet, medicine and the like. During the 1960s, anthropologists increasingly moved beyond this model, as the world changed, including the worlds of indigenous peoples. Studies of peasant societies increased, a much broader undertaking, which required refashioning the holistic ideal toward more narrowly targeted objectives. The use of anthropological methods to study modern, western societies had begun in earnest by the 1980s, but what I was undertaking was still sufficiently different that some of the department's faculty were wary.

With the guidance of Professor Jon Anderson, I adopted a cultural analytic approach that looks beyond structure to the often confusing and contradictory patchwork of ideas, metaphors and myths by which people seek to comprehend and shape their world. My plan was to focus on what people have to say about their experiences as UN employees.

Because radically cultural methods were so new, the forms of data necessarily messy and the methods of analysis only able to yield imprecise, tentative results, I found it difficult to explain satisfactorily to others, including colleagues, what my work in Rome entailed. I was, of course, still sorting this out for myself. Assuming all went well, I would interview employees of one or more international secretariats and observe occasional international conferences. But this was not a "bureaucracy study." I was not interested in describing the structure and performance of any particular organization. To do that would have been to conduct a study driven by prevailing understandings about how bureaucracies work, which would have shown nothing new. My objective was to learn informants' own real life ways of understanding and constructing their world. I wanted to build an analysis from their own terms.

I flew to Rome in September. On my arrival, an overconfident taxi driver took me from the airport directly to the house of the Crozier Fathers, apparently thinking that he might deposit me at any of the places where English-speaking clergy reside. I repeated the address: "San Gregorio al Celio, *numero uno.*" This time, after stopping to ask directions, we found the right street, but when I saw the building with blankets and clothes hanging from the windows and occupants shouting at each other, I tensed up. Surely this could not be San Gregorio's! I made my way up a dark path to a door, where I knocked, but was unable to rouse anyone. My driver pushed on another half-block, stopping in front of the church of San Gregorio, with its mountain of marble stairs. After ringing, Father Andreas, the guest master appeared. What a relief! A friendly young priest who spoke English. He helped haul my luggage up the steps.

My room was so tiny I managed to get just inside with the luggage. I was across the hall from Andreas, on a corridor that had been truncated by a partition. On the other side of the partition were, I soon learned, "deinstitutionalized" mental patients who would be on the streets but for this facility, which was run by Mother Teresa's Missionaries of Charity. It was to that section of the building that I had first gone and knocked, without response. In the months that followed, the sights and sounds of these troubled neighbors, who occupied half the building owned by the Camaldolese, would become a familiar backdrop to daily life. Sometimes there would be shouting and scuffling of such ferocity that it seemed the pugilists might come crashing through the wall into my room.

The Camaldolese Congregation with which I lived is one of the oldest religious orders in the church. An order of hermits, it was founded by St. Romuald in the tenth century near the swamps of Venice. Now based in Tuscany, the Camaldolese maintained the house in Rome to educate their men preparing for ordination. By the 1980s, with dwindling numbers, they divided the building so that the Missionaries of Charity could have a place to care for the poor. In the fall of 1986, San Gregorio's housed only eight seminarians.

The only non-Italian in the house, I found myself immersed not only in the Italian language, but in the life of an extended Italian family. This was a wonderful experience and proved to be just the right counterpoint to my days in the international secretariats. The food was consistently the best that I have found in any institutional setting. Fresh bread was delivered daily and I often had the delicious job of slicing it before pranzo, the large, midday meal. The wine was passable. Desserts were served and I came to realize how underappreciated in the United States is this vital aspect of Italian cuisine.

I settled well into life with the Camaldolese. They were easygoing men who dressed casually, enjoyed life and prayed with fervor and beauty. The priests were scholarly men whose sermons at daily Mass were always deep and interesting. The brothers included men trained in engineering and pharmacology. There was also one sweet busybody, the beloved house eccentric, who, after a few months, declared exuberantly that I was "a good man."

San Gregorio is a medieval church that was altered with baroque touches in the seventeenth and eighteenth centuries. It was built on the family estate of Gregory the Great, who was pope from the late sixth to early seventh centuries. Gregory was from a noble family that lived in this section of the city with others of its class. The building looks directly across the Via di San Gregorio to the Palatine hill, where the imperial family lived, until the fifth century.

Saint Gregory is a figure of historic importance to Anglicans, because he commissioned Augustine to evangelize Britain. The Venerable Bede, an eighth century English monk, dates Gregory's interest, indeed, his fascination with Britain to the day he discovered in the market place in Rome some Angle youths being sold as slaves. Bede writes that they had "fair complexions, handsome faces, and lovely hair." When Gregory learned that they were from Britain, he asked whether these islanders were Christian or heathen. On learning that they were heathen, Gregory sighed deeply and lamented that "the author of darkness should have men so bright of face in his grip." Gregory made a pun based on the name of their nation, Angles (*Angli*), declaring that they were "angelic." (A noble precedent was thus established, long before I nicknamed Larry, "Angelique.") So taken was Gregory by these young Angles that he sought permission from the pope to travel to Britain to evangelize it. The pope was willing to let him go, but the citizens of Rome were not. Eventually, after his own election as pope, Gregory commissioned Augustine to go on the mission instead. This famous story recalls a time when the frank expression of same-sex attraction carried none of the stigma we know today.

This episode is depicted in one of San Gregorio's side chapels. Guide books report that San Gregorio's has been a favorite site of Anglican and English visitors for centuries. I never saw any evidence of this myself and, in fact, I found the presence of tourists at San Gregorio, despite its central location, to be something of a rarity. In the hallway outside the sacristy, however, I noticed a woodcarving with a plaque identifying it as a gift from the Anglican monks of Holy Cross Monastery in West Park, New York, where I had often visited as an undergraduate. On inquiring about this I learned that the Camaldolese have a special relationship with the Order of the Holy Cross. In fact, they had formed a joint Anglican/Roman Catholic monastery with Holy Cross monks in Berkeley, California. This discovery confirmed my sense that I had chosen the right residence.

San Gregorio was a setting that stirred my imagination and nurtured my soul. I was very happy there. Although my weak grasp of Italian and shyness held me back from much of the conversation, I found that these men simply enjoyed being together in a way that contrasted sharply with the stiff and generally indifferent settings of the rectories where I had lived. In Washington, I was made to feel the odd man out for my dislike of the reactionary and authoritarian trends in the Vatican. At San Gregorio, the Vatican was viewed with bemused detachment and generally regarded as a place that, lamentably, may not even be considered Christian. After ten years of finding myself spiritually and intellectually isolated by the provincialism of American clergy, San Gregorio's provided a welcome oasis.

San Gregorio's was also the most convenient location I could have chosen, from the standpoint of my field research. FAO was a ten-minute walk away. So also was the entrance to the Metropolitana rail line that I took to another center of my research, IFAD (International Fund for Agricultural Development).

I embarked on my field research with much uncertainty. Would the assurances that I had been given of access to IFAD and WFP (World Food Programme) pan out? In the early weeks, there were unexplained delays, which made me anxious. During those weeks, however, I made considerable inroads with people at FAO. A friend in Washington had given me the name of FAO's general counsel, Mr. Roche. Once this British gentleman got past the puzzling notion that this time the anthropologist was there to look at them ("Am *I* a specimen?"), rather than to go out to some third world site to study *others* (non-Westerners), he took to the idea. Mr. Roche gave me entree, through the director of personnel, to every level of the organization, from the managerial to the secretarial. FAO, which I had been prepared to find inaccessible, turned out to be the centerpiece of my research.

Eventually approval came for my work at IFAD and WFP, as well. I established a routine of interviewing one or, at most, two people a day and then returning to San Gregorio to record my notes in computer files. I also had the opportunity for considerable participant observation within these secretariats — eating lunch in FAO's cafeteria or sipping a coffee on the roof terrace. I soon became a familiar face that security guards waved through the checkpoints.

VI

In October, the Vatican's Congregation for the Doctrine of the Faith issued a "pastoral" letter on homosexuality, commonly referred to as the "Halloween Letter." Authored by Cardinal Josef Ratzinger, the future Pope Benedict XVI, the letter declared homosexuality to be something other than a morally neutral condition; it is, he claimed, an "objective disorder," because it represents "a more or less strong tendency ordered toward an intrinsic moral evil." Gregory the Great would have been astonished by such assertions.

The letter also included language of astonishing benevolence toward perpetrators of violence against gay persons: "neither the Church nor society at large should be surprised when... irrational and violent reactions increase," in response to increased social tolerance of homosexuality. Here was a line of reasoning that resonates with a familiar rhetorical strategy employed by fascist regimes: blame the victims of violence. This document and its implications would weigh heavily on me in the future, after returning to parish ministry. At the time of its release, I found it little more than an unpleasant distraction. I was working on my doctorate and enjoying the freedom of a sabbatical. With a doctorate, I reasoned, I would enjoy sufficient independence to speak and write on topics, including sexuality, where I departed from the official line, because I would be doing so as an anthropologist, rather than a theologian. Such thinking now seems naive, but it is worth noting that the Vatican itself harbors its own interest in cultural study.

Tucked away in the Vatican's bureaucratic recesses is a small agency dedicated to exploring anthropological approaches to contemporary society, the Pontifical Institute for the Study of Culture. I met with its Secretary, Father Hervé Carrier, S.J., who holds a doctorate in sociology from The Catholic University of America. He was rector of the Gregorian University, when I was a theology student, and had overseen the restructuring of its academic programs, as well as the liberalization of policies on student dress and the admission of women. I met with Father Carrier to learn more about the Vatican's interest in culture.

The Institute was the creation of Pope John Paul II. The Vatican's interest in culture dates from Vatican II's document on the church in the modern world, *Gaudium et Spes*, which emphasizes understanding the human person as a cultural being, rather than the abstract "rational being" of scholastic, philosophical definition. It was John Paul II, however, with a philosophical background in phenomenology, who brought to the Vatican an organized interest in the subject. The Institute was the pope's pet project. Other parts of the Vatican bureaucracy, for example, the Congregation for Education, were obliged to interface with the Institute to identify culture-related goals to include in their missions.

I found the Institute's work and objectives both misguided and arrogant, on the one hand, and yet profoundly heartening, on the other. Methodologically, they were two generations behind, conceptualizing "culture" with the exaggerated holism that had been the hallmark of anthropology's past focus on villages of indigenous peoples as if of isolated specimens. Worse, it was evident that the ultimate objective was to manipulate or manage culture, a goal that most anthropologists would consider scientifically spurious, even if the ethical dilemmas entailed could somehow be overcome.

By its very existence, however, the Institute plants seeds that one day could produce some real change within the church. An official interest in anthropology registers a notion that is radical for the clerical culture, namely, that it is important to know what is happening in the world. Cultural anthropology is a form of intentional, disciplined listening. The higher clergy are not good at listening. Perhaps the phenomenologist-pope had something more to offer than restorationist conservatism after all.

Father Carrier spoke with the ebullient confidence of a man with a mission. The bishops in Africa and Latin America, he explained, have all adopted strategies to study the cultures of the peoples they serve. Even the Diocese of Rome, he claimed, has an auxiliary bishop whose primary job is the study of culture. The bishops of the United States, he lamented, have been slow to see the relevance of this. My work at FAO, however, he found most encouraging. He offered to help, although he admitted that the Institute's UN connections were with UNESCO, rather than the agencies in Rome.

Father Carrier asked how I present myself in the agencies. I explained that I introduce myself as "Father Murray," because that makes it somewhat easier to get past secretaries and to set up interviews, but that I wear jacket and tie, rather than the Roman collar, on site. He remarked approvingly that this is precisely the type of work the church needs to be doing. He predicted that my bishop, Hickey, a "smart man," would likely be supportive of my career as an anthropologist.

I was elated to find such views expressed at a locus so central to the church's bureaucracy. It gave me hope, as had the opening of the Vatican's Gallery of Modern Religious Art, thirteen years before, that, behind the grim walls and heavy-handed pronouncements exist active minds with genuine interests in the contemporary world. Father Carrier's ringing endorsement of my work gave me hope that I had indeed found my niche as a priest.

VII

My work on the UN system reached its modest eureka-moment, as I waited one day on the platform at the Metropolitana station in suburban EUR for the train back to town. I had just come from a council session of diplomats, a sort of mini-General Assembly. These are prodigiously dull events, and that day's session had been no exception. Delegates representing different countries stand, one by one, to speak on various issues. Most participants know each other's positions in advance. Everyone knows that the real work takes place behind the scenes, not in meetings where the media are watching. "So why do they bother?" I wondered. And then it hit me: the gathering of UN diplomats in assembly is its own purpose. The exchange of information or lack of it is quite beside the point. What happens in the big, general assembly-type meeting is that the nation-states of the world are recognized and recognize each other. The mechanism that holds it together is addressing the assembly. This is pure ritual. When delegates address the assembly they essentially tell stories about what brings their country to its particular perspective. The point of telling the story, of speaking, is not to construe events so much as it is simply to speak, to exercise the prerogative of a nation-state to make an articulation before the "world," which, for them, is the world of nation-states. By doing so, every time they assemble, the nations of the world, through their diplomats, reconstitute "the world" as they know it. Such sessions are meaningful to participants in their own terms, not because of objective outcomes.

This insight concerning diplomatic councils opened up for me the foundations of secretariat life, which, in theory, must strive to transcend differences of nationality, ethnicity, and language. How and why that transcendence is supposed to work was what I wanted to know. I now understood that ritual is the key. In the appointment of a secretariat's executive head (the secretary-general of the UN or the director-general of FAO, for example), the members designate an individual who is uniquely entrusted with the responsibility to represent and enact this transcendence. Whether anyone believes this or not, the executive head ritually embodies this special (I would say "sacred") state of transcendence. While controversy and tension surround the entire system, the possibility that staff can actually have such an "internationalist" outlook is the core belief around which secretariat life is structured. What makes the system work, however, is not measurable evidence that it actually does, but the ritualized role of the executive head, whose existence confers on the secretariat's bureaucracy its legitimacy as "internationalist."

This realization was a crucial moment in my field research. It is fulfilling to find connections between one's own work and the works of other social theorists and ethnographers. The breakthrough moment means that one has seen some wrinkle of the social fabric in a new light. I knew, as I stepped onto the Metropolitana that day that I had accomplished a quintessential rite of passage. I would come away not only with mounds of data, but with a theory, a kernel of insight, a fresh perspective. From that moment I was an anthropologist.

While I was in Rome, my dear friend, Robert Nicolich, died of AIDS. He succumbed quickly, I learned, from a letter sent a few days after by a mutual friend. During a hospitalization in November, his heart gave out. I also learned, during this time, that Michael Peterson, a priest of the Archdiocese of Washington, was dying of AIDS. Michael, a psychiatrist who had been ordained a few years before, founded the St. Luke's Institute, a treatment facility for clergy and religious. I learned of his death on the morning of my return to Washington. Archbishop Hickey generally received high marks for his compassionate regard for Michael, during his final weeks, and his openness with the public about the cause of death. In 1987 AIDS was still homophobically stigmatized as a disease of gay men. Without admitting anything about the sexuality of this nationally prominent priest who had served as a consultant to the American bishops on human sexuality, Hickey demonstrated well the Roman Catholic Church's skill for burying the dead with dignity.

CHAPTER 5

BEGINNINGS

I

I returned to St. Matthew's, where I was to remain another four years. This would bring my assignment at St. Matthew's to eleven years, a long stretch for a parish priest, especially an associate, and, for me personally, a long stretch indeed in a place where the pastor treated me with disdainful indifference. I was, however, growing indifferent to his indifference. I was even glad to be home.

In June of 1987, Hickey expelled Dignity/Washington from Georgetown University, where the community had been meeting for Sunday Mass in St. William's Chapel. The expulsion offered a show of compliance with both the letter and spirit of the Vatican's "Halloween Letter." Hickey had already been passed over once for the red hat. Now was the time to redouble efforts at demonstrating unqualified loyalty to the Holy See.

The place of homosexuality in church politics had been made clear the previous November, when the pope sent the American bishops a letter that stressed the importance of maintaining "full communion with the successor of St. Peter." I wonder what mere *partial* communion might entail. No matter, the Vatican was ready to unleash its arsenal in the pursuit of "full communion." Unprecedented Vatican intervention in the affairs of the Archdiocese of Seattle, where a tolerant stance toward homosexuality was a factor, had precipitated a restless mood among the bishops. Hickey had served as the Vatican's investigator of Raymond Hunthausen, the Archbishop of Seattle. Hunthausen had personally welcomed a national Dignity convention to Seattle and made his cathedral available for a convention liturgy. Hickey's willingness to serve as the Vatican's point man did not sit well with fellow bishops, who resented Vatican interference in diocesan affairs. I saw Hickey in Rome, in the fall of 1986, just after the bishops' meeting when matters had come to a head. He was angered by what he took to be the disloyalty of some in the American hierarchy to the Holy Father. And, as it happened, he was in Rome to join Vatican curialists in a chorus of dismay over the persistence of such wrinkles of independence in the American hierarchy.

Hickey's expulsion of Dignity/Washington from Georgetown, had, therefore, been foreshadowed by his investigation of Hunthausen. He ordered the expulsion without bothering to consult or inform his official lieutenant on homosexual Catholics, Father John Gigrich. John had been officially designated by Hickey as the Archdiocese's Coordinator of Ministry to Homosexual Catholics. In exchange for this empty title John stated his agreement that all homosexual genital behavior was sinful. That declaration cost him dearly. He lost the support and respect of many in Washington's gay community. More than that, I believe he lost his self-respect. John's life took a significant turn, from that point on. He became narcissistically self-preoccupied and seemed never to achieve a state of happiness beyond the occasional display of laughter forced in rapid-fire explosions through a reluctant windpipe.

John was miffed by the expulsion, but remained stoically loyal. There was a particularly pathetic performance, when he went on WAMU's Diane Rehm Show to discuss the expulsion with the Vice President of Dignity, Elinor Crocker, the mother of a lesbian. He ranged back and forth, going to ludicrous lengths to put a positive spin on the situation. Speaking of the Vatican's harsh letter on homosexuality, for example, he came up with this: "there are not always the attempts that there should be locally to translate... into non-technical terms so that people really understand and can still see the compassionate face of Jesus behind the technical terms, the technical jargon. I think it is sometimes there." Really? I was embarrassed for John, as it became apparent that he had made a Faustian bargain for an empty title that afforded him no advantage whatsoever in advancing the church's position or pastoral work in this area.

II

In 1988 I completed my dissertation. I now possessed the credential that I had long sought. I felt empowered. Free. I could build a new life for myself. I would continue to work as a priest, but with a new measure of independence.

Cardinal Hickey and I discussed my future in the Archdiocese. I had no interest in becoming a pastor, but suggested some alternative areas where my skills might be helpful: cultural diversity, tracking cultural trends, and conflict management. Hickey seemed willing to consider some alternatives to parish ministry. He said he would get back to me.

After several weeks, it was not Hickey himself, but his Director of Priests' Personnel, Bill English, who contacted me. The Personnel Board and the Cardinal had decided that I should find my own job. After getting a job, I would then be reassigned to another parish, where I would reside and engage in parish ministry to the extent that my schedule permitted.

I was astonished. I had never heard of such a thing, especially for a diocesan priest. It seemed that all I could ask for had just been handed to me. Or had it? Was this not also a backhanded way of marginalizing me? Was I, in effect, being fired? What troubled me was that the Archdiocese of Washington, the organization to which I had dedicated my life, had not managed to find a place for me. Why had the opportunities that I discussed with Cardinal Hickey been set aside? Why had I not been consulted about this new arrangement, prior to being presented with it as a *fait accompli?* Did they know that going out and finding my own job was what I wanted? What did it mean? What were the limits? Could it truly be *any* job that I chose?

III

John Gigrich dropped dead while shaving, one morning in late 1990. A housekeeper wailed that he should not have died like *that*, on the bathroom floor. As the paramedics hoisted him into the ambulance, I exchanged sad glances with one of the block's veteran street persons, whom John had often helped. George Washington University Hospital telephoned shortly after to confirm what we already knew. The cause of death was later identified as a pulmonary embolism.

Lou Quinn and I went to John's rooms to fetch his will and any other pertinent papers. The will was brief and, I noted, left a significant chunk to the Archdiocese of Washington for the support of ministry to homosexual persons. I could have kicked John in the teeth for being so obtuse. The wording left the Archdiocese free to use the bequest in any way, including support of ministries such as "Courage" that promote celibacy and chastity as the only acceptable norms for gay persons. The likelihood that Archdiocesan officials would use the funds in support of a ministry similar in philosophy to John's was nil. John always trusted church officials to be better than they were. My criticisms of their actions he inevitably countered with intimations that they were smarter, wiser, more forward-looking and generous than I imagined, appearances notwithstanding.

John's instructions that his body not be carried into church, but cremated as soon as possible, were disregarded by Archdiocesan officials. He had not wanted a funeral Mass, as such, that is, a service with the body present, but only a memorial Mass. His requests were unusual for a Catholic priest, but should have been honored. The failure to do so is, of course, typical for the Archdiocese, as John should have known. The interment was a private affair at Arlington National Cemetery. He somehow qualified for a military cemetery, perhaps because of his work for many years as a civilian employee of the Department of Defense. Since priests of the Archdiocese are normally buried at Gate of Heaven, in Silver Spring, his choice was striking.

John's death, although sudden, concluded a period of several weeks of bizarre behavior, during which he became withdrawn and sullen. He did not take meals with the rest of us. He sat alone in his room throughout the day. He refused to say Mass. When Lou gently urged him to try, he snapped angrily, "You don't understand. I can't!" Lou suggested that the priests of the house drop in on John, sensing that something was very wrong.

When John died, I immediately telephoned his close friend, Bill Neitz. Bill and John had met after a Dignity Mass some years before. In recent weeks, Bill had taken John to doctors' appointments. I was not aware of any grave illnesses, although John had been scheduled for prostate surgery the following week. The operation was serious, but not life threatening. John, however, had become irrationally distressed about it and had upset one sister with darkly pessimistic talk about his prognosis. When I reached Bill, I found him as surprised by the news as we at the rectory had been. Bill then recalled a conversation with John the evening before, about a prescription of pills that had just been filled. John said, "This should do it." "Do what?" Bill asked. But John did not elaborate. This was unsettling news. The announcement that a pulmonary embolism had been the cause of death indicated that the medical professionals were satisfied that they knew. For me, John's death remained shrouded in mystery. Whether he took pills that somehow triggered his demise, I have no way of knowing. The real puzzle lay in his dark mood during the weeks that preceded it. He had become like someone dead. And then he died. What happened?

This question haunted me for months. I periodically asked friends of

John for their observations. Several agreed that since the mid-1980s he had become much crankier. But none could shed light on the final weeks of deep depression.

Eventually, however, a crucial piece of that puzzle came to me from a psychologist, who knew John well. She recalled that someone associated with an ex-gay ministry had set John up. The man claimed that John had put his hand on his knee during a counseling session. Whatever happened, the allegation that John had made a pass at a counselee seemed preposterous. Indeed, it appeared to me that John had been completely celibate during the time I knew him. I could, however, readily believe that someone from the religious right had targeted him. John must have been devastated. This certainly made his sharp decline in the weeks preceding his death more understandable. This story was one more example of what a treacherous and harsh environment the Archdiocese of Washington can be for a priest who works with the gay and lesbian community.

IV

John's death coincided with my own transition out of St. Matthew's. We had arrived together in 1979 and I was to leave a few weeks after his death. During the fall, I had already begun teaching at American University. I also accepted part-time work with a consulting firm, one of the "beltway bandits" that thrives on government contracts.

During this period, my interest in the gay community began to take on a sense of urgency. It was no longer enough that I had gay friends, that I enjoyed companionship in gay clubs or that gay men and lesbians sought me out for counseling. I was angry. Angry at the way the Reagan administration had been standoffish about the AIDS epidemic and at the president's refusal even to say the acronym, AIDS, in public. Angry that the Catholic Church had done nothing to help and much to hurt gay people. I was angry that I had felt obliged to stuff my feelings throughout my life. John's death added fuel to the fire. I was angry that John had been made to jump through the "church teaching" hoop to secure an empty title.

With John dead and my departure from St. Matthew's imminent, I was concerned about the many gay persons who worshiped there. It troubled me that St. Matthew's would likely become less gay friendly. I therefore decided to speak to the subject of homosexuality in my farewell homily. If I could find the courage. After so many years of public silence, it would not be easy to speak out. I prayed for guidance and strength.

In prayer, I did something I had not done in many years. I asked for a passage, by opening my Bible at random, a kind of divining technique that I had learned from the charismatics. My finger fell on Paul's Second Letter to the Corinthians, chapter 3, where, starting at verse 12, I found words that were astonishingly pertinent:

> Our hope being such, we speak with full confidence. We are not like Moses, who used to hide his face with a veil so that the Israelites could not see the final fading of that glory. Their minds, of course, were dulled. To this very day, when the old covenant is read the veil remains unlifted; it is only in Christ that it is taken away. Even now, when Moses is read a veil covers their understanding. 'But whenever he turns to the Lord, the veil will be removed.' The Lord is the Spirit, and where the Spirit of the Lord is, there is freedom. All of us, gazing on the Lord's glory with unveiled faces, are being transformed from glory to glory into his very image by the Lord who is the Spirit. (*New American Bible*)

The issue for me was not simply whether to speak about homosexuality, but whether to come out. I had labored for fifteen years as a priest, but with a "veiled face." I had celebrated Mass, preached, absolved from sin, anointed the sick, buried the dead, and officiated at weddings, all from behind a veil. Something fundamental about my identity had been hidden. What would people have thought, if they had known I was gay? Would they have thought less of my ministry? Would they have rejected me? What I reckoned with, in a new way, was that this hiddenness has nothing to do with the gospel and, indeed, is contrary to the freedom about which Paul waxed enthusiastic. I was determined to make my own the words of verse 12: "we speak with full confidence."

But how? How could I speak out without being shut down? I had images of speaking out in a homily, only to have Lou Quinn intervene in some way. I knew he would be listening from his study on Saturday, during my evening Mass, but would leave for Fort Lauderdale the next day. Would he telephone the Cardinal? Would he go so far as to cut off the sound system? To preclude such interventions, I delivered a nice, general, farewell address with no reference to homosexuality. The next morning,

Lou commented on my sermon to Bernie Gerhardt, saying that it was a relief that I had not said some of the things that I might have been inclined to say. He was referring, I believe, to my disdain for himself. That left me with the 5:30 P.M. Mass on Sunday, as well as the 10 A.M. Mass the following Sunday. These were the Masses where I said what was in me to say.

I told the congregants that a "quiet" ministry to gay persons had been an important aspect of my life at St. Matthew's. I spoke of the challenges entailed in being gay and indicated that the church must do much more to support this population. I spoke of St. Aelred, an eleventh century English abbot and gay man who had been sexually active in his youth. I spoke of the many gay persons who had participated in the life of the Cathedral parish and of that parish's proximity to Dupont Circle, a major locus of gay life in Washington. I said that my departure from St. Matthew's would also mean separation from this neighborhood, where gay persons were so naturally a part of my life and ministry. I concluded by declaring that because of a "burden of love that will not go away, my pastoral commitment to the gay community will not decrease, but, on the contrary, will be intensified and conducted much more openly than in the past."

The moment was electrified. The congregation was stunned. They had just heard what they did not expect to hear in church: an honest, passionate statement from their parish priest. They had just heard a sermon on a topic that Catholic preachers avoid the way cats recoil from spiders. They knew that this took courage. They knew that my heart was fully in it. They also knew that, without saying the actual words, I had just come out as a gay man. The response was overwhelmingly positive. Several parishioners thanked me with tears in their eyes. They thanked me for saying what they had never heard in church before, their name, and for saying that it is good to be who they are. Many others, though not gay, welcomed my words and expressed their support.

At the 10 A.M. Mass the following Sunday, I repeated the homily, after making some changes to allow the gospel text for the day to serve as the springboard for my remarks. This time, a few people, perhaps three or four, got up and left the church, as soon as they heard the word, "gay." Since this was the weekly Latin Mass, which draws a crowd that generally is averse to things modern, at least in church, it was surprising there were not more departures. Those that did take place actually strengthened my resolve and enhanced the moment, like a touch of just the right seasoning that adds zest to a pasta sauce.

Once again, the moment was electrified. Once again, the outpouring of gratitude and support: "It's about time." "Thank you for speaking about me." A local gay activist, Tom Chorlton, happened to be there that Sunday with his mother. He was thrilled. The publisher of the *National Catholic Reporter*, Bill McSweeney, was also present and requested a copy of the sermon for his editor.

I had taken several steps forward. These were steps not only into a more public commitment to the gay community, but into the life of faith. I was taking a risk with my career by publicly taking a gay-affirming stance, however well-founded in church tradition or nuanced. In fact, my words had been very carefully chosen and I prided myself on the fact that a close scrutiny of the text would give church officials, however antipathetic, nothing doctrinal with which to accuse me. I glanced at the lights of incoming phone calls several times, during my remaining days at St. Matthew's, expecting a call from the chancery at any moment. It never came. But that was not because my sermon had not come to their attention. It had. I would be questioned about it four years later. I was correct in thinking they would notice. I was now tagged as a troublemaker. A performance such as this confirmed my outsider status. Perhaps they would not shut me down. That might prove to be difficult. But neither would they advance me or entrust me with any increase of responsibilities.

I received phone calls, letters of support and a poem that had been written anonymously by someone who had obviously listened *very* carefully to my sermons on this and other occasions.

I felt invigorated by this exercise in personal integrity. I had stood before people who had known me for years. Several must have suspected I had a certain affinity for gay men, while others probably gave it little or no thought. But to hear such words from one whom they had long known as a celebrant at Mass, father confessor, counselor and teacher, was something new. Their responses might well have been negative. This moment was a decisive turning point in my life and ministry. I emerged from behind the veil. My commitment was to truth and compassion, core values of the Kingdom of God. These were baby steps, but I was for the first time experiencing what it means to have faith in the sense of trusting that it would be okay to take a significant risk for truth. God would be there. I was discovering that I do have the courage of my convictions. A new level of self was emerging.

V

I rejoined Dignity, after the move to St. Andrew's. Following Cardinal Hickey's order of expulsion from Georgetown University, the community had moved to St. Margaret's Episcopal Church on Connecticut Avenue, near Dupont Circle. It had been over ten years since I had been to a Dignity Mass. I was immediately impressed by the size of the congregation. There were some four hundred persons present. At Georgetown, average attendance had been less than half that number. The choir had grown considerably in size and was accompanied by multiple instruments — organ, piano, guitar, violin, flute, and clarinet. At the end of Mass, someone from the community's AIDS ministry walked to the altar to receive a pyx containing eucharistic bread for distribution to the sick. I was on holy ground. This was a Christian community, a gathering of deeply committed Christians, friends, joyfully gathering for worship week after week. The liturgies were thoughtful and prayerful. The sermons were deep and passionate. This was a community that had been tempered by the AIDS epidemic and by the official church's rejection. Dignity/Washington had grown much, much stronger.

I felt myself the prodigal son. These were my people. This was where I belonged. I knew well a number of the faces scattered through the church, from my former involvement with the chapter. They had stuck it out over the years and must have been deeply gratified by the growth that had taken place.

But where had I been? I had conveniently left Dignity behind at about the time I moved to the Cathedral, a place where I might have reasonably expected, as Cardinal Baum suggested, consideration for advancement. I had remained silent and out of sight, when my friends were expelled from Georgetown. And I had left the AIDS ministry to John Gigrich.

Was I being too hard on myself? Probably. I had no legal, ethical or moral obligation to be a member of this group. It is also true that I had spent the 1980s working on a doctorate and had, at times, been stretched thin by my commitments. Nonetheless, the feelings of remorse were very keen. They had to do, I suppose, with a broader sense that I had failed the gay community through cowardice and complacency. For several Sundays,

I sat quietly on a side pew during the Dignity Masses reflecting on this. My old friends received me back very warmly and graciously. I just took in the sense of being back home and how good it felt. Eventually, someone asked if I would celebrate a Sunday Mass for Dignity. This was certainly not an urgent request. Dignity had a pool of a dozen or more priests who rotated as celebrants. I readily agreed and was scheduled for April 28th.

I put my heart into preparing for that Mass. When I finally did stand before the Dignity congregation, I compared the experience of this Catholic community in exile to that of the Archdiocese:

Comparisons are often odious, but I think we know what we have here and how it compares with what we find in too many parishes: people coming late to Mass and leaving early, a sense that they want to get this over with, minimalist liturgies that seldom stir the heart, lip service to the assemblage being a community, hymns which have become so familiar they are sung, by the few who sing, without a moment's thought as to their meaning, an assortment of tepid parish activities that do not inspire or challenge or seek in any significant way to reach out to new people.

The branches are drying up. Not much fruit is being produced and frankly, many are blissfully unaware that they are supposed to be producing something or doing anything other than replicating the familiar routine, year in, year out. Vocations are down. Many have left, turning elsewhere for spiritual sustenance. Giving is down. Churches and Catholic schools are being shut down, as the barren branches begin to be pruned away. And the principal solutions proffered by those who have presided over this decline are for more of the same: extensions of their own authoritarian control; to control yet more of what we say and think and do; to discipline and silence voices that question, that challenge, that dare to disagree; to demand still more complete and more complexly worded pledges of allegiance and oaths of fidelity. The idea here is really a very simple one. They think that all they need do is lock our lips shut and then they need not concern themselves much about what's actually going on in our hearts and minds.

But however frenetic the activity of the designated keepers of this vineyard, there is no disguising the fact that they have lost touch with the moral, intellectual and psychological reality of the lives of many, many of their people. The official branches are increasingly barren, while others are proving fruitful, the ones that are branching out on their own, or that, like Dignity, have been stripped from the vine only to take root elsewhere and spring up to bear more fruit than ever, an abundance of fruit, an embarrassment of fruit.

I added that I could "no longer minister quietly to the needs of individuals while failing to address the root causes of many of those needs in the unjust, ignorant, prejudicial, hurtful and hateful, homophobic attitudes that have been institutionalized in our church and in our society." The congregation's response was warm and enthusiastic. I was where I needed to be. I was home.

VI

St. Andrew's was what I expected. Its church building, like St. Jane de Chantal's, had been constructed for eventual use as the school gymnasium. Having grown accustomed to the sumptuous decor and hushed, devotional tone of St. Matthew's, I found this new worship space jarring. Steel fire doors on either side, near the sanctuary, opened and slammed shut throughout the first part of the Mass, as parishioners utilized them for entrance from the rear parking lot. As celebrant, I found myself precariously perched, at the beginning and end of Mass, on a steep and narrow step placed just before the building's highest and poshest seat, from which I read the beginning and closing prayers. Just before me was the altar, over which a life-sized, wooden crucifix hung, suspended on two chains. I occasionally mused that the Mass — and my life — would come to a swift and dramatic conclusion should any link in those chains prove weak.

As in Bethesda, I was once again in an ambience of screaming babies, restless toddlers and snickering teen-agers. Late arrivals were common, although, for some reason, St. Andrew's lacked the tradition of early departures I had found at de Chantal. There was, on weekends, a general hubbub at Mass that greatly challenged any effort at thoughtful reflection. So far as I could see, this suited most parishioners just fine. Adults at St. Andrew's generally lacked programs, educational or otherwise, that would have encouraged significant examination of their lives or world. Their participation in church was focused on their children. The fact that the church was attached to a school building, the school being the larger of the two, represented in the physical order the way many parishioners related to their religion.

For his part, the pastor seemed to be in accord with this mind-set. Prior to Dave's arrival in 1984, St. Andrew's had been riven by factions that

represented polar opposites in the approach to church, indeed, to life. These
factions represented the residual influence of former pastors, alternately
liberal and conservative. In the heyday of the liberal pastor, laypersons had
easy access to the rectory, gathered around the altar during Mass, and took
charge of many parish ministries. Then came the conservative pastor, who
halted the egalitarian spirit for a return to unambiguous clerical control.

Dave Conway had been assigned to St. Andrew's as a healer.
Apparently he had been successful. During my two years there I found
hardly a ripple of the former tensions. On the other hand, the lack of
programming for adults was probably a result of the burnout experienced
by many from the days of the conservative-liberal rift. Why try to learn
anything new or to share one's thoughts, when the end result is unpleasant?

Dave was described to me, by my fellow associate, Mike Quill, as a
"gentleman." Mike was an enthusiastic and grateful booster of Dave. They
worked well together. As an associate in name only, I was not quite a part
of the team, but I found that Mike was right. Dave was gentlemanly in
manner, conversation, attitudes and aspirations. A tall, ruddy-faced, largely
baldheaded man of Irish descent, he dressed nicely, in the manner of
suburban casual — slacks and Lascoste T-shirts.

The rectory, which sat at the edge of the athletic field, was at a bit of a
remove from church and school, separated by a parking lot. One of Dave's
proud accomplishments had been the refurbishment of this thirty-year old
building, which had fallen into bad repair. The halls had been tastefully
carpeted. The common room had been very comfortably furnished and
equipped with television and video. Dave made frequent use of this room
to receive guests and foster some sense of priestly fraternity in the house.
Hors d'oeuvres and cocktails were occasionally served before dinner.
Saturday night was the focal point of the week, when the priests, joined by
the two seminarians who assisted on weekends, would trundle out to any of
Dave's dozen favorite restaurants for an ample meal that inevitably
included cocktails, appetizers, and desserts. Dave relished his role as host
to this weekly ritual and often added, upon returning to the rectory, "Thank
you, Mr. Hickey," an ironic slap at the Cardinal. I never knew how these
outings were funded. I suppose some Archdiocesan bureaucrat might have
objected, but quite frankly, if this is the price of building a bit of morale
and camaraderie among "the troops," it is a bargain. Knowing Cardinal
Hickey's own love for a good meal shared with fellow priests, I think he

would have agreed.

I never knew why Dave held such antipathy toward Hickey, but I supposed it had something to do with his own friendship with Cardinal Baum, Hickey's predecessor, who by that time was heading up the Vatican's unfortunately named Apostolic Penitentiary, the office that dispenses indulgences. On my initial visit to St. Andrew's I noticed that while a portrait of Cardinal Baum adorned the foyer, none of Cardinal Hickey was to be found. I suspected that this was intentional and Dave later confirmed that it was. This led me to think of my assignment to St. Andrew's as a kind of internal exile. It was a tacit acknowledgment that I had been tagged an outsider and sent to live with others who held views which, in one way or another, were institutionally incorrect.

VII

Exile enabled Dignity/Washington to develop a mature responsibility for its own faith life. For example, the community decided to implement gender-inclusive language in the liturgy. This may seem a small thing to persons unacquainted with liturgically oriented churches, where any change in worship activities typically arouses strong feelings and, inevitably, divisions. There were seemingly endless twists to the inclusive-language discussion in Dignity/Washington. For example, what to do with the invocation, "In the name of the Father, and of the Son, and of the Holy Spirit"? What are the theological ramifications of altering language with regard to such basic doctrines as the Trinity? What are the ramifications of not changing our language? What does "gender-inclusive" mean? Does it require something beyond gender-neutrality? Does it call for finding ways to integrate feminine terms and images into worship?

Dignity drafted experimental creeds and prayers. Evening discussions and an all-day forum were held. Yes, there was disagreement, but what I found more impressive were the earnestness, passion and intelligence with which the community engaged these issues. Catholic parishioners, however, do not have the opportunity for this level of participation in decision-making. They enjoy the relative peace and security of having the fundamentals of parish life and worship decided for them at considerable distance. Their opinions are neither desired nor elicited. Dignity, not having that dubious luxury, finds itself compelled to draw on its own resources. The result is the excitement of rediscovering the depth and resources of the Catholic tradition as the community reappropriates and adapts them for itself.

Dignity, in exile, has also been free to explore how to celebrate and support committed gay and lesbian relationships. The community formed a task force, on which I served, to study the issue. We met with couples to elicit opinions about what they would have liked or found helpful, to celebrate and affirm their relationship. As a result, we formed the Pastoral Team for Holy Unions to provide pre-Cana instructions for couples, retreats, potlucks with talks, and guidance for couples in organizing and celebrating their commitment (most prefer the traditional terms, "wedding" and "marriage") ceremonies. I was the director of this effort for its first two years, which meant that I presided at several holy union ceremonies, preached on the subject at Dignity Sunday Masses and generally stuck my neck out on an issue about which I felt strongly.

Dignity inspired me with hope that Catholics elsewhere might learn to take charge of their own spiritual lives. Quite apart from the question of sexual orientation, there are the millions who find themselves disaffected from the rule of church officials. If they could experience the depth of worship, loving support and intellectual and moral challenges of being in a community such as Dignity, they would rediscover the excitement of Catholicism.

My own creative energies, which had lain dormant under the restraints, some real, some perhaps only imagined, of my life as a priest in the Archdiocese, were awakening. It was exhilarating to have an opportunity to leave cynicism and hopelessness behind and to put my analytical and organizational skills to use in crafting new and much needed ministries.

During my years of "quiet" ministry to gay and lesbian persons, I often encountered persons who needed a healthy alternative to their current living situation. These included gay persons who had been kicked out of their homes by their families, suffered physical and sexual abuse, addiction and unemployment. In the spring of 1992 I decided to act on my dream of providing a place of refuge and transition for gay persons in crisis.

I drafted a proposal for an organization and shared it with friends. An attorney and his life partner, a certified public accountant, offered their services *pro bono*. Others expressed an interest in attending an organizing meeting. Just prior to the first meeting, Brian Gallagher, a member of Dignity, took me to lunch at Mrs. K's Toll House, a Silver Spring restaurant that is a favorite of begloved, elderly ladies for its antiques and gardens. In this unlikely setting, Brian presented me with a $2,000 check. That first donation gave credibility and momentum to the effort. At the first meeting of its board, we agreed to call ourselves "Among Friends."

VIII

Among Friends clarified my thoughts about what I wanted to do and where I wanted to be. St. Andrew's and its good people were neither. It makes all the difference when ministry comes from the heart, that is, from love rooted in a calling. Church bureaucrats lose sight of this, as they seek to fill slots, when assigning priests. The Mass is, after all, the Mass, and one priest's Mass, in Catholic theology, accomplishes the same outcome as any other priest's Mass — the consecration of bread and wine. If I was in St. Andrew's, it was because it served a convenient purpose for both the Archdiocese and me. But real ministry, the moments when I gave the best that I had to give, took place at Dignity. What felt right, what felt like magic, happened there, not at St. Andrew's. The people of St. Andrew's deserved better. I deserved better. I was ready to move on.

My reassignment returned me to the city, this time to St. Stephen's, a parish that neighbors St. Matthew's. Prior to moving to there, I informed the pastor, Tom Sheehan, of my involvement with the gay community. We were seated at the kitchen table.

"That's good, Paul. And that's very much needed here."

I leaned forward, straining to catch the words. Tom was a pale, white-haired Irishman in his mid-sixties. He spoke, or, rather, mumbled in a thick brogue. There was a pathos about him. He was frail, exhausted, overwhelmed, and seemed often on the verge of tears.

"Well, I felt that you should know this, because it's possible there may be an occasional mention in the newspaper of things that I am doing. For example, I am working now on an interfaith conference on ministry to gay persons that will take place this coming fall."

"No, none of that is a problem. Dear God! Someone has to do something to help these poor people. Damien Ministries used to meet in our church, and to hear these young men talk about having AIDS and how they coped was very moving. Back in the seventies Dignity even held some dinners here, until the Archdiocese told me I could no longer permit it."

The move to St. Stephen, Martyr Church was a return not only to the city but to a neighborhood that I had once known well. St. Paul's Episcopal Church, the parish where I had been a member at the time of my "going over to Rome" in 1968, was a block away. Foggy Bottom had changed during the intervening years. The neighborhood had been gentrified. Modest row houses morphed wondrously into pricey town houses. The former, African-American residents had vanished. The Kennedy Center and the Watergate complex now dominated the Potomac waterfront.

Only a week before my arrival at St. Stephen's, the organizing committee of the Gay and Lesbian Pride Day festivities presented me with an award. I rode in the parade, with other award recipients, on the back of a convertible, waving to the crowds. It was only two years before that I had worked up the courage to march in the parade myself. Now I appeared on stage and briefly addressed the crowd, as founder of a fledgling, gay organization. Would I be seen by parishioners of St. Matthew's, which was only two blocks from the parade route? Would television coverage include a shot of me? I considered the possibilities, but found myself willing to face any consequences.

IX

The various strands of my life were coming together. My steps into gay community work were meeting, happily, with acceptance and support from fellow priests. Prior even to discussing my gay commitments with Tom Sheehan, I mentioned them to Bill English. He was supportive and indicated that the Archdiocese would seek to place me in a parish with a gay population. When, after a few weeks, he suggested St. Stephen's and then the pastor there also proved to be receptive, my life seemed suddenly to be in harmony with the cosmos. Perhaps, finally, I would be able to bring it all together — ministry, vocation and gay identity.

Within two months of my arrival at St. Stephen's, I signed a year's lease for a small office suite for Among Friends. It was on the second floor of a dilapidated house of 1890s vintage that was owned by a realtor, whose offices were housed in the same building. This space served as the center where we began to learn more about our target population, while raising sufficient funds to open a house.

I handled most of the incoming calls to Among Friends. Gay people in crisis, I found, do very much want places to turn for help where they can be themselves without explanation and fuss. One man called several times from a small town. He had read about us in a newspaper. He was in a relationship that had become physically abusive, but did not know where he would live or how he would work, if he tried to leave it. He thought Washington might have more opportunities for him. A forty-year-old lesbian, who still lived at home, where she suffered verbal abuse on a daily basis, wanted desperately to make a break, but knew nothing about the lesbian community in Washington.

Although not a religious organization, Among Friends was my ministry. The same love that had coursed through me years before, at the Court Jester, I recognized, was with me in Among Friends. It demanded the best that I had to give.

X

With Among Friends, which was about a half hour's walk from St. Stephen's, I had, in essence, a full-time job without pay. At St. Stephen's, I had, in essence, a part-time job. At the parish, in addition to the basic ministerial duties – Mass, confession, baptisms, and such — I was responsible for developing educational programs. Tom Sheehan and Jack Davin had suggested the educational focus. Jack was a former executive, who had been forced into early retirement for health reasons.

Jack and I did not hit it off. I found him a well-intentioned man who disregarded the input and observations of everyone other than Tom. This was, I suppose, the competitive mode of behavior that had served him well in the world of management. Because he had been a high-level executive, there was a presumption that his managerial skills were vastly superior to those of parish clergy. Tom regarded Jack as the savior who would set the parish on the right course, during a critical, transitional moment. For my part, I saw that he had little understanding of either the theology or realities of pastoral work, which often builds slowly, with little to show by way of quantifiable results.

A case in point is the parish council. Although required by Archdiocesan policy, St. Stephen's did not have a parish council, an elected, representative body of parishioners. Tom attributed this lack to the disruption caused by the parish's construction of a new rectory and parish center. He believed that the parishioners were insufficiently acquainted with one another to be trusted with the responsibility of voting for council members. Moreover, he claimed, he wanted to promote new and younger leadership in the parish. He and Jack selected thirteen individuals to serve on the newly created council.

A series of meetings with the appointees began, under Jack's tutelage. And tutelage it was. Over several months Jack droned on at the monthly meetings, with the help of an overhead projector and easel, flow charts and sheaves of photocopied materials, about Catholicism, parishes, parish councils, and committees. When, in the spring of 1994, he upbraided the newly appointed council members for their seeming inactivity, I blithely suggested that they needed an opportunity to talk and begin to make some decisions for themselves. My message was unmistakable: it was time for Jack to step aside and let the council begin to function. Jack brushed my remarks aside, unwilling to admit that his overbearing presence had itself become an obstacle to the maturation of the body he presumably sought to create.

Not surprisingly, Jack became an antagonist. He differed with my approach to the education ministry. I began by building an infrastructure, a parish committee that could share meaningfully in the responsibility for developing and running the parish's educational programs. That way, the ministry would not depend entirely on myself. It would be the *parishioners'* ministry and would be able to continue in the event of my departure. I desired, as well, to test different types of programs, with a variety of schedulings (weeknights, Saturday morning, Sunday) to see what worked. It was also clear that we needed to find ways of broadening the parish's appeal, to reach beyond the aging and dwindling population of registered parishioners.

The education committee had some modest successes and, indeed, proved to be the only entity at St. Stephen's organizing parish activities other than Sunday Mass. Nevertheless, Jack was clearly dissatisfied and, I believe, formed the same opinion of me that he had of the council, namely, that not enough was happening.

Tom dissolved the council at the start of its August meeting. Most council members were baffled by this unexpected development. Many were hurt and angered. Tom did not attempt to assuage their feelings. The only explanation proffered, the one that gained momentary acceptance by the council's leadership as a kind of political correctness, was that the "right chemistry" had been lacking for the council to work together.

In September, Tom told me over a Friday evening dinner that St.

Stephen's could not afford a "third priest." Somehow *I* was the third priest. No personal or professional deficiency on my part was intimated. It was simply a matter of finances, he muttered. I learned through a colleague, however, that he had made vague references to my not doing enough around the parish.

It was true that I had invested considerable time elsewhere, especially with Among Friends. For me, that was ministry in the truest sense. I had, after all, informed Tom about these endeavors before moving to St. Stephen's. What had gone wrong? Why had he not discussed his concerns with me? Had the extracurricular involvements turned out to be more than he expected? I wanted the truth. But I was not in an ambience that fosters speaking the truth. I was in the Roman Catholic Church.

PART II

LIVING TRUTH

CHAPTER 6

BINDING

"Priests at St. Stephen's crash and burn. That's how Father Sheehan operates. Something in him needs to push his fellow priests into crisis. He's the kind of person that thrives on crisis. It has happened over and over. Father Jeff was one of them. I knew what was happening, because I became Father Jeff's friend and he confided in me."

Ben, an attorney, had invited me to dinner at his home, a nearby condo. The vermicelli, clumped from overcooking, was difficult to lift from the bowl onto my plate. Ben is a plain man with little use for the social lubricants of urbanity. His best insights tend to come in awkward clumps, like his pasta, but with a bit of parsing and sorting, prove to be acute and even prescient. When we had this conversation, a month before Tom's disclosure of his plans for my separation from St. Stephen's, I had no idea how close I was to a crash and burn scenario.

"Well, Ben, I understand what you are saying. I appreciate your concern. But Father Sheehan and I are getting along fine, although I would like better communication. It's hard to get him to say what he's thinking. We *should* have staff meetings. But I don't see any problems between us."

"No crash and burn scenarios, then?" Ben pressed his concern.

"None that I can see."

And so we left the matter that evening.

Two months later, the alarms began to sound. Tom's announcement that St. Stephen's could no longer afford a "third priest" was very distressing. To my mind, the assignment to St. Stephen's had worked out well, given my lowered expectations of parish life.

In late August I presented Tom a list of programs the Education Committee proposed for the coming year. Our meeting was curious. He stood at the kitchen counter cleaning parts from a clock he had disassembled. I read off the items: prayer and scripture series, book discussions, an evening on Anglican-Roman Catholic relations, an interfaith concert, the Rite of the Christian Initiation of Adults, special events for the elderly.

"Very ambitious," Tom mumbled, his attention more focused on restoring the workings of his clock than on my efforts to restore life to his moribund parish.

With the recently abortive attempt to form a parish council, the Education Committee's offerings represented the only splash of life left in the place. Tom's response to the committee's proposals was quite beside the point. My intention was not to impress. I wanted to build both parish leadership and a broader clientele for our activities. I sought not only Tom's approval, but his interest and active support. His support was crucial not only to the success of programs during the coming year, but to the development of long-range goals.

Given the professional populations of the parish's surrounding neighborhoods — Foggy Bottom, West End and Georgetown — St. Stephen's needed to offer some sophisticated fare. A bit down the road I hoped we might offer an array of courses as part of a cohesive program in spirituality or lay ministry. First, however, we needed to develop the infrastructure to plan, publicize and conduct our programs. I envisaged the coming year as a time to test market various concepts and see if we could draw from beyond the core of the parish's dozen or so regulars, who would attend whatever we scheduled. This was what I had hoped to discuss with Tom.

I did allude briefly to these ideas, but found no opening to expand on them. My interlocutor, a thin, ashen man, bent over his clockworks, looking aged well beyond his sixty-six years, managed only a barely audible "very ambitious" by way of response. Such experiences were disconcerting, but did not suggest impending trouble. From Tom, a cryptic, withdrawn man, this was what I had come to expect.

The rectory, as it happened, was walking distance from my office at the Among Friends Center, where I spent two or three afternoons a week. Given Tom's acceptance of my work with the gay community, the convenience of living in such proximity to much of gay Washington made my assignment to St. Stephen's fortuitous.

The summer of 1994 was an especially productive time. During those happy, peaceful weeks, the thought of quitting the Archdiocese came to mind once again. My relationship with the Archdiocese seemed like a marriage that had failed. Perhaps we could have a no-fault divorce. I did not wish the organization or its leaders ill, but my profound disagreement with their approaches to Catholicism and ministry would never go away. I needed a change.

St. Stephen's made the ideal point of departure, because of its location and flexible schedule. Knowing that the job search would take some months, I set the following June as my deadline for finding a job and moving out on my own.

Tom knew none of this, when, in early September, he sat across from me at dinner, preparing to drop his bomb. Words of any kind from him were rare. At lunch and dinner, day after day, we greeted one another at the table and then set about chomping salad greens, slurping soup and cutting into our steaks without any conversation whatsoever. Unnerved by this, during my initial months there, I would mention topics of current interest — a neighboring pastor's illness, the Vatican's harsh treatment of a theologian, the difficulties experienced by the friends and family of a man who had died from AIDS. From Tom's briefly muttered responses, sometimes accompanied by compassionately exclamatory moans and sighs, I inferred that we shared common perspectives in at least a few areas. Nevertheless, these were perfunctory responses and conversation between us never took flight. After a while, I began to test not speaking at all, to see whether, indeed, we might pass an entire meal in silence. We did. By the end of my first year, I yielded entirely to Tom's preference for no conversation.

And so we sat across from one another at the dining room's splendid mahogany table, our meals served from the kitchen by a Peruvian woman who interrupted the uneasy quiet with barely audible squeaks of "excuse me" and "thank you," as she delivered and removed dishes, always with a sense of unease, as though she loathed entering this ambience even for brief moments. During the course of each meal, Tom would invariably light up one or two cigarettes. Before slicing into his pizza bread or making the last stabs at his salad, he fortified himself with a few puffs of tobacco. His colorless countenance became a disturbing mystery. I wondered what was going on behind it, as I glanced across at his head, which seemed too intent on the task of adding relish to a hot dog. I accepted that this was how it would be between us. Rectory life never had much appealed to me anyway. Living with Tom only confirmed that I had made the right decision: to get out and, for once, create my own living space.

Then, one quiet summer evening, he dropped his bomb. It was Friday, September 9th. Tom scrunched his face into a wrinkled mass, a grimace I suppose, in anticipation of some unpleasant response, to announce the news:

"St. Stephen's is in trouble. We are not able to pay our bills. We find that we just cannot afford to have a third priest."

Being of a frame of mind to leave the Archdiocese anyway, I offered supportive words. Tom seemed a pathetic creature who was somehow overwhelmed by circumstances beyond his comprehension. I *wanted* to offer my sympathetic support:

"Father Val, of course, is essential, because of his hospital ministry. Clearly I am the most expendable member of the staff."

Tom intoned his own sympathetic note in response to my generous, self-sacrificial gesture:

"And you haven't even had your vacation yet."

"Before we decide anything, perhaps we can make some arrangement. When I was at St. Andrew's, I was on half-salary, because I had a job outside the rectory. I think I could find another job within a few months. Let me put out some feelers and see what I can do. Let's meet a week from now and I will propose something specific."

Tom nodded what I took to be his assent.

Tom's announcement was distressing. A move at just this moment would upset my plans to leave the Archdiocese or, at least, set back those plans by several months. In addition to the inconvenience of packing and moving, there were the uncertainties of how compatible another assignment would be with Among Friends. I regularly put in some twenty to thirty hours each week on the organization. Indeed, one transitioning strategy was to raise the revenues of Among Friends to the point where I could draw at least part of my income from it. For the other part, I hoped to get some part-time contract work. The uncertainties of my status at St. Stephen's placed these plans in jeopardy.

Two weeks later, we resumed the discussion in his office. Tom said:

"The Finance Council has turned down your proposal."

"But I haven't yet made a proposal. What I suggested was that I get back to you after exploring some options. I wanted to see if I could come up with a solution that would both relieve the parish's financial burden and enable me to continue on here."

Tom's office was a small room where clutter abounded. Antique clocks under the desk. Stacks of papers and books on the desk, the air convection unit, the round table at which we sat. Sunlight streamed in through the window. With the air conditioning cut off, the atmosphere was close and warm. Smoke from Tom's cigarette curlicued upward through the light. I saw immediately that I was not going to get through. He had made up his mind. I continued, in the stubborn hope that what I considered reason would prevail:

"I have inquired into the practicalities of setting up a day-care program. Given our location, I think this makes a lot of sense for us and it can be highly lucrative, in addition to providing a needed service."

"I can't do that to Cornish," Tom said.

"Cornish" was Father Richard Cornish Martin, then rector of nearby St. Paul's, which ran a day-care program.

"Have you spoken to him?" I asked. "Perhaps they have a waiting list. Perhaps we could serve a different market niche. If they do toddler care, we could do infant, or vice versa. It might even be mutually beneficial for both parishes to have programs."

Tom scribbled a note and agreed to call Cornish.

"Or we could do elder day-care, I continued. We already have parishioners who work with the elderly. The need for this in this neighborhood is probably significant. It's a natural for us."

Tom's demeanor remained indifferent.

"Let's set some goals," I persisted. "I think I can get some consulting work within a few months. Let's say that within six months I will cut the expense of my compensation by the parish in half. At the same time, I can help you to explore increasing revenues by obtaining a grant. I am sure you can get money from the District for an elder care program."

Tom scribbled more notes. He said he would ask the Finance Council. I left his office confused and annoyed by his indifference. There was not a word of concern about what my departure from the parish would mean to me.

The following Monday I received a telephone message from Bill English. From this I knew that Tom was moving quickly. My efforts to negotiate had been in vain. When I returned the call, Bill's soft, earnest voice was reassuring.

Bill and I met in my office, a few days later. I suggested that we begin by stating our respective understandings of the situation. After I provided a quick chronology that began with Tom's announcement that one priest must leave the parish, Bill said that much more had been said to me than to him.

I suggested that there was more here than Tom was admitting. The Finance Council's annual report had just been printed that week and it showed a slight surplus for the fiscal year just finished and projected a similar one for the year ahead, without any change in the lines pertaining to priests' salaries and benefits. The budget also included something new: ten thousand dollars for the salary of a "director of education," and twelve hundred dollars for educational expenses.

"This may not be an especially robust financial picture," I observed, "but there is nothing here that says, 'crisis.'"

"If a pastor says there is a financial crisis in his parish, the Archdiocese has to accept that," Bill said.

Bill was a company man. Despite his earnest handholding and sympathetic talk about the Archdiocese's need to update its personnel practices, he had been thoroughly absorbed into the hierarchical culture of the Archdiocese. Of course, the pastor is right. If Tom says there is a financial crisis, "the Archdiocese has to accept that." He's the pastor and I'm not.

"But I doubt whether finances are the reason," Bill continued.

"What do you mean?"

"I believe that you find money for what you want. If Tom wanted to keep you, money would not be a problem. You should have some kind of meeting with Tom, perhaps with Ray Kemp present. Ray is good at asking blunt questions that get to the things that would otherwise not be spoken."

"Has Tom suggested that there are underlying issues?" I asked.

"No, he has said nothing negative about you."

"Well, Bill, I must tell you that this situation completely baffles me. I have found Tom to be supportive of my work, including my ministry with the gay community. I have put together an Education Committee in the parish, which is currently the only source of programming here at St. Stephen's. Tom even called our plans for the coming year 'ambitious.'"

If there were a financial crisis, I argued, it had been building for months, at the least, and the priests of the house should have been consulted much earlier.

"Paul," Bill responded, "the Archdiocese still has not decided anything."

Later that day, I met with Ben. I was not yet at crash and burn, but things were heading in that direction. Ben, however, brought a fresh perspective:

"You have rights. You are not as powerless in this as you think."

Not powerless? I was hungry for those words. Did this attorney think I might have some kind of legal recourse? Ben was an outsider to the ways of clerical culture. I had seen too much mistreatment of staff by church officials to believe the "rights" of ordinary citizens extend to church settings. I recalled a meeting I once had with a lawyer, a theologian and a sociologist in the late 1980s. A Catholic periodical had asked me to expand on a proposal I had drafted to establish an organization that would investigate and publicize abuses of power within the church at all levels — parish, school, diocese and national office. The proposal had resonated with several influential persons and this group had convened a brown-bag luncheon to explore it further.

The lawyer noted how difficult it is to prosecute and litigate misconduct by church officials. The separation of church and state means that experiences of improper termination, harassment and prejudice in church organizations are often viewed as untouchable by the courts. (Things have changed dramatically, since the 2002 explosion triggered by a chain reaction of sexual abuse scandals involving Catholic clergy and cover-ups by several American bishops.) My proposal, however, had not been to call for legal action, but for the *shaming* of church officials by shining a spotlight on deeds they would prefer to keep hidden and challenging them with their own rhetoric. The project failed to go forward, but the lawyer's lecture on the lack of rights within the church had been instructive. As Ben now alluded to my rights, I realized how foreign the concept had become to my thinking about the church. I wanted to believe him, but I suspected he was being naive.

Feeling as vulnerable as I did, to speak of rights seemed to promise nothing practical for my immediate needs. Had I had sufficient resources to cover a few months' rent, I would have bolted right then. But I needed several more months from the Archdiocese, before I could manage a reasonable transition. At the same time, I had made a considerable investment of time and resources in Among Friends. This fledgling organization needed much more from me in order to survive. Reassignment to another parish might dramatically curtail my ability to donate time and energy.

What made my sense of powerlessness particularly acute was the fact that these were not issues I could very well bring to the discussion with the

Archdiocese. Church officials were not likely to view sympathetically a request to help me transition out of their service.

Ben suggested that I keep a journal of all that happened in this affair. In it I would keep notes about conversations, phone calls, and observations of even small details of uncertain significance. Ben said I should choose someone to periodically read, sign and date each page. This would provide useful evidence, should it be necessary to go to court.

Keeping a journal felt a bit conspiratorial, which, I suppose, is why I took to the idea at once. While I continued to be skeptical that I had any enforceable rights, keeping a journal did afford some sense of control. Even if no laws had yet been broken, they might be. My journal would provide the "paper trail" that showed how persons, events and ideas fitted together.

A few days later, on Sunday morning, Ray and I met in my study. He did not want to meet in my office, where, as he put it, the "walls have ears." Ray had a special rapport with Tom. Tom's face always brightened into an unaccustomed smile on those infrequent occasions when Ray momentarily stopped into the rectory, usually as he passed through the dining room, after celebrating the evening Mass. Ray already knew about my plight.

"I'm not surprised," he said. "Some of the old biddies in the parish have found out about Among Friends. They read about you in the *Blade*."

"Oh? And how did they happen to read about me in the *Blade*? Are they subscribers?"

Ray chuckled:

"One of them said to me, 'You know, Father Murray has another job.' I believe pressure built to the point where Tom just decided to get rid of you."

"But I told him about this before I came here. In any event, I am not being treated fairly here. Tom should have discussed this with Val and you and myself months ago. Maybe we could have done something. I agree that this parish is in trouble, but Tom's lack of leadership is the main cause of that trouble."

"Dying flowers," Ray said.

"What?"

"Dying flowers. Flowers are always left in the sanctuary here long after they have wilted. This is the image of this place that sticks in my mind."

"There's something else you should know, Ray," I continued. "In

August, I decided to leave the Archdiocese. A transfer now comes at the worst possible moment. I need some time to make my transition. A move would complicate things badly."

"Have you told Tom?"

"It's not easy to tell Tom anything," I said. "At least, not for me. He's so introverted I find it hard to tell what he's thinking or how he is reacting to what I say. I don't see what difference knowing this would make."

"You mean, he might wonder why the parish should foot the bill for your transition?"

"Exactly."

"Well, I think that's more likely to make an impression on him than the justice argument. A guy taking a leave is the sort of thing Tom would have some sympathy for."

"You mean because of his own anger at the Archdiocese?"

Ray nodded. He offered to speak to Tom and asked for permission to mention to him my plans to leave the Archdiocese. He thought he could get Tom to agree to keep me on for some months, with June 30th as the target for my departure.

Two days later, Ray called to say that the outcome of his discussion with Tom had not been favorable. Tom held fast to the financial rationale for getting rid of me. When my work with gay people was mentioned, Tom had even become wistful about the need for it. He was, however, indifferent to my plans to leave the Archdiocese.

Ray had also spoken with Bill English. They both found Tom's understanding of the process of reassigning a priest poor. Normally it takes at least a few months. Tom seemed to expect that I would be moved out of St. Stephen's immediately on his say so. Ray said that I could probably count on not moving before the first of the year.

I asked Ray to meet with Tom and me. I had an uneasy feeling about Tom. He was a volatile mix of incomprehension and uncommunicativeness. Perhaps we could clear the air a bit, as well as get across to him that I would continue to be at St. Stephen's for a few more months. Ray agreed and planned one of his momentary stops at the dinner table for the next Friday evening, when both Tom and I would be there. He would suggest that we schedule a time to meet.

"Why, Ray?" Tom asked with a kind of wail, as though he had been unexpectedly punched in the stomach.

Tom's face contracted into a mass of wrinkles at Ray's gently worded suggestion of a meeting. He was like a turtle, ready to pull into his shell at the barest provocation.

"Meet to discuss what?" Tom bellowed.

Gesturing toward the housekeeper in the kitchen, he continued:

"The parish doesn't have the money even to pay her."

"In the spirit of the gospel of the day, Tom. In the spirit of reconciliation. So that Paul's remaining weeks here can be as productive as possible."

Tom relented and we met the following Tuesday. At that meeting Tom recited his familiar woes about the parish's financial crisis. Since Val provided an essential service, he was the obvious person to remain on the staff.

I thanked Tom for having graciously welcomed me to St. Stephen's and for the support he had shown my ministry to the gay community. I went on, however, to protest the impersonal way I was being pushed out:

"I feel like a piece of machinery being unbolted from the floor and tossed aside."

In a debriefing by phone the next day Ray said that he agreed with what I had said about being treated like machinery. He also called attention to something I had scarcely noticed:

"The Finance Council. What's their role in all of this? Tom said they were asking why you are still here. Obviously they are very close to the decision-making process."

"Yes, now that you mention it," I said, "Tom keeps referring to them. For example, he said he would ask them about my proposal to earn part of my income from an outside job. Also about starting day-care."

"I wouldn't start packing my bags yet," Ray said. "These people don't have a clue about how the Archdiocese works."

However the Archdiocese works, its engines were gearing up to extract me from St. Stephen's, with or without my consent, and set me down again God knows where. Does God have something to do with all of this? The assumption that the decisions of bishops are guided the Holy Spirit and enjoy a kind of divine authority has permitted the processes by which priests are assigned to remain veiled in mystery, not unlike the machinations of the Wizard of Oz. I know of one former priest of the Archdiocese of New York, a man with strong academic credentials, who was told by

Cardinal Cook, "God does not want you to be anything other than a parish priest."

There is, indeed, a case to be made from Catholic tradition that the bishop's voice is in some sense the voice of God. This, however, must be taken together with other vehicles of God's voice, including the members of the church, the scriptures, tradition, and creation itself. For a bureaucrat, the temptation to abuse this tradition is very great. Armies, governmental agencies, and big corporations all have their own versions of it: it must be so, because we say it is. The Catholic hierarchy, however, includes divinity in its palette. It employs the sacred patina to justify actions taken even for the most patently self-serving reasons. The consequences of such a coupling of bureaucratic exigency and the sacred can, of course, be dreadful.

In the weeks that followed, it became evident the Archdiocese had made a decision to oust me from the parish. Tom's rationale became the Archdiocese's rationale: financial crisis. Never mind the objective truth of the assertion. And so the personnel mechanism began to roll in its fixed roulette.

In mid-November, Bill English met with me, once again, to discuss reassignment.

"Please do not take this the wrong way, but you do not fit into the typical parish assignment," Bill said, wincing defensively.

If he was bracing for an argument, I was not about to give him one:

"Well, no problem there. That's what I have been telling the Archdiocese for many years. I don't fit into parish ministry as I find it in the Archdiocese of Washington. Yet I love being a priest and believe I have something to offer. Just not in a way that confines me to a parish."

"Have you considered joining a religious order?" Bill asked.

"There's something to that," I said. "But at this stage of my life, and nearly twenty years into the priesthood, I am not inclined to make that change. But it is true that my life probably would have been much easier had I joined an order, such as the Jesuits, that fosters the development of individual gifts."

Bill winced a bit more and with obvious hesitation said:

"Ray shared with me that you had told him in confidence that you plan to leave the Archdiocese in June of next year. I cannot use that if I do not hear it from you. It would help to know that, because it would bear on any decision about a placement."

I sat for a moment in silence. I had not expected this. True, I had consented to letting Ray disclose my intentions to Tom. No doubt Ray meant well, but I was not ready to entrust Archdiocesan officials with any of this. Bill looked at me, his eyes gentle, solicitous, understanding. What to do? By admitting it, I would cross a threshold I was unprepared to cross. I wanted to negotiate with the Archdiocese for a reassignment that would be based on my qualifications and experience. Who knew what might, at long last, come of that? I continued to hope that somehow I might find my place, my niche, in the Archdiocese. On the other hand, not admitting to the truthfulness of what Ray had reported to Bill would mean doing something that I find personally unbearable: dissembling, pretending that we did not know some crucial fact. Perhaps my distaste for disingenuousness comes from the struggle to claim my same-sex feelings and to be pleased, finally, with letting others know my identity as a gay man. Simply covering over the truth was not an option. I found, instead, another aspect of the truth to bring forward:

"Ray and I spoke several weeks ago. This whole affair has been such a distraction that I have not been able to think about other things. It is true that I discussed leaving in June with Ray, but reassignment places that in doubt. My position today is that I continue to hope to resolve my differences with the Archdiocese. What difference does this make to what you have to do?"

"Temporary assignments, until a fixed date, are sometimes made."

"I don't like the idea of that. I can tell you now that I will not accept a short-term assignment."

Bill's earnest solicitude began to feel like calculated probing, a kind of dissection of the soul. Bill went on to say that he had personally investigated the finances of St. Stephen's and concluded that there really is a crisis. I replied:

"Yes, I agree that a crisis of sorts exists, but it is the result of mismanagement. Instead of moving me, the Archdiocese should investigate the practices of those who brought us to this point. Meanwhile, I am being pushed out without any regard for how this affects me or where I might best fit in. I intend to meet with Cardinal Hickey as part of this process to express my views on this."

"I have no problem with that," Bill responded. "But if you meet with the Cardinal, then you should be prepared to answer questions about Among Friends."

There was a momentary silence. The kind of silence in which the hum of the fluorescent lights overhead suddenly becomes bothersome. This was the first mention of Among Friends by any official of the Archdiocese. I had avoided mentioning specific organizations, when I had told Bill about my involvement with the gay community. I drew a breath and calmly replied:

"Among Friends helps gay and lesbian persons in crisis. I am proud of how far we have come, in just two years. I will be happy to discuss this with the Cardinal, though I don't see why he should be concerned with it."

"The Cardinal has an interest, because any ministry in which a priest is involved must be approved by him," Bill said.

"I do not hide the fact that I am a priest in my work with Among Friends, but neither do I emphasize it. I often present myself as 'Doctor Murray,' as a way of overriding 'Father Murray.' The truth is, the Catholic Church is such a negative in the gay community that being a Catholic priest is not much help."

"There was an article that appeared about Among Friends in the *Blade* last year. I recall it mentioning your being a Catholic priest," he solemnly countered.

After the meeting with Bill, in debriefing sessions with an expanding circle of confidantes, I asked repeatedly about Bill's motives in bringing up Among Friends. What did that have to do with anything? He introduced it only when I mentioned meeting with the Cardinal — about which he professed to have "no problem," which meant, of course, that he did have a problem with it. Clearly it was a warning. But of what kind? It might have been a friendly warning, a way of cautioning me in advance that if I chose to go to the Cardinal, who already knew and wondered about this organization, the subject would inevitably come up. Or it could have been a threat: if you challenge my authority and go over my head to the Cardinal, then I will retaliate by bringing Among Friends to his attention.

I was inclined to credit the friendly warning interpretation. Bill had become more aloof and bureaucratic during his tenure as personnel director, but that was to be expected. His was a sensitive job and he worked, after all, directly for the Cardinal. His pastoral instincts, however, were still discernible. He impressed me as basically a simple, good-hearted man who cared about the goals and struggles of his fellow priests. It was hard to imagine Bill being sufficiently Machiavellian to introduce Among Friends into the picture as a way of tripping me up.

When it came to the gay issue, I had crossed certain thresholds. And when I crossed them, I knew that there would be consequences. I had even expected them long before this. Whether Bill's warning had been friendly or ominous I was beyond the point of being cowed. No more wrenching in the gut at the thought of exposure. I was proud of what I was doing.

Four weeks later, Bill announced the Personnel Board's recommendation: that I move to St. Anthony's, a parish in northeast Washington, near Catholic University. This was, he said, a temporary assignment, "until you can be clear about what you want to do." They were giving me until July 1st.

Although Bill had disregarded my plea not to be given a temporary assignment, I was impressed that this was not a mean-spirited appointment. Dick Burton, the pastor of St. Anthony's, welcomed the prospect of utilizing my background to beef up his parish's adult education programs and he was also a strong advocate for priests engaging in specialized ministries. It was the kind of place, Bill suggested, where I might work out an arrangement to reside at the parish while pursuing other work.

But I knew I would not go there for what would be a horizontal move, at best, and at considerable expense and inconvenience to myself. What most troubled me was that the Archdiocese had passed on the opportunity to make an offer, to recommend a job, where I would be integral to some facet of church life. Instead, this felt much like being shelved, pushed to the periphery, where I would have time "to decide."

I telephoned the Cardinal's secretary, Father Barry Knestout, to schedule an appointment. I was to meet with Hickey in his office at the Pastoral Center on December 30th.

The impending meeting with Hickey heightened the sense of crisis. This was crisis in the full sense. "Crisis" is derived from the Greek word for decision. Personally and professionally this crisis had precipitated a moment of decision. There were too many variables at work, most of all the Cardinal's reaction, to predict specific outcomes. But I had already made, more than I realized, the most important decision: to be a person. I was done with being a cog in somebody's machine. Done with hiding. Done with being afraid. Done with letting others decide how I should live and work.

From my own investigation I learned that my assignment to St. Stephen's had itself been tentative from the start, although no one had bothered to inform me. This was because when Bill English first proposed my transfer to St. Stephen's, Tom took the matter to the Finance Council, which was undecided about whether the parish would be able to handle an increase in staff. Bill knew this, but the assignment had been made in the usual way.

Wondering just what lay in store at St. Anthony's, I arranged a luncheon visit with its pastor. Dick Burton was a radiant blimp, about sixty years old. He led me on a dark, creaky staircase up several flights to what was supposed to be my new home. I thought of the former occupant of these rooms, Mike, whom I had often seen staggeringly drunk in clubs, and wondered how he negotiated those stairs at night. Mike was a thoughtful, intelligent man, whose health problems were well known in the Archdiocese. Was I, in their view, another Mike, another difficult soul needing to be shelved in this remote loft?

Dick opened the door, admitting that he had never been in the rooms before. They were spacious and bright. Large windows provided a marvelous view of the city. Furniture was needed, he observed, but the parish would take care of that. I would be sharing the floor with a priest who, he said, I would never see.

"Never see?" I asked.

"Never," Dick replied seriously. "He celebrates an early Mass. That's the only time he comes out. He lives off cans of Ensure that he keeps in his room."

The feeling of being warehoused was confirmed.

Dick obviously enjoyed being pastor of St. Anthony's, an economically and racially diverse parish that also included many academics and diplomats. Dick said he had frequent dinner guests and was looking for ways to tap into the parish's impressive pool of talent. He thought I might help with that. He was trying to make me feel welcome.

After lunch at a nearby tavern, we strolled briefly through the neighborhood, as he chatted on about the possibilities. Dick knew that I was ambivalent. When we parted, I thanked him for lunch and for his generous offer:

"Dick, I want you to know that I'm still trying to decide what to do. It has to do with my relationship to the church. With my personal history in the Archdiocese. It has nothing to do with you or St. Anthony's. I know I could be as happy here as I could any place, but I have to think just now more broadly about my future."

Dick nodded with understanding:

"Yes, Paul, I know. Sometimes I have those kinds of thoughts, too."

He paused and, staring off to nowhere in particular, added:

"You reach a point of no return, you know."

The visit to St. Anthony's fortified my resolve not to be shuttled about at the whim of others. Yes, St. Anthony's would be an engaging assignment, under different circumstances. But I was being sent there for the wrong reasons: appeasement of an erratic pastor with a history of treating associates badly, church officials who refuse to discuss career development, a personnel director who has found the top floor of St. Anthony's a convenient site for shelving problems.

It was a cold, sunny day when I drove to the Pastoral Center for my meeting with Cardinal Hickey. Hickey was already seated behind the desk, when I was escorted into his study. This was not his real office, a place where papers stack up and books are studied. This was an executive's showcase office: couch and chairs overlooked by a portrait of John Carroll, first bishop of the United States; one corner ablaze with colorful, full-sized flags of Maryland, the District of Columbia, the United States, and the Vatican; a glistening curio cabinet; and next to the windows, the Cardinal's desk, polished and clear.

Cardinal Hickey greeted me with his customary, two-handed, gripping handshake and big smile. Usually there would have been a few minutes of pleasantries, tidbits about Rome or recent travels. Instead, we moved directly to the business at hand. It added to the sense of gravity that he was seated behind the desk. He pulled out the leaf to take notes, which he wrote in a meticulous hand by fountain pen throughout the meeting. The air of formality was unlike the mood of any of my previous meetings with him.

At the Cardinal's invitation I launched into a detailed narration of the events that had led to the decision to transfer me from St. Stephen's. He was surprised that the parish had budgeted for me only through September and that the pastor and Finance Council had expected I would be transferred by a given date. He was impressed that I had held a meeting to afford Tom the opportunity to state whether there were any reasons other than

---

financial for proposing my transfer.

It was apparent that my complaints about my treatment by Tom Sheehan had found receptive ears. I knew something of the Cardinal's own history with Tom, who had a well-deserved reputation for being prickly and enigmatic.

When I turned to the question of my reassignment to St. Anthony's, once again, to my surprise, I found a sympathetic response.

"Your Eminence, I object to being given a temporary assignment. I told Bill English that I would cooperate with a transfer, but I need a real assignment."

"Yes," the Cardinal responded, "I myself do not understand the reason for assigning you to St. Anthony's only until July. What is supposed to happen then?"

"The reason July has taken on some importance is based on something I had said to Ray Kemp. I told him that before any of this problem came up, I had decided to take a leave from the Archdiocese. I was planning to begin a job search, with a goal of being out by June. When Tom disclosed his intention of moving me out by the end of September, I knew this would disrupt those plans and set my job search back by several months. I gave Ray permission to repeat this to Tom and Bill English learned of it, as well."

The Cardinal busily took down page after page of notes on his small pad, without registering any perceptible reaction.

"In other words," the Cardinal paused thoughtfully, "you are asking to put down roots and instead you are being offered only a temporary assignment?"

"That's correct, your Eminence."

I was heartened to find my point of view, at long last, gaining some credence.

"Well, I believe we need to revisit this decision, the Cardinal said as he scribbled a note beneath a grave demeanor. And how is it for you to live at St. Stephen's?"

"I enjoy it very much. I have begun to develop some educational programs. I enjoy being in the city. Many of the parishioners I already know from St. Matthew's."

"And Father Sheehan, how are you getting along with him?" he asked.

"Father Sheehan is probably the most introverted man I have ever met.

As Bill English put it, he has his 'limitations,' and I try to work around them. I am probably as happy at St. Stephen's as I have been at any parish."

The Cardinal nodded. He seemed favorably impressed. I was encouraged by his intensified scribbling. It appeared the meeting was going my way. He then set down his pen, looked down at his desk and quietly, with halting voice, introduced the next topic of discussion:

"Now, Paul, what is this I hear about a group of some kind? What is it called, Among Friends? For homosexuals?" His voice dropped on this final word, as though barely able to get it out.

"Your Eminence, I will be happy to fill you in, but what have you heard?" I asked.

"Not much. Someone brought it to my attention just a week or two ago."

I briefed Hickey on the genesis of the idea in my ministry and the history of the organization. I explained the range of services — job search group, peer counseling, referrals, workshops — and he listened intently.

"There is more to this than I had thought. But Paul, what about the teaching of the church?"

"Your Eminence, we are providing services to gay men and lesbians in need and crisis. I don't hide the fact that I'm a priest, but I am not there to talk about religious beliefs. So church teaching just does not come up."

"Well, I know that when we give food to the poor, for example, we don't ask the recipients about their lives," the Cardinal admitted. "Do you have any literature about Among Friends?"

"Certainly, your Eminence."

"Could you drop some of it off for me at St. Matthew's? I will be there on New Year's Day. I'm going on retreat right after that and can take the materials with me to pray over this. I'll get back to you the following week."

I delivered some materials about Among Friends to the Cathedral. I included a portion of a grant proposal that argued the need for our services, by citing the results of various studies:

30 per cent of suicides among youth annually are committed by gay and lesbian youth. By the age of twenty-one, 29 per cent of all gay and bisexual males have attempted suicide. 32 per cent of the respondents of a sexual minority survey report experiences of antigay violence that include being chased, having an object thrown, being beaten, having property vandalized,

being robbed, raped, assaulted with a weapon and spat upon.

The question of my transfer was now in the hands of the Cardinal. I did not expect much of a delay. I had gone to him primarily to discuss my future in the Archdiocese. I did not expect him to reverse the Personnel Board's decision to move me from St. Stephen's to St. Anthony's, but I wanted him to know what I thought about it.

In February, the parish's Education Committee sponsored a joint presentation between Father Joseph Lund, an Episcopal priest, and myself, on Anglican-Roman Catholic relations. This was one of the rare moments when my parents attended a parish function that I had organized. Tom Sheehan put in a brief appearance, as people arrived. It happened that my parents were introduced to him in the elevator by a parishioner. Tom failed to introduce himself in return. Later, in the Parish Hall, when I attempted to bring Tom and my parents together for a moment, he muttered that they had "already met" and made a quick exit.

This behavior was unmistakably rude. Since my parents are not Roman Catholic, it mattered to me that they feel a part of my life and work. Achieving this had never been a problem, until that evening at St. Stephen's. A few days later, my mother remarked that she did not feel insulted, because she could see from his eyes that Tom is a sick man.

The differences between Tom and myself were taking on an intensely personal tone. Ray Kemp confirmed this, a week later, over dinner:

"I believe that Tom has made up his mind against you."

"Does he say why?" I asked.

"All he says is that you are 'not helpful.' This seems to be fixed in his mind. I don't believe there is anything you can do to change it."

That same month four priests of the Archdiocese were accused of pedophilia. They were men who had served the Archdiocese for many years. Two were close to retirement.

One of the accused, Tom Schaeffer, who was chaplain of a nursing home, I knew from St. Andrew's. He was a close friend of the pastor, Dave Conway, and a frequent dinner guest. Dave permitted him to leave his laundry to be done by the rectory help. The laundress was once reduced to tears, because Tom insisted that his French-cuffed white shirts be more heavily starched than she thought possible in the absence of professional equipment.

Lurid details of the men and their alleged deeds with boys, which went back many years, were trotted through the news media again and again. The four were called in and confronted by the Vicar General, Monsignor William Lori. They responded candidly to his questions in discussions they believed were confidential. Had they known that Bill would report these conversations to prosecutors, they would certainly have insisted on first consulting with attorneys. In addition, Lori informed *The Washington Post* of the meetings and their outcomes. These unprecedented measures represented a new effort to deal with such accusations openly and immediately, in contrast to the secretiveness and denials of the past, for which the church had been widely criticized.

Bill Lori was a young priest who had served as Hickey's secretary for several years. As Hickey approached the age of retirement, Bill was to be rewarded. Bill Kane was unceremoniously removed from the Archdiocese's top administrative job, outside of being Archbishop, to make way for Bill, who was quickly made a monsignor and, a few months later, a bishop. Having assisted Hickey for many years, he had come to share many of his traits. Their sermons were interchangeable compilations of paternalistic anecdotes, formulaic statements of doctrine, including *de rigueur* allusions to Mary, and reminders of the importance of church authority. The only difference was that Hickey's style was his own, while Bill was an emulator. Bill did a good imitation of Hickey's somewhat naive, somewhat out-of-fashion, overly proper, but nevertheless fundamentally kind demeanor. At the core, however, Bill remained solidly and simply an administrator.

February 1995 was a tough month for the Archdiocese, due to the loss and dismay associated with the four priests who had been charged. Cardinal Hickey organized a dinner for priests of the Archdiocese to boost morale. Arranged on short notice, the dinner invitations were sent out via pastors, who were to pass word along to their associates and resident priests. Tom informed Val and Ray, but not me. I did not learn of the event until after it was over. This was a breach of priestly fraternity that I found unbelievable. I had been denied the opportunity to participate in the most important and emotional gathering of my colleagues since ordination. I knew that Tom was not fond of me, but this was plainly vindictive.

As Tom's animus toward me became more transparent, his habitual reticence took on a menacing aspect. At meals, he now refused to make even polite responses to my occasional remarks. If I asked about plans for the vacant building across the street, he did not know. If I inquired about Holy Week liturgies, he would get back to me about it, but not do so. The deacon related that Tom celebrated Mass once in a highly distracted and confused manner, losing his place several times, just after having angrily denounced me in the sacristy. Ray Kemp made himself scarce, seldom celebrating Mass at St. Stephen's, as a "silent protest," he said, against Tom's treatment of me.

I tried to understand what was troubling Tom. Was there something more I should have been doing in the parish? And if so, what was it? Certainly nothing had ever been suggested by Tom. Or was it simply my homosexuality, after all, that was the cause of his consternation, despite his ostensibly enlightened stand?

On one occasion I came upon Tom in the inelegantly named Work Room, a catchall storage area, where he was poring over documents. He looked up at me in quizzical bewilderment, with eyes that asked, "Oh, are you still here?"

I attended a meeting of the Finance Council. If this body was to have such import in determining my destiny, I decided I had better know what they were discussing. On entering the conference room, I found Mary Nenno, the council's chair, sorting through papers. Mary was a retired government accountant. She had a quiet, reasoned way about her. As chair of the Finance Council, she cast herself as an advisor to Father Sheehan, but that masked the reality of his deep dependence on her judgment and driving willfulness. Before the start of the meeting, Mary announced she had "bad news" for me.

"I have just examined the figures for the first six months of the fiscal year and we are running a deficit of $12,600. That just about equals your salary and benefits. It is clear that this cannot continue. Have you been in touch with Monsignor English?"

"There have been discussions."

"Well, I am confident that the Archdiocese can find another position where your skills can be utilized."

I did not respond. However she thought of her role at St. Stephen's, I was under no obligation to discuss my business with her. My presence messed up her books and she apparently believed I remained only out of obstinacy.

Eventually, Tom arrived and the meeting began. When we got to the six-month report, Mary related what she had been telling me prior to the start of the meeting. At that, Tom slammed some papers on the table and, in a voice shaking with bile, declared:

"I have sent the six-month report to Bill English. Bellwoar, Mendenhall. I should have known."

"What do those names represent?" I asked.

"Third priests!" Tom shouted. "There is a pattern. The Archdiocese never sends a third priest when one is needed."

Tom's explanation for reciting this list of names was not convincing. Why had he not simply said that priests are not assigned when they are most needed? The obvious implication was that these men all had something in common. We had all failed to measure up to his expectations.

"Okay, I'll say it publicly!" Tom continued. "Father Murray has met with Cardinal Hickey and they were to have a second meeting, when the question of his reassignment would be decided. But after many weeks, there has been no second meeting."

He paused and, with lowered voice, said:

"This is affecting my health. I am considering taking an early retirement."

"Oh, Father, no!" Mary intoned her lament at the unthinkable prospect.

"What else can I do, Mary?" Tom inquired plaintively?

I was astonished at the spectacle unfolding before me. I sat quietly, offering no comment. I considered leaving the room, but decided to remain. Eventually I joined the discussion, as we moved on to other, less personal, topics.

A week later, when I found that I had received no paycheck for the month, I asked the parish secretary, Celia, about it. She led me into the elevator and waited for the doors to close to inform me that the bookkeeper said I had to ask Father Sheehan about it.

I went to Tom, who was seated at the round table in his office. Although I stood in the doorway, I noticed that his office was extraordinarily warm. The temperature must have been at least eighty degrees. Heat radiated from the room. Tom's pale face looked up with a quizzical wrinkle. I asked:

"Tom, where is my paycheck? It's the last day of the month."

"You saw the letter I wrote to Bill English."

"No, I did not see any letter to Bill."

"Yes, you did," he contradicted me. "I put a copy in your box."

Tom grinned. It was a broad, deliberate grin. There was a fiendish merriment in his face, an enjoyment of my discomfiture.

"I said it at the Finance Council and I wrote to Bill that there would be no more paychecks for you."

I had some fleeting recollection of the phrase, "no more checks," being spoken during his outburst, but it had not registered that by this partial utterance he meant I would no longer be paid.

"You can't do that," I said. "I have been assigned to this parish by the Archbishop of Washington and I will remain here until he transfers me. This is plainly unjust."

"Yes, I can do it. I am the pastor and canon law gives me this right."

Then, in a voice that was much louder, by design, no doubt, to let whoever was within earshot hear what he had to say:

"And don't speak to me of justice! You have been unjust to the parishioners. You have only done the minimum here, the schedule of Masses and confessions."

"I wanted to do more, but discussion with you was never possible. If we had continued to have regular staff meetings where ideas could be discussed, it would have helped."

"When we did have meetings, you didn't say much. All you did was sit on your hands."

"That's because you and Jack completely dominated them by using up the time to go over lists of names of people I had not even met, when you were putting together a parish council. There was never time to bring up anything else."

Knowing I had Mass in ten minutes, I concluded the conversation. I calmed myself. Tom's position was ludicrous. Obviously the Archdiocese would not permit a priest to go unpaid. Obviously the Archdiocese would not tolerate such a challenge to its authority.

What was most disturbing about the episode was Tom himself. He was coming unhinged. His fiendish grin lingered in my mind. His dislike of me had taken hold as a passion. What would he do next?

I celebrated the evening Mass, putting the unpleasantness behind with an ease that surprised me. I trusted that God had some sort of hand in this affair. It was disappointing that the move to St. Stephen's, which a year before had seemed such a triumph, had quickly soured. It did seem that Hickey was taking a long time getting back to me. I assumed that the pedophile priests scandal preoccupied him. St. Stephen's and I were minor items on the agenda.

Tom's craziness, or at least, some of it, represented a calculated effort to speed things up. The paycheck incident turned out to have been a ruse. Bill English told me the next morning that he had already secured funding from the Archdiocese for my salary and benefits. The Archdiocese would funnel the funds through the parish, which would continue to issue my paycheck. Tom knew that. It was, in fact, issued the next day. Tom simply wanted to make his point.

Two weeks later, when a call came from Bill Lori, I felt very uneasy. This was a henchman who enjoyed his work. With Hickey I felt some personal connection. But, for that very reason, if he had unpleasant news, it was likely to come from Bill.

Bill wanted to "continue the conversation" I had begun with Hickey. We met at his office a week later. Since he had recently become "bishop-elect," I congratulated him on his appointment as one of Washington's auxiliary bishops. My congratulations were not even halfhearted. The elevation of Bill was just another example of a hard-boiled, administrative type with little pastoral experience or sensibility moving up. Bill responded with the ritualistic protest of surprise at the development. There was, of course, no surprise in it. Hickey had requested Bill's selection as bishop more than once and it had been turned down by the Vatican, until this last time. As a result, Washington was now saddled with an auxiliary bishop who was in a position to serve as Hickey's alter ego, until his assignment as head of his own diocese. Sensitivity toward the gay community not being an attitude rewarded by the Holy See, I anticipated a tough line from this ascendant, young hierarch.

Bill locked the doors of his office, because, he said, he did not want any interruptions. A sketch of FDR leaned against the wall, waiting to be hung. A window was open a crack, cooling the room with damp morning air. As I gazed out the window, I thought how isolated and small the Pastoral Center seemed. It was too quiet, too removed from the humming traffic onto which the Archbishop's office looked, when the chancery was on Rhode Island Avenue.

Like Hickey, Bill took notes on a small pad with a fountain pen. We discussed St. Stephen's. He was annoyed that the Finance Council had gone beyond its purview by getting into priest personnel matters. He was angered at Tom's presumption in refusing to pay me. He said:

"Even if a parish has to go into debt to pay a priest, it must do so."

"Tom said that he had the right to do this under canon law."

"Tom is a clever man, who reads many books, but he is wrong. If we allowed this kind of thing, the Archdiocese would be in chaos."

For an hour we spoke in this vein. It was clear that we were of one mind on the St. Stephen's affair. Then we came to Among Friends and homosexuality.

Bill had not looked through the materials I had given to Hickey. He was not even aware of them. This annoyed me, because it meant he had not bothered to study the facts about the difficulties experienced by gay and lesbian people. Bill evinced no concern for people. All that mattered was the mantra, "church teaching."

"This is, in many ways, a new subject for the church," I suggested. "The church has only recently accepted that there is such a thing as a same-sex orientation. John Paul is the first Roman Pontiff to speak of homosexuality in a way that acknowledges it is a personal orientation and not only a particular behavior."

"Under Pope Paul, the Congregation for the Doctrine of the Faith's 1975 declaration on sexual ethics, *Personae Humanae*, mentioned the homosexual orientation," Bill countered. No such document could have been released without the pope's approval.

"Nonetheless, this is a very recent development in church history and my point is that once we take in this fact, inevitably it will have an impact on church teaching and pastoral practice, though we are probably talking about decades from now."

"You may well be right," Bill conceded. "But we must work within the framework of contemporary church teaching."

I wondered what that does to the idea of truth. Bill was saying, in essence, that we must remain within the constraints imposed by the political correctness *du jour*.

Bill asked me to meet with Monsignor Lorenzo Albacete to discuss my views on homosexuality. I reminded Bill that I knew Lorenzo long ago, before either of us had entered the seminary. He started work at *Triumph* just as I was leaving.

"Yes, I know," Bill said, though, in fact, he looked surprised. "That is why I thought he would be a good person for you to talk to. I believe you will find his thinking has developed very much since then."

Throughout this discussion, Bill asked me several times what I would do if the Cardinal asked me to step down from Among Friends. Each time, I replied:

"I hope the Cardinal would not put me in that bind."

Bill refused to accept this as an answer to his question. Once again, as we parted, he repeated it:

"What would you do, Paul, if the Cardinal asked you to step down from Among Friends?"

"I hope that His Eminence would not put me in that bind."

"I want you to think about that question," Bill insisted.

Meeting with Lorenzo, I found, was not an easy accomplishment. He seldom answered or returned telephone calls.

I checked with a mutual friend, Michael Winters, to find out more about Lorenzo. Michael was the wry, loquacious, bright, funny and conspicuously gay manager of a Dupont Circle restaurant. He was working on a doctorate in church history and beginning a career as a writer on the Catholic church. Michael liked to present himself as a conservative, which, I suppose, gave him a certain cachet with the hierarchy, but beneath the carefully orchestrated self-presentation he was, in reality, and, of necessity, socially progressive.

Michael was thrilled that Lorenzo was being pulled into my business with the Archdiocese. He had endless admiration for Lorenzo's wit, brilliance and, certainly not least, connections. Lorenzo, Michael gushed, was a personal friend of the pope. Indeed, John Paul II was said to have summoned Lorenzo within a day of his election. They continued to see each other often for casual visits, to discuss philosophy, the arts, literature, and current affairs. Apparently church politics was out of bounds. At the same time, Lorenzo was, according to Michael, one of the few persons who could speak bluntly to Cardinal Hickey and enable this man, whose views seemed stuck in the 1950s, to see other possibilities. As I twisted strands of fettuccine onto my fork, Michael leaned across the table to advise me:

"When you meet with Lorenzo, be as outrageous as you like. In fact, the more outrageous the better! Tell him whatever you want about the gay thing. He knows me. I have told him about relationships I've had. He understands."

Lorenzo met me at the front gate of St. Stephen's. We drove four blocks to the entrance of the swank Ana Hotel, where a valet parked his car. Now in his mid-fifties, Lorenzo had become notably rotund. His appearance was a bit disheveled. His black suit shined in spots. The few remaining wisps of hair were combed into meaningless service across his scalp.

Lorenzo was the epitome of the jovial, ecclesiastical *prepotente*. This is a familiar type, in Rome, that combines immense influence — or the appearance of immense influence — with a carefree enjoyment of life and people. Lorenzo wore well the massive body, the thick Hispanic accent, the sardonicism, the affluence, the connections. I was at once both charmed and wary.

We were seated in a solarium that looked onto the courtyard, where the waters of a central fountain pounded away. Coffee was poured. Food orders placed. Lorenzo broke open a muffin, peeled foil from a pat of putter, and, after completing the labor of combining butter and muffin, took several eager bites, crumbs dropping onto his black vest, as he launched into a monologue about how what I was attempting to do for gay persons was no different from what Monsignor John Kuhn had been doing for many years, since establishing Anchor Mental Health, an organization that serves the mentally ill. My problems stem, he explained, from church officials' attitude toward the population I am serving. Lorenzo made clear that he did not share this negative attitude. He recalled that in Puerto Rico he became acquainted with a gay man whose lover was in the hospital dying from AIDS. Lorenzo had been very impressed by their love for one another.

He mentioned our mutual friend, Michael, and chuckled about Michael's primness in ending a relationship, because the man was not Catholic. I responded that many gay persons who are serious about religion or spirituality seek partners who share their interests and values.

Lorenzo lowered his voice, as his tone became more serious:

"My own approach is to support church teaching, whatever it is. Who am I to question it? If they say the world is flat, then I support it! And then, on an individual basis, to look at these things."

"I believe that church teaching on homosexuality will develop," I said, "now that the church has accepted the notion of sexual orientation. That is what I have told Hickey and Lori."

Lorenzo advised against telling *them* such things. He was implicitly distancing himself from them and opening an avenue where we might find common ground. He continued:

"The Holy Father is strongly committed to evangelization. He is distressed that an excessive moralism is overtaking his legacy. We should be presenting the attractiveness of Christ. The reason so many in the church are hung up on telling people what not to do is that they don't believe their own doctrine. If they believed, then they would simply present Christ and leave the Spirit to do the rest. That's the way it was with the apostles. They began by being attracted to Christ. Who knows what they did when they went home at night? But the Spirit was at work in them."

I was incredulous. Lorenzo was saying what I had long been thinking, especially about trusting the Spirit to do its work in people. And what was still more astonishing, he claimed this represented the thinking of the pope. I had anticipated some intellectual arm-wrestling over church teaching. Instead, I found myself drawn into a delicious conspiracy to neutralize "them," Hickey and Lori. They were hopeless squares who understood only a paint-by-the-numbers approach to church governance.

Lorenzo made allowances for the fact that I myself might not be comfortable with his own approach of easy assent to church teaching, even when the church says the world is flat. He said:

"I will write to Hickey and tell him that we met and talked. I will recommend that he permit you to continue your work. And before I send the letter I will fax it to you so you can look it over. If there is anything in it that offends your conscience, then I will change it."

At the conclusion of breakfast, I bid Lorenzo farewell beneath Ana Hotel's lustrous awning and walked back to the rectory. I certainly felt buoyed by our meeting. It impressed me, once again, with the thought of how complex the Catholic Church is. Behind the seemingly immovable surfaces lies a resilient flexibility. Even the rigid conservatism that characterized the pontificate of John Paul, it turned out, had an unsuspected, sophisticated, enlightened core. But why was that core so masked? And if the pope was concerned about an excess of "moralism," who bore responsibility for this more than himself?

My crisis had devolved into a succession of meetings with church officials. The putative financial crisis of St. Stephen's faded from view as homosexuality took center stage. Sympathetic observers debriefed me, after each event, contributing insights based on their particular interest — the law, St. Stephen's parish, Catholic clergy, priests in the Archdiocese, homosexuality and Catholicism. While it was a personal drama, my conversations with higher-ups provided a tiny window into the world of those who set — or presume to set — the standards and conditions that define Catholicism for everyone else.

The hierarchical church's stance on homosexuality, in particular, is a painful enigma that intertwines with the hopes, anxieties, angers, and spiritualities of many gay men and lesbians, including non-Catholics, former Catholics, and practicing Catholics. In a world where gay people have become increasingly visible, through both the tragedy of AIDS and the energy of organizing as a community, no institution, from the family to the White House to AT&T, has remained unaffected. Can Catholic officialdom really remain unmoved by such a profound change in the culture? Behind all their talk of the unchanging nature of church teaching, what is really going on with the bishops? One gay man put it this way:

"I have a stake in what happens to you, because that tells me whether the church wants anything good for gay people. Or do the bishops insist on remaining in denial and ignorance?"

My meeting with Lorenzo had, indeed, taken the process to a new level, one that provided a glimpse beyond the Archdiocese into the Vatican itself. At this level, the drama transforms into pure farce. Cardinals and bishops become men to be managed. "Church teaching" provides a cover for acting on one's real convictions.

This was not where I wanted to be, at least, not for very long. Socially, intellectually and spiritually, I found myself more than ever at the boundaries of Catholicism. At St. Stephen's, I hosted an evening of interfaith music with participation from Jewish, Muslim, Buddhist, Russian Orthodox and Catholic communities. I was increasingly drawn to interfaith settings. They express the hope that we can transcend organizational rigidities and accretions. Gay ministry is inevitably an ecumenical, interfaith affair. It happened that I was also chairing the steering committee of an interfaith conference, "Sharing Our Rainbow of Light," on ministry to gay men and lesbians. The conference was to take place during the fall at Foundry United Methodist Church, where both President Clinton and, until shortly before the 1996 presidential campaign, when he decided to pander to the evangelical right, Senator Bob Dole, worshiped.

My work was personally fulfilling and spiritually uplifting beyond anything that I had experienced in parish ministry. Ironically, being a Catholic priest afforded me the opportunity to develop this ministry, while at the same time underscoring my vulnerability. While my work brought me into spiritual fellowship with Unitarians, Jews and Presbyterians, I was in daily contact with a pastor who barely acknowledged my existence, while forcing me to engage in an enervating chess game with church officials who had the power to shut me down.

I knew what Hickey's decision would be, before I met with him, at the end of May. He would leave me free to do my work at Among Friends. I learned this first from Lorenzo, who was confident that Hickey would comply with his own recommendations.

Hickey received me in his office with the characteristic, too tight handshake. His demeanor was relaxed, compared to what I had seen before. It appeared that Lorenzo was right. But we were seated, again, rather formally, as if for interrogation. Hickey behind the desk. I at the side.

He questioned me, once again, regarding my beliefs about homosexuality:

"Now, Paul," he began, "in a gentle, cautious tone, suppose a young man came to you and said, 'Father, I am in a relationship with another guy and it is really good.' What would you tell him?"

I was amused that the example was of a man. Homophobes invariably focus their attention on the sexual behavior and proclivities of gay men, rather than lesbians, when arguing their objections. This is because homosexuality means to them, at bottom, the violation of masculinity. When two men have sex, one usually penetrates somewhere into the other's body and the other "submits" to it. It is the act of submission by a man that gravely offends deeply rooted understandings about what men are. And within the Catholic Church's patriarchal culture, the investment in conventional understandings about masculinity and male dominance is very great.

I answered Hickey:

"Your Eminence, I would look at what this young man was saying anthropologically and phenomenologically. That means that I believe we in the church must listen and listen deeply to the experience of others, before we presume to speak. I would want this man to tell me what the relationship means to him. What does it mean within the context of his life? What has his experience of love been?"

Hickey paused and said:

"You will not go as far as John."

The allusion was to John Gigrich, who had made the devil's bargain of espousing the Church's official teaching on homosexuality in exchange for a title. Hickey was observing that I was refusing to follow John's path. He continued:

"John had his approach. Father Harvey has his approach. And you have your approach."

These words bespoke a new and unaccustomed level of respect. Father John Harvey is a conservative theologian who founded a national organization, "Courage," to promote sexual abstinence among homosexuals. By placing me alongside John and Father Harvey, Hickey was acknowledging that I had become an actor in my own right in this arena. I had my "approach" and he would let it be.

Atop his desk were the printed materials about Among Friends that I had left for him months before. He picked them up and, with a reluctant sigh, said:

"You make a compelling case. I am inclined to give you permission to continue this work. Do you want to continue to reside in a parish?"

"My identity and work as a priest are fundamental to who I am. I would like to continue to be involved in work in a parish."

Among Friends, it seemed, was not something he was merely permitting me to do. He was *assigning* me to it! By asking about residence in a parish, he implied that my life in a parish should not be an encumbrance to my *real* work. He even remarked that ideally the parish where I reside should be near the Among Friends Center.

At the conclusion of our meeting, he pulled me into a vigorous, two-cheeked embrace. As he did so, I felt an emotional surge. Tears of relief that the pressure was off. A crisis had passed. But also, something else. I felt the pain of generations of gay persons who had suffered because of the Catholic Church. I carried their pain with me to a conversation with a cardinal, a "prince of the church." I felt privileged to have had the opportunity for this discussion with someone so highly placed in the hierarchy. It was a moment to which I had been called.

CHAPTER 7

LOOSING

Washington summers are notoriously hot and slow. The summer of 1995 was no exception. In July I was mugged one sultry night by two young men on my way home from Mr. P's, a neighborhood bar. I suppose it was careless of me to be on the street alone at that hour, but I had long lived in the city without incident, passing street corners where clusters of liquored men laughed darkly and walking at night on too quiet, tree-lined streets of tall, Victorian town houses.

My muggers pursued me for two blocks, peeling off from a group of their cohorts who had been lurking in an alley. I knew at once that I was being followed, but drew false confidence from the fact that I was walking along M Street, which is reasonably well trafficked. That night, however, it was eerily calm. I reached Twenty-fourth Street, an intersection bordered by three large hotels, each loudly claiming luxuries above and beyond the others'.

Surely I was safe in that zone of privilege. Surely my pursuers would wilt in the radiance of Twenty-fourth and M. I stopped and turned to face them. They were African-American. One, tall and trim, had a handsome face. His companion, who stood back somewhat, had the bulk and look of an experienced mugger. Perhaps this was a tutorial of sorts. The pursuit had started the adrenaline pumping, at least, in me. My breathing grew shallow. The handsome one asked for the time. I said I did not have the time and started across the street toward a hotel entrance.

"Come here!" he growled, in a tone of ferocity unexpected from such a pleasant face. His tough-looking companion stayed back. My assailant grabbed my arm, knocked my knees from behind and pinned me to the pavement in an instant. His body covered mine. The contact was strangely intimate. I did not feel myself to be in bodily danger. I did not detect a mean spirit in my assailant. The wallet was slipped from my back pocket. He backed away. As he started off with his companion, I called out a futile "Nooooooo!", reaching out for them, as though they were running off with my most prized possession. In fact, they had nothing of value, not even cash, which remained undisturbed in a side pocket. My calling after them had more to do with metaphysics than property. An injustice had been done! How could they do this? How could they be this way?

My cry came from some profound, instinctual place that does not understand the violation of one person by another. This is the same place that was bewildered by the cruelty of the boys who chased me home from Nottingham Elementary School, years before. It is the same place that did not comprehend Lou Quinn's indifference to his staff. It is a place in the heart that recognizes sin. "Sin," in the fully textured, Biblical sense that speaks to humankind's separation from God. Not only in the sense of infractions against statutes. Sin, rather, as the world askew, at odds with the creator's intentions, people behaving in erratic ways that violate the dignity of other persons.

This experience sharply increased my sense of vulnerability. It would have been nothing for my assailant to stab me. I was completely at his mercy. The quick jab of a knife into the throat could have come so easily. Moreover, my customary watchfulness had availed nothing. I doubted whether I could have done anything to prevent the robbery, from the moment when the pair chose me as their target.

But I felt myself vulnerable in a still deeper sense: I was alone. I was alone that night because I was alone in life. I was out late, because I wanted not to be alone. And if I had someone in my life, I told myself, I would not have been walking down M Street alone.

Not that such reasoning makes much sense. These were reflections triggered by a mugging. I was not particularly angry toward my assailants. People who do such things have no idea who they really are. They have no idea that they are created out of love and for love; that they are children of God. Drugs were undoubtedly the motivators here. These guys were not even very good at mugging. What they did accomplish, however, was to increase my sense of vulnerability. I had to take more precautions, I told myself. I began to take the dangers of streets seriously. I was drawn into talk about those dangers with the elderly denizens of Foggy Bottom, who approved my sudden conversion to vigilance. I told myself life in the city is dangerous. Life as a gay man makes it more dangerous. And life as a gay man alone still more dangerous.

During the summer, the board of Among Friends decided to move ahead with opening a house to provide a place where gay and lesbian persons could stay a few months. I wanted a homey atmosphere for it, so I was delighted when we settled on a stucco house in a tranquil, blue-collar neighborhood in upper northwest Washington. There were trees, a front porch, and a back deck. It was of a size that could easily accommodate four clients, with room for a resident manager.

Moving into a house was a financial risk. We had received a bequest of twenty-five thousand dollars from the estate of Brian Gallagher. For Brian and for all of us who had committed so much to starting Among Friends, housing was at the heart of the dream. The sooner we set up a house the sooner would people in the community understand what we were about. The community's support, we believed, would follow.

At the same time that this expansion of Among Friends was taking place, strains in my recently crafted understanding with the Archdiocese were surfacing. Bill English tried to find a residence for me at several parishes. Pastors were turning him down. One preferred to live alone. Another had "no furnishings" for a resident. One place had yapping Chihuahuas and was too far outside the city. What most disturbed me about these potential placements was that none represented the least effort to match my personal attributes to the needs of a parish. Where St. Stephen's had been a place where my reflective, academic style of ministry had been well received, Bill now proposed assignments where I knew I would have little to offer and, according to the pastors, was not needed.

The Archdiocese, it appeared, would tolerate my work in the gay community, but at a cost. Indeed, they had changed the subject on me. I had gone to see the Cardinal, the previous December, to protest being pushed out of St. Stephen's, where I did have a meaningful ministry. Among Friends, instead, became the focus. I pointed this out to Bill English, after a spate of unsuccessful efforts to place me:

"Bill, why don't you just leave me at St. Stephen's? Since the Archdiocese is now paying my salary, Tom's concerns about the expense of a third priest on the staff have been addressed."

"Paul, you have, in effect, been fired by Tom. It's better for you to get away from there."

"But I am doing good ministry at St. Stephen's. I doubt whether I would have much to offer in the places you've come up with so far, beyond saying the magic words at Mass."

"You need to be more flexible about the kind of parish where you go."

Why could I not draw these people into some kind of honest discussion about my life as a priest? The closest they came to honesty was the admission that I was being "fired" by Tom. But for what cause? It was obvious to me, as it was to some of the core parishioners at St. Stephen's, people who knew Tom well, that he had developed an irrational fixation on me. Why did the Archdiocese choose to be complicitous with his dysfunction?

I felt a bit stupid coming so late to this realization. There was a part of me that kept hoping for the Catholic Church to live up to its promise. That it would be a place of genuine regard for persons. A place of justice. That its officials would be more than careerists and bureaucrats.

As I reviewed my twenty years as a priest, and my life, before that, as a seminarian, I saw that my problems with Tom were symptomatic of deeper ills. The underlying issue was a disconnection between the Archdiocese of Washington — and, perhaps, the Roman Catholic Church itself — and myself.

Recognizing this disconnection was more important to me than analyzing it. Was it cultural? Did it have to do with transferring an Episcopalian's frame of reference to Roman Catholicism? Did it have to do with a WASP trying to fit into a world dominated by Irish Catholics? And had I been attracted to all of this and held by it over the years out of some psychological need to be controlled? Whatever the explanation, it did seem that it was time for us to state the obvious and go our separate ways.

I wrote a lengthy letter to Cardinal Hickey about the "failed marriage." The placements with uncommunicative and abusive pastors. The refusal to discuss my career development. "I dare not allow concerns about my future life within the Archdiocese to be brushed aside," I wrote, "lest I, too, fall victim, as have others, to the consequences of a 'smothered rage.'" "Smothered rage" was borrowed from an essay by Thomas Merton on the consequences of basing religious life on institutional conformism, rather than personal freedom. The sick energy that fueled the bizarre and destructive behavior of several of my pastors and colleagues was, in my view, precisely such a rage.

I would move into the attic room of the Among Friends House, which was quickly taking shape. Donations of furniture, pictures, carpets, beds, linens, and kitchen supplies came together, as if on cue. One day I remarked that I wanted a Futon in a particular spot, though we did not have one. Within a week someone called to donate a Futon. It was impressive to experience so directly the earnest desire of people, especially gay people, to be of help to their brothers and sisters in need.

The attic room was a narrow space, only nine feet wide, but ran the full length of the house and had a sliding glass door at one end that opened onto a small deck. It was very quiet. I would have, for once in my life, my own space.

The Washington Blade sent a reporter, Wendy Johnson, to cover the opening of the house, the first of its kind in Washington and, so far as we knew, in the nation. Wendy's first question, on entering the house, was:

"Are you gay?"

"Yes," I replied.

It had taken a lifetime to reach that simple, affirmative response. Yes, I am gay. Proudly so. Proud to announce it in print. Proud to do so calmly, without a lot of fuss. I knew that she would make use of this in the article. Gay priests are not a rarity, but gay priests who say so publicly are. Being out goes with the territory of running a gay organization. Without being open about myself, there was no way that Among Friends would have any credibility.

I had an appointment with Cardinal Hickey the week after my interview with the *Blade*, but just before the article's publication. It was at his house, a mansion in a neighborhood of mansions, near Tenley Circle. This was the house where a predecessor, Cardinal O'Boyle, had lived. Hickey had moved there from his apartment at the Pastoral Center, anticipating retirement. He mentioned O'Boyle having died in the house, apparently thinking ahead to his own declining years.

We met in his study, a restful, glass enclosed room that had been added on to the second floor. The house's original, stone exterior imparted an attractively rough and casual feeling that I did not expect in the workspace of one so rigidly proper. On his desk was my personal file, a garden of colorful tape flags poking out from the side. My recent letter was on top with markings in yellow. The second paragraph, where I detailed my love of priestly ministry, notwithstanding difficulties with the Archdiocese, blazed in a halo of yellow ink. The atmosphere was more intimate than it had been sitting at the desk in his study at the Pastoral Center.

Sitting back, Hickey raised his hands to press the fingertips together. He started haltingly, weighing each word before speaking it:

"Paul, I've read your letter. And to prepare for this meeting I have read every page in your file. I want to know if your decision is final or if there is any room for dialogue."

"Your Eminence, I would not have bothered to write such a lengthy letter, if I were not open to dialogue. Dialogue is what I have always wanted. I love the priesthood. I value my work as a priest. That, in fact, is why I can't go on this way. I feel that what I have to offer has no chance of development in the Archdiocese. Bill is offering goofy assignments to places where I'm neither wanted or needed."

Hickey reviewed the history of my various assignments. He said he knew some of these had been difficult for me. Smiling, he declared that it was not our purpose to assess blame.

I brought out what was for me the central point:

"Your Eminence, what I want to know, what I need to know is what I am building toward. What is my career path? Where do I fit in?"

"Well, normally a diocesan priest eventually becomes a pastor. I don't think you want this and I suspect that even before your ordination you knew you did not want it."

"That's probably true."

"You should have been confronted with that."

"But, your Eminence, many priests do other things. At one point, I was recommended to serve as director of the Office of Social Development by Sean O'Malley, when he left that job. That interested me, but you chose someone else, saying that I was too gentle to confront pastors on their racism. I inquired about a university chaplaincy, but was told I was too conservative. There are many things that priests do, besides parish work. Why can't I get some discussion going about where my talents can best be utilized?"

After a thoughtful silence, Hickey replied:

"We are here to help people, wherever we are sent."

After another pause, he continued:

"As I review your file, I see some consistent reports about you."

"What are they?"

"Well, you have relational problems. You are introverted."

"Your Eminence, of course I am introverted. That's who I am. It isn't going to change. That is part of the reason I do not feel I would make a very good pastor. But I do get along well with people and have much to offer, even in the parish setting."

"You expressed anger to Lou Quinn."

"Yes, I did. And he deserved to have anger expressed to him. He treated his priests and staff with callous indifference."

"And the Archdiocese paid for two years of psychological counseling for you. Perhaps you would like some more counseling?"

"I chose to go into counseling myself for personal growth. It was a healthy, positive choice. I do not see any need for counseling at this time."

This was as close as I would get to honest discussion with the Archdiocese. There was nothing substantive against me, just vague observations about "relational problems" and a history of "counseling" suggesting that I was somehow weak. Hickey was certainly not willing to concede anything about how I had been treated by the Archdiocese. He then took a more personal tack:

"I don't understand why you are doing this. When the Archdiocese has agreed to support you in your work. Why not do that for five years and then see where things stand?"

"There is something to that, I conceded. Leaving at this time would impact severely on what I am trying to build. Let me think about that some more."

I was leaving the meeting with nothing concrete, and yet I agreed to reconsider, to meet again. Hickey could be so gentle, simple and considerate that I somehow did not want to disappoint him. At the same time, I knew that the *Blade* article would appear at the end of the week. In addition, the following week the Sharing Our Rainbow of Light Conference would take place. I was to introduce a nationally prominent speaker, John Shelby Spong, Bishop of the Episcopal Diocese of Newark. I expected media coverage of the conference. The month ahead would test my relationship with the Archdiocese as never before. If we could survive these bumps in the road, perhaps we did have something to talk about, after all.

In the front hall, the Cardinal insisted on helping me on with my raincoat. He then held my head with surprising firmness between his hands and, drawing me close, said:

"I regard you as part of my family."

I was drawn into a double-cheeked farewell, before being released. On leaving, I noted the jack-o'-lantern on the top step and asked whether children actually go trick-or-treating in that neighborhood.

"Oh, yes!" the Cardinal responded, with giddy glee. "There are always a few!"

The image of this goodly Cardinal distributing candy to children presents itself easily. It is the kind of role he relishes. Hickey wants to believe his world is peopled mostly by children eager for the tokens of affection that he dispenses out of his beneficence. His problems come with the notion of adults claiming recognition as his equals and insisting on adult talk.

The *Blade* article appeared two days later. While it accurately reported about the house, the story focused on my struggle with coming out and my commitment to serve gay people. Wendy Johnson had alluded to stresses with the Archdiocese.

Everyone who knew me, gay or straight, seemed to know about the appearance of the article instantaneously, from the moment of its release. At St. Stephen's word shot through the network quickly. Multiple copies of the paper were obtained at a nearby music store, by the heartier types, for distribution to the parish's core, elderly women ensconced in the condominia of Foggy Bottom. Tom Sheehan, I learned, actually came to my defense with an influential parishioner, a woman, who assumed that a public declaration of gayness also meant that I was bringing young men into the rectory for sex. Tom assured her that this was not the case and that the differences between us had nothing to do with my being gay.

My simple declaration caused, I learned second hand, a stir in the offices of the Archdiocese, as well. The *Blade* article circulated there as quickly as it did in the parish. The stir had to do with what would happen to me. How quickly would I be suspended?

The conversations, the speculations, the gossip, became very tedious. Most of the talk focused on the politics of the situation. Would Hickey, as a "good administrator," choose simply to let the moment pass? Or would he risk taking actions that might exacerbate tensions with the gay community? How could he act against me, since I had done nothing wrong and, indeed, sought to help a community the church had long ignored?

Was the marriage over? Was it time to go our separate ways? This time it was Hickey's turn to make a decision. For my part, I was at peace. There was nothing I would have done differently.

"The Cardinal will be with you shortly. He sits there," Barry Knestout said, indicating by implication in which of the two wing-backed chairs I should sit.

So we would not be at the desk. Did that mean our meeting would be somewhat casual? Why had Barry dispensed with the ritual of removing my overcoat and hanging it in the waiting room? Instead, it had been draped over a chair in the Cardinal's study. Was I being kept out of the waiting room, where the door was shut, for a reason? Perhaps there was someone there they did not want me to see. It was hard to keep my mind from racing through such speculations. I was anxious. I was waiting. Perhaps my judgment would be affected, as it had been by being followed for two blocks, before being assaulted.

Hickey entered the study. Brief greeting. Not two-cheeked. Some mention of Rome. Then:

"Paul," the Cardinal slowly intoned in his nasal voice, "it has been a little over a month since we last met. What are your thoughts now?"

"Well, your Eminence, I have been thinking about what you said..."

I spoke on as Hickey opened a folder and removed a clipping of the article from the Blade. He started flipping it back and forth. This gesture so absorbed my attention that I almost did not hear my own words. It happened that Tracks, a large disco club, had a full-page ad on the reverse side that included the largely unclad body of a young man. The Cardinal flipped the clipping back and forth. Was he was calling attention to the article about me or the provocative ad? Obviously he was in no mood for humorous speculations. Ironically, as I drew on his own words urging me to reconsider, I knew that he would now just as soon be rid of me.

"... and I see the wisdom of delaying any departure, for now, because I do enjoy the basics of priestly ministry — celebrating Mass, hearing confessions, preaching."

"I saw the article in the *Blade* the same day it came out. I must say it wasn't very prudent. Now I can't place you in *any* parish. I don't know what the circulation of this paper is, but people would talk."

Cardinal Hickey was shaking. I had never seen him so angry. We sat in silence for a minute. It would be of no use to try responding. For example, to point out that gay priests are nothing new and that problems are more likely to arise from concealing one's identity than from being open. He continued:

"And the sentence that most troubled me was where you said the church is an environment where you find it's difficult to deal with the truth openly. You say this the next day, after meeting at my house."

More silence. I saw that he had taken my interview as a personal affront. Wanting, somehow, to protect him, I said:

"Well, your Eminence, I did not mean to cause you distress. The same could be said of most bureaucracies. They are places that don't much welcome the truth."

He nodded. I continued:

"The church does, of course, have a special obligation in this regard, since it is supposed to be in the service of the gospel."

His face tightened. My words were not helping. No words would help.

"I am going to have to reconsider your work with Among Friends."

He went on to mention the Archdiocese's liability risks in permitting me to run Among Friends. A lawyer had advised him that the Archdiocese has no way of protecting itself against possible lawsuits. It may simply not be possible to permit me to continue, for that reason alone.

"I will think about this some more," Hickey said. "I will pray, Paul, and see what my conscience will allow."

As I drove away from the Pastoral Center, I considered that for the first time in my life I had been treated as a pariah. Not for anything that I had done wrong, but only because of who I am. It hurt; but it also felt good. Good to be free. Good to be in solidarity with my gay brothers and lesbian sisters, who have experienced the same and far worse. Good to be unambiguous in my commitment to truth, integrity, justice and compassion.

The Among Friends House had, by this time, received its first client. As word of the house's existence spread, queries came from therapists, social workers and potential applicants. A young man had been outed to his parents, who consequently wanted him out of their home. A man in the terminal stages of AIDS, who had closed out his apartment to move back in with his fundamentalist Baptist parents, attempted suicide, when they decided to force him to choose between visits with gay friends and continuing to live with them. Someone needed a way out of an abusive relationship, but had no place to live.

If forced to choose, I would not turn my back on these people for the opportunity to continue with the dull routine of dispensing sacraments that is the reality of most parish ministry. On the other hand, if forced out of the Archdiocese, I doubted whether I would be able to keep Among Friends going, since I would have to find gainful employment.

When Hickey and I next met, in early January, he announced his decision. We were, again, overlooked by the portrait of Bishop Carroll, as we sat in the wing-backed chairs.

"I'm afraid I must tell you what you don't want to hear," Hickey said. "I must ask you to sever ties with Among Friends."

He paused. His voice was firm, rising slightly in pitch the way it does, when he is being firm. He seemed to be bracing for a reaction. Anger, perhaps? Tears? But I sat comfortably still, gazing at him.

"Paul, I have discussed this decision with my auxiliary bishops. I wanted to be sure I was not reaching some kind of wild decision on my own. And they all agree that *you* should not be in *this* ministry."

Securing the agreement of his three auxiliaries locked the decision into place in a way that underscored its finality. Indeed, I had never heard of such a thing. Hickey would be seventy-five in a few months, the usual age of retirement. A decision such as this would be difficult for a successor to undo, even if he were so inclined. Moreover, personalizing it — "*you* should not be in *this* ministry" — added a nasty touch. It implied knowledge of personal characteristics, proclivities perhaps, that caused prudent minds to conclude I was unsuitable for this work. I was now officially deemed tainted by the unanimous consent of the top officials of the Archdiocese.

I was either to take a parish assignment or leave the active ministry. Hickey urged me not to decide then and there, but to think it over. I thanked him for that and told him that I preferred not to respond immediately. I said:

"Your Eminence, I want to tell you about a man that I anointed on the day after Christmas a year ago. You may recall that we had an ice storm on Christmas night. The roads were particularly hazardous. I returned late to the rectory from my family's house and found a message on my answering machine from a friend, Barbara, who was calling on behalf of a man who was dying of AIDS. I returned her call and said that I could not go out just then — the location was across town — because of the ice, but I would see him the next day.

"It turned out that it was just as well I had delayed a bit, because the man, Dana, had been in a coma and rallied into consciousness just minutes before I entered the house. We spoke for a few minutes and I anointed him and gave him holy communion. He was grateful. Even, it seemed to me, too grateful. On the way out, I learned why.

"A friend told me that Dana had grown up in rural Maryland. The pastor of his parish told him he could not be a server at Mass, because he was black. As a young man, when he realized he was gay, Dana went to this same pastor for counseling. He was told that he would go to hell, because he was gay. Eventually, in his mid-thirties, he contracted AIDS. While visiting his family, he went, once again, to this parish, where the same man was still pastor. Dana extended his hand, but the pastor slapped it away. This happened on the front steps. The slap so startled Dana that he stumbled backwards and fell down the steps. He loved the Catholic Church and had never given up his faith, although he felt rejected by the church. That was why Dana was so grateful. To him, it was unbelievably wonderful to have a priest enter his home and give him the sacraments."

"Yes," Hickey responded, "it must have been very rewarding to administer the sacraments at such a moment."

"Well, your Eminence, the predominant emotion I was feeling at that time was anger. Anger at the way this man had been kicked in the teeth three times — for being black, for being gay, and for having AIDS — by the church that he loved with all his heart. I don't even know why I am telling you this story, but I wanted you to hear it."

We ended our meeting. I was to get back to him. I knew, of course, what my decision would be. It was a relief, finally, to have the question of my future in the Archdiocese resolved. The marriage was over. I would be leaving.

The Cardinal had, at last, put me into the bind that I had, months before, told Bishop Lori I hoped not to face. My departure from the Archdiocese was now a foregone conclusion. Nevertheless, I faced several options about how to negotiate the separation and I wanted to leave on my terms.

During this period I gained a new respect for the role of lawyers as "counselors." Several lawyer friends did provide invaluable counsel about strategies for approaching negotiations with the Archdiocese. It became evident that while the Archdiocese was declining to create a paper trail, it was insisting that I make one by stating my intentions in writing. This protected them, in the event of a lawsuit, because they could easily recraft recollections about what they had said to me. It was, I learned, important that I not simply capitulate on the assumption that I had no rights.

It did, at first, seem that I was without a trace of anything resembling a right. I was losing my job and home simultaneously. Since I was not a rent-paying tenant, I lacked the rights that can delay eviction. Because the Archdiocese is self-insured, I did not have the option usually available to employees to extend health care coverage after termination by assuming the premium payments.

I was, in fact, being terminated due to the blatant homophobia of my employer. I had not denied church teaching. I had never failed to fulfill my duties as a parish priest. I had committed no crimes. Coming out as gay was the sole cause of my troubles. And even at that, Hickey had not brought himself to the point of saying, "so, you are gay," or in any way discussing it with me. The talk had been, rather, of public reactions, liability and my fitness for this ministry. Everything from the Archdiocese was oblique and opaque, a strategy to isolate, without directly engaging real issues. They hoped I would make things easy, either by going away or by allowing myself to be cowed into submission.

After a few weeks, however, it became evident to me that my position was not so weak as I had, at first, imagined. I was on the side of truth, integrity, justice and compassion. They were on the side of fear, intimidation, dissimulation and expedience. "God is on our side" is, of course, the tiredest of clichés. This was, however, the refrain of those who were pinning me to the ground. At bottom, it is, they would claim, about "church teaching," that is, "Truth," as they define it.

I wondered how the Cardinal could have gotten himself into such a weak position. True, I was the one who would be looking for work, health coverage, and a place to live. But he was in the unenviable position of opposing works that are self-evidently good solely on the basis of transparent homophobia.

As news of my predicament spread, people wanted to respond. At first, I was cool to the idea, because I was trying to buy what time I could through delay. Publicity and protest, I feared, would only make things more difficult. As I came to understand the moral weakness of the Archdiocese's position, however, I decided that if friends and supporters wanted to write letters, I should not prevent them from doing so. If I was going to leave the Archdiocese, I wanted it to be part of the record that some felt they had benefited from my ministry and many disagreed with the Cardinal's decision. I did not, however, expect letters or any other form of protest to cause some reconsideration.

Determined that my ministry would continue beyond the confines of Roman Catholicism, I began to explore alternatives. Over a few lunches at a downtown restaurant, Bob Fagan, a onetime colleague at St. Matthew's, explained how his own ministry of weddings and counseling continued, despite having left the Archdiocese and getting married. He encouraged me to join CORPUS, an organization of resigned priests. I might join my friend, Bruce Simpson, in starting a congregation in the Old Catholic Church, a small but international tradition of Catholics who differ with Rome over papal infallibility and church structure. In Europe, Latin America and North America, there are, as well, thousands of Eucharist-centered communities that have emerged from or remain just at the boundaries of Roman Catholicism. Like Dignity, many of them differ with Rome on some specific issue of church teaching, but nevertheless continue to worship within the Catholic tradition. While these are generally small groups, the cumulative effect of such efforts is to render the boundaries of Roman Catholicism increasingly vague and porous.

Since I had long held an interest in independent communities, I was intellectually and spiritually prepared to make such a transition. I might be on leave from what the Archdiocese calls "active ministry," but my ministry would continue to be affirmed and fully "active" in any meaningful sense of the word.

I also considered reaffiliating with the Episcopal Church. The issues that had prompted my departure from Anglicanism in 1968 had long since faded into insignificance. I admired the capacity of the Episcopal Church to accommodate a wide spectrum of views, especially on homosexuality. To be sure, the debates there are often acrimonious. Moreover, I had several gay Episcopal priest friends, who found it necessary to remain closeted. Nevertheless, openly gay priests were working in several dioceses, including Washington. Bishop Spong telephoned to say he would be "proud" to have me as a priest in his diocese. I was deeply moved by his gesture, which was also a keen reminder of my inability to form any similarly affirming ties with the leadership of the Roman Catholic Church.

In early March, Cardinal Hickey said I would have only until Easter, which was about a month away, to decide what to do. His choice of deadline, the symbolic core of Christianity, was profoundly ironic. Just as the Son of God had been arrested and killed at the behest of religious leaders who found his views dangerous and heretical, only to rise again to new life, so my life was to be dismantled at the behest of religious leaders. I was confident that however distressing the dismantling, I would pass through the process into a new life that would be better, because it would be free and truthful. I wondered how it would feel to preach and worship as I chose, without constantly looking over my shoulder.

The Washington Blade ran another article about me under the headline, "Priest faces tough decision: Paul Murray must give up church or work in Gay community." This article disseminated news of my dilemma widely. Friends, casual acquaintances and strangers called or approached me with words of support. At Mr. P's a redheaded Adonis, his generous smile magnified by the perpetual chewing of gum, eagerly shook my hand. He introduced himself, "Mike," and said he had read about me in the paper.

"What you are doing is very important," he solemnly declared. "I just want to thank you for standing up for us."

A brief, but special moment. For those who have eyes to see, an anointing as sacred as any imparted amid the gilded sparkle of pontifical ceremonies. DJs, bartenders and drag queens rallied to my defense. Their concern confirmed in my heart the sense of calling, the "burden of love," that I felt for this community. A gay man in his thirties, an insightful, sweet lush, noticed me singing along to gay pop star Jimmy Somerville's, "Hurts So Good":

"Look at you! You know the lyrics. This also is your world. You belong to us as much as you do to the Catholic Church."

The campaign of letter writing spread. I was pleased that the Archdiocese was receiving letters from persons of very diverse backgrounds: a nun, gay couples, a man coming out after thirty years of marriage to a woman, Methodists, Jews, Episcopalians, including a priest and a bishop, lesbians, former Catholics, returning Catholics.

In some cases, the letters were virulent. One, from a writer who had personal knowledge of the Cardinal's inner circle during the 1980s, recalled the outright campiness of several of those priests, even in ceremonial settings. He suggested that the news media might take an interest in the blatant hypocrisy inherent in the way I was being treated. Another threatened demonstrations in front of the Cardinal's residence.

I did not want demonstrations or the publication of exposes, nor did I think it likely that such things would ensue, whatever the outcome. I recognized, however, that through no fault of my own my situation provided a convenient symbol of the Catholic hierarchy's hypocrisy and homophobia. I knew well the depth of pain and hurt that many carried because of this. Non-Catholics, as well, often hold strong feelings about such matters, because of the visibility of the Catholic hierarchy's opposition to initiatives to protect gay and lesbian persons from discrimination. As I saw the possibilities for turning my expulsion into a teaching moment, it was clear that the Archdiocese had left itself without a patch of morally defensible ground. My heart was at peace. The life that I had known and crafted under very confining circumstances was about to come apart. I had no illusions about the difficulties I faced, both practical and emotional. But peace had taken hold in a way that was unshakable. Indeed I felt very fortunate. I had stumbled unawares into the Kingdom of God. I had found my heart. Jesus said, "the kingdom of heaven is like a merchant in search of fine pearls; on finding one pearl of great value, he went and sold all that he had and bought it." (Matt 13:45-46. *New Revised Standard Version*)

All that remained was to decide my mode of departure: withdrawal or expulsion. Leaving quietly had the advantage of allowing, perhaps, some negotiation of the terms of my separation, for example, the extension of health care coverage, until I was fully employed. The alternative was to make my expulsion a *cause celèbre* through the use of the news media. The eviction of a priest from his residence would make an irresistible story. My experience could serve as a lens through which to refract the struggle of gay and lesbian persons in the Catholic Church.

Although I knew it would be emotionally demanding, I was inclined toward confrontation. The more I considered my "choice," the clearer it became that it was an impossible one. I felt myself to be a priest to the core of my being. I had done nothing that should cause me to quit the priesthood. At the same time, as a gay man, I was not about to deny my calling to serve the gay community for the sake of appeasing a homophobic bishop. This was a choice between my right arm and my left arm. I could not make such a choice. The Archdiocese would have to choose and their choice would be executed in the sight of a watchful public.

On Palm Sunday, the Cardinal's secretary called with news that Hickey wanted to see me. The appointment was set for Tuesday. When I arrived at the Cardinal's residence, I already had received word informally that Hickey had decided to back off. By this point, I was exhausted and wary from the ordeal. After endless rounds of conversations with lawyers, canon lawyers, resigned priests, active priests, gay activists and well-wishers, I was skeptical that any news from the Archdiocese could be good. Would I find his offer acceptable? What kinds of conditions would be attached?

Barry seated me in the small, front parlor. The room was furnished with straight-backed, studded leather chairs that reminded me of the Spanish Inquisition. Hickey entered and greeted me warmly. I had lost weight since we had last met. Weight loss in a gay man during those years often signaling cause for alarm, he wanted to know if I was well.

"The weight loss is intentional, your Eminence. My physician said it would help to bring my blood pressure down."

We sat. Hickey placed a slim folder on the table.

"Paul, I want you to know you have been on my mind every day since our last meeting. I have read all of the letters that were sent by your supporters. The first wave was protesty, but then came a second wave of letters sharing personal stories. I have also thought about the story you told me about the black man you anointed the day after Christmas. Then I woke up early one morning thinking about you. It was four-fifty. I got up and meditated. I jotted down some ideas, while I prayed, about how we might work things out so that you won't have to leave Among Friends."

The Cardinal paused. His eyes moistening, he continued:

"I know that I must meet my maker sooner than I would like. I will have to give an account for how I treated my priests and people. I know that the church has not done the right thing by gay people."

My eyes began to moisten as well. I noticed every breath I drew. Brilliant sunlight suffused the room. Dust motes gyrated in the still air. I felt enormously privileged to be a party to this conversation. I was witness to the conversion of a Cardinal!

Hickey continued:

"We have been much more censorious toward the sexual sins of gays than we have toward those of straight persons. Paul, the work that you are doing is needed. You should be doing this work. Before discussing ideas I have for a new arrangement, however, I must show you a letter that might send your blood pressure soaring. It was sent anonymously."

He handed me the letter. It was written by an ostensive supporter who claimed to be a gay, Roman Catholic clergyman. Capital letters erratically expressed points of emphasis. The syntax was disjointed. The style of the letter suggested a very confused state of mind.

The author warned the Cardinal about two things. First, that I am too closely affiliated with the leather community, as evidenced by the fact that I celebrated Mass for a leather club called, "The Defenders." The leather community, the author opined, is into sado-masochistic behavior and is, therefore, Satanic. Second, that I am an alcoholic still in denial about my drinking, as evidenced by my frequenting Mr. P's, a "seedy, leather bar."

I looked up from the letter. Its author was plainly too irrational to merit much concern, but I knew the Cardinal wanted some response.

"It is true," I admitted, "that I go to Mr. P's. The owner happens to be a parishioner of St. Matthew's, where I met him. Mr. P's is not, however, a leather bar, although leather men sometimes go there."

"Paul, you're going to have to help me out. What is a leather bar?"

Where to begin? Could he truly be *that* isolated from the world? I provided a brief, historical sketch of the leather world as one of the expressions of gay male culture that had proliferated during the 1970s, in the wake of the Stonewall riots. As I spoke, I observed Hickey taking notes on his small pad. I imagined these notes going into archives from which, decades later, they would eventually be retrieved by researchers investigating the Roman Catholic hierarchy's approach to the gay and lesbian movement during the late twentieth century.

As for alcoholism, I said that because denial is one of the symptoms of this disease, we must all be humble in the face of such a possibility. I did not drink alone at home, I noted, because I had seen that become a serious problem for many priests. Hickey nodded his concurrence. The objective evidence, I said, did not support the suggestion of a drinking problem.

The Cardinal returned the letter to its folder. He said, with apparent relief:

"That's enough time on an anonymous letter. Let's discuss the compromise that I believe will enable you to continue."

He handed me a letter, which he had prepared, but not yet signed. For the most part, it represented a return to the terms on which we had previously agreed. I was to communicate periodically with Lorenzo Albacete and take theology courses at the traditionalist John Paul II Institute. One condition that leaped out, however, was that I pledge "to teach, counsel and write only in accordance with the teaching of the Magisterium on faith and morals." I asked what this meant.

"I know that you do not agree with Ratzinger and the Congregation for the Doctrine of the Faith," Hickey said. "I am not asking you to kneel down on Rhode Island Avenue in front of the Cathedral," he chuckled. "You have a way with words," Hickey reassured me. "I know that you can come up with wording that you can live with."

Hickey explained that he needed some way of keeping the right wing "*Wanderer* crowd" at bay. He asked me to understand his position as a cardinal and the way in which our arrangement might be viewed as a capitulation, if it became publicly known. On the other hand, he expressed understanding about my need not to alienate the people I sought to serve. I was impressed by the collaborative tone. Bureaucratic correctness had given way to two men, two pastors, working together to make something happen.

As we concluded our meeting, the tears resurfaced. With this memoir in mind, I said:

"Your Eminence, I have been reflecting extensively on my life these past few months. I hope some day you will know what led me to the decisions I have made."

With that, we stood and Cardinal Hickey placed his hands on my head and blessed me, something he had never done before.

As I drove from his house, to enter the stream of rush hour traffic on Wisconsin Avenue, I realized that I had just been a party to a work of God's Spirit. This was a humbling, yet not entirely welcome thought. For some weeks I had been bracing for a clear, if painful, break from the Archdiocese. I had begun to enjoy the notion of liberation that would mean from professional and personal constraints. Perhaps, I thought, I might find a lover, something I would never do without the ability to acknowledge the relationship openly. Instead, I found myself drawn back into the ambiguities of compromise. But this seemed a compromise I could live with. At the same time, it even seemed likely that whatever agreement we cobbled together — and the negotiations were to continue — would last only a short time. But if God was calling me to this moment, to push forward somewhat the Catholic Church's understanding of gay and lesbian persons, I needed to see it through.

A brief correspondence followed over the next two months. I agreed to some of the conditions and remained silent on others. The Cardinal did not press me on the latter. He accepted the statement I crafted on church teaching: "I happily reaffirm, at this time, my adherence to the Catholic tradition and Church teaching. Indeed, I consider this tradition, which Thomas Merton describes as the 'one unchanging life that was infused into the Church at the beginning,' to be at once the source, substance, message and goal of my work and pastoral ministry. I fully expect this commitment to continue to be evident in my teaching, counseling, and writing in the future." This language is broad enough to satisfy the scrutiny even of radical Protestants. At the same time, as the Cardinal anticipated, it omits any mention of homosexuality.

Two weeks later, in response to a letter sent by a supporter expressing gratitude for the outcome that permitted me to continue my work in the gay and lesbian community, Bishop Lori wrote:

> His Eminence appreciates your kind remarks concerning decisions reached with respect to Fr. Paul. At the same time, I would note that he has asked Fr. Paul to assure him, in writing, of his acceptance of the Church's teaching with regard to homosexuality. This Father Paul has done.

The bureaucrats had been clever. They knew that I would not lie. No problem. They would do the lying. When I saw Lori's letter, it was as though I had been mugged by thugs out for a quick fix, once again. Not of crack or smack or crystal. Their drug is control. Control over the speaking, writing, teaching, learning, thinking, living and praying of others. Control, above all, over the appearance of having control. But as before, in my street mugging, I was none the worse for the experience. In the end, I lost nothing.

TWO MONTHS LATER

"Come in, come in, Father! I'm Sebastian. Please go ahead and sit down, while I pull myself together. Would you like anything to drink? We have some fresh lemonade."

This was clearly a sick room, complete with adjustable hospital bed and tray and the clutter of countless medicine bottles. I took my place in a pink, vinyl chair that tilted back on the support of chrome arches. Frank, the young man who had shown me in, fetched two glasses of lemonade and quickly disappeared down the hall. The apartment was massive, extending the full length of the building. Beneath were a warehouse and, fronting

Fourteenth Street, dingy retail establishments — used furniture, a convenience store. The apartment was a hidden oasis of comfort and elegance.

Sebastian was clad in powder blue pajamas. In his thirties, I guessed, though AIDS had obscured the indicators of age — skin, eyes, hair. It was a look I had seen often before. The look of soul pulling away from flesh. He stood up unsteadily from the bed and pushed his arms into the sleeves of a white, terry cloth robe. After blowing his nose into several tissues, he worked his way toward the matching loveseat opposite my chair. Once seated, he took a moment to catch his breath from the exertion. Looking directly at me, he declared:

"What a *lovely* face you have! You can tell so much about a person from their face. And I can see that you are a very kind person. How long have you been a priest?"

"Twenty years. It was my anniversary just a couple of weeks ago."

"I once considered the priesthood, you know, when I was young. But I knew it would never work. Too gay, you know. Too interested in sex. Too wild!" Sebastian threw his head back and laughed vigorously, until a cough interrupted.

"How did you happen to call me?"

"My friend, Robbie, the guy who owns this apartment, saw the story about you in the *Blade*, when you had your flap with the Catholic Church. I wanted to see a priest, but it had to be someone who would understand."

"Well, Sebastian, I'm happy to be here, but there are actually many good priests who would understand. I'm not so unusual, except, perhaps, in sticking my neck out in public."

"Robbie, I know, told you how sick I am. In fact, last week there was a scare, when I lost consciousness for a while. That's when Robbie decided we shouldn't wait any longer. This disease, I tell you, has been a roller coaster. A blood transfusion two months ago brought me back from the brink. It was great for a few weeks to have my energy back, but I don't want to keep returning from the brink. I'm ready. I wanted to have a priest here for, you know, last rites. I want to be anointed. I want to go to confession. I want you to bless me. All of those good things."

Despite his ashen skin and gaunt face, Sebastian retained a core of energetic graciousness. His elegant voice exuded a deep, satisfying warmth, like cognac. He continued:

"Father, most of all, I called you here to be a witness."

"A witness?"

"Yes, I want to tell you about myself. I want to tell you, because I know you will understand what I mean when I say that God has blessed me. And I need to tell that to someone."

"Sebastian, take your time. That's why I'm here."

"My life has been the theater, for the past seventeen years. Much of it here in DC, where I grew up. All I have cared about are acting and my friends, and all of my friends are theater people. I never made much money, so I've lived always in rooms or shared houses with friends."

"What kind of productions were you in?"

"Oh, I love it all and I've done it all — comedy, drama, musicals, Shakespeare, avant-garde, even some cabaret. I've been in plays at the Kennedy Center and at small community theaters. It's been my whole life. I was born for it, which is why, I suppose, I was drawn to the priesthood. The robes, the music, the drama of liturgy — church is theater. And I know I could have made it great theater! But, as I explained, that was not to be my trip in life — not this time, anyway."

"You believe you've been here before?"

"Oh, absolutely! Many times, Father. Not that I know much about my past lives or even want to know about them. This is who I am now. What matters is that I learn from this life what I need to learn. You have some ideas about this, too. I can see it in your eyes."

"I've never known what to make of the idea of past lives, Sebastian. Yes, I've had some inkling, some little intuitions that I've been here before. Of course, as a priest I can't think such thoughts out loud, though I know many Catholics who have similar beliefs. But whether I've been around before or not, I find the notion that life is about learning and that some of the issues we have to reckon with here are set in advance very compelling. For example, I've long had a sense of destiny about being a Catholic priest, living for a time in Rome, and even the difficulties that I've had with church officials. For some reason I was supposed to have these experiences. And it goes both ways, I think, that is, the Archdiocese was supposed to have me as a priest. Cardinal Hickey was supposed to deal with me. God has, I think, a keen, often ironic, sense of humor."

"I know the Catholic Church has been a tough place for you, but it's obvious that you are a priest. I mean that's what you are at some deeply personal level. And I think you are a good one. That's the paradox, isn't it?

Father, God will take care of you, as he has taken care of me. Just be true to yourself and the rest will take care of itself. Even this apartment, for example, has been provided by my dear friend, Robbie. We're not lovers. I've never been very good at relationships. The longest one lasted two years. My friendships have been so much more important than my sexual relationships. Not that I wouldn't have liked to have a lover. It just seemed to be part of my life's script that I would not develop many attachments — personal or material."

Sebastian paused, his lower lip trembling momentarily, before continuing:

"About three years ago, I got a part in a Broadway production. My career might have taken off in a big way, then, but that's when I discovered I was sick. I had my first bout with pneumonia. So, I had to give up the part. I've never made any real money and now I have nothing. But my friends have taken care of me every step of the way. They have really been my church. I have found so much love and encouragement in them — more than I found in 'the church,' if you know what I mean."

"Yes, Sebastian, I know exactly what you mean."

"With the church or without it, I have always known that God — a loving, joyful, wonderfully creative God — is here with me. I used to be kind of wild. Sex with lots of partners. Drugs. Nothing heavy mind you, just marijuana and, for a while, coke. None of those things ever dominated me, thank God. I lived a completely worldly, materialistic life, without becoming, you know, defined by it. My spirituality, my sense of God, was always there. God helped me to accept life for what it is and to let go, when I needed to let go, especially now. Above all, love, knowing that I am loved, loving others, accepting others' love, has been the foundation of my life. Now, at the end of life, I have this great condo. And I have it, because of love. I am blessed because I have been able to open to this love, which I have found everywhere. That's why I am ready to return to God. I wanted to tell that to someone, before I go, someone who would understand. My friends are wonderful, each in their own unique way," Sebastian chuckled, "but they don't understand spirituality. They have it, obviously, from the way they care for me and each other. Many of them have been so hurt by the church's rejection, because they're gay, that talk about God of any kind puts them off."

"But Sebastian, I sometimes wonder what difference it makes when we do talk about God. Religion, church, I can tell you, is a terrible bother, at times, and what it's become is far removed from the gospel and anything that the ministry of Jesus of Nazareth represented."

"Father — Paul — we are forgetful. People forget. We have forgotten where we came from and where we are going. Prayer, talking to God, and ritual lift us momentarily out of what we're doing, to remember, if only dimly, the big picture. To remember what really matters. I have not been a churchgoer since I was about twenty. In a way I loved it, but I could also see that many of the clergy don't believe their own words. In theater, we have to study our lines and rehearse them over and over, until they become a part of us. The same thing happens in church — people saying their lines, acting as though they believe. And then, perhaps, one day, like magic, it takes hold. For some. Not that they were hypocrites before. They believed they believed. But when it hits, when you *become* the part you are acting, well, that's when all the words light up and become *true*."

"I've had some glimmers of what it is to speak truly to God. I think back on how pious I was when I was young. All the hours I spent in prayer. The prayer techniques. I really had no idea what I was looking for. I had no understanding that God is here, now, in all of us. I have learned that much more recently in unexpected ways and unexpected places. Funny, now that I think about it, I realize, like you, that I am not able to share these things with many people, especially my fellow priests. They just wouldn't get it. Still, given that church has been so disappointing to you, and has not been a part of your life, I wonder why you had the idea of asking for a priest."

"Ritual has its place, Paul!" Sebastian declared with solemn exuberance, as though letting me in on a secret. "This is *my* celebration and I have invited you to share in it with me. Confessing my sins and being absolved. Being anointed with oil. Receiving the holy bread. Ritual has its place. I know God is with me, no matter what! I know I don't need forgiveness from a priest. But it is good to express these things in rituals, to feel them, to share them. I want to hear you say I am forgiven. I want to feel your hands touching my head with holy oil. To taste the holy bread."

I opened my thin ritual book, its pages translucent from the oils of anointings past. What an honor to be with this man, this wise, gay brother, at this moment. How refreshing his trust in God. No hat-in-hand trembling before the lip of eternity. Sebastian was ready to leap in. No last minute doubts about turning to holy mother church, "just in case." Here, rather, was a man who knew exactly how to use the church's resources. The church was here to meet his needs the way he understood them, not the other way around.

I thought of my fellow priests, my bishops. I wished that they could share this experience with me and glimpse the joyful faith of this man. We celebrated the coming of God's Kingdom that day, my brother Sebastian and I. He took a few sips of lemonade to wash down the wafer. The rites completed, we lingered, savoring the blissful moment.

APPENDIX

The appendix includes correspondence between Bishop Kevin Farrell and myself regarding his accusation of heresy against me. He alleges other, less serious, delicts against church law, as well, including membership in an association of noncanonical priests, mostly married men. This correspondence took place during the spring of 2004. I had, by this time, left Washington and been teaching and working as Catholic Chaplain at Bard College for six years. The tone and reasoning of Bishop Farrell's letters disclose the hierarchical worldview that I engage, struggle to comprehend and from which I finally diverge.

- letter from Most Rev. Kevin Farrell. March 31, 2004. Includes suggested form for a resignation letter addressed to the pope.
- my response. April 27, 2004.
- letter from Bishop Farrell. May 26, 2004.
- my response. June 29, 2004.

To date, there has been no heresy trial.

ARCHDIOCESE OF WASHINGTON

Archdiocesan Pastoral Center: 5001 Eastern Avenue, Hyattsville, MD 20782-3447
Mailing Address: Post Office Box 29260, Washington, DC 20017-0260
301-853-4500   TDD 301-853-5300

Office of the Vicar General
Phone: 301-853-4520
Fax: 301-853-5346

March 31, 2004

Reverend Paul E. Murray, Ph.D.
Professor of Religion
Bard College
Annandale-on-Hudson, New York 12504

Dear Father Murray:

Thank you for meeting to meet with Msgr. Mellone earlier this month. Thank you, also, for your letter to him of March 11, 2004, which he has referred to me for a response.

The concerns of the Archdiocese of Washington are basically fourfold. They relate to: (1) your public position on matrimony in relation to Church teaching; (2) your public availability for sacramental ministry on the "rent-a-priest" website; (3) the potential for simulation of a sacrament because you have no faculties; and (4) your relationship as a priest to the Catholic Church because of the concerns already expressed. Let me comment briefly on each of these.

Regarding the first point, you are aware of the Church's teaching that matrimony is possible only between a man and a woman, whether considered in natural or divine law. Thus, the positions regarding marriage as evidenced in your teaching materials and conference presentations can technically be considered in the category of heresy. This, of course, results in automatic excommunication with potential additional penalties for clergy including possible dismissal from the clerical state (Canon 1364).

The second and third points are directly connected. Since you no longer possess any faculties to function in priestly ministry, your continued listing on the "rent-a-priest" website is unwarranted because you know that any attempt on your part to function as an official witness at a marriage on behalf of the Church would render it invalid (Canon 1108). This being the case, any such function on your part would also be deliberate simulation of a sacrament (Canon 1379).

Finally, since your recent actions and public positions clearly render you liable for certain canonical penalties, unless you are willing to publicly terminate

Page Two
Reverend Paul Murray
March 31, 2004

the actions in question and retract your positions regarding matrimony, the Archdiocese of Washington will have to proceed with a formal declaration and imposition of appropriate penalties. This, of course, might have some negative consequences in your current teaching position. Therefore, if you are convinced in conscience that you must continue in your current actions and positions, I urge that you prayerfully consider requesting voluntary departure from the clerical state. It might enable a transition to legitimate cessation of priestly ministry while also allowing you to continue as a professor at Bard College.

With this in mind, Paul, I have included a possible letter for you to submit to the Holy Father requesting such a dispensation. You could use this one or a similar one written in your own words. In either case, I ask that you give me some specific indication of your decision no later than April 30, 2004, or approximately a month from now.

With an assurance of my prayers and with kindest personal regards, I am

Sincerely in Christ,

+ Kevin Farrell

Most Reverend Kevin Farrell, V. G.
Auxiliary Bishop of Washington

Enclosure:

Paul E. Murray
Bard College
Annandale-on-Hudson, New York 12504

April 30, 2004

Most Holy Father,

My name is **Paul Edward Murray**. I was born in Washington, D.C., on August 4, 1947. I was ordained to the priesthood for the Archdiocese of Washington on June 29, 1975 by His Holiness, Pope Paul VI.

I voluntarily seek departure from the clerical state. I do this freely and according to my conscience. I am not being coerced in any way.

Since 1998, I have been on leave from the Archdiocese of Washington to teach full time at a small, non-sectarian college in New York State. I have also functioned as the Catholic Chaplain there.

In the last several years, and especially recently, I have found it difficult to support the teaching of the Church regarding homosexuals and also in relation to marriage as restricted to a union between a man and a woman. Because of my positions, I have been in communication with the Archdiocese of Washington during the last few months and have come to the conclusion that I cannot in conscience continue to embrace and teach what the Church teaches regarding these matters. I believe, under these circumstances, that seeking voluntary departure from the clerical state is important for my own good as well as for the good of the Archdiocese and of the Church. I believe my request for laicization is appropriate given my present circumstances and theological positions. I do not currently have plans to enter into marriage, but it is possible that I may wish to do so in the future.

Therefore, after prayerful consideration and with great reverence remaining for the Sacrament of Holy Orders, I humbly ask Your Holiness to grant a dispensation from the obligations of the clerical state, including celibacy.

I remain your obedient servant in Christ,

Paul E. Murray

His Holiness
Pope John Paul II

BARD
A College of
the Liberal Arts
and Sciences

Annandale-on-Hudson
New York 12504
Telephone 914-758-6822

April 27, 2004

Most Reverend Kevin Farrell, V.G.
Auxiliary Bishop of Washington
Archdiocese of Washington
P. O. Box 29260
Washington, DC 20017-0260

Dear Bishop Farrell:

I am in receipt of your letter of March 31, 2004. I write in response to the concerns that you express concerning my ministry.

The first regards my public position on matrimony. You state that my positions in this area "can technically be considered in the category of heresy." I find this assertion astonishing and categorically deny that I have ever denied church teaching regarding the sacrament of holy matrimony.

The second and third concerns regard the posting of my name on the "rent-a-priest" website, a service of CITI Ministries, Inc. I posted my name on this site only recently, in early February of this year. In our meeting on March 5, 2004, Msgr. Mellone mentioned your concern about this posting and related it specifically to officiating at weddings, as though this was the principal purpose of having one's name listed there. I assure you that is not my purpose. I have, to date, received not a single request from a couple for a wedding through that posting. Rest assured that if I did, I would consider myself ethically obligated to disclose my condition of not enjoying faculties from the Archdiocese of New York; thus, there can be no danger of a "deliberate simulation of a sacrament."

My posting with CITI Ministries is principally an expression of solidarity with these fellow priests who are almost entirely or entirely of a "noncanonical" status, in the sense of once having resigned or departed from their respective dioceses and religious communities, but who now wish to resume priestly ministry. Because most have married, they find themselves unable to function within the approved structures of the church. As I remarked to Msgr. Mellone, I attended a CITI convention last Fall and find the pastoral experience, insights and spiritual depth of these men compelling. I believe their services are greatly needed and that the Church can only be enriched by embracing and reincorporating them into its ministry. My posting serves, additionally, as a way of making myself known to marginalized and alienated Catholics in this region, so as to offer them spiritual support.

The fourth concern is, in fact, your suggestion that I request voluntary departure from the clerical state. My commitment to priestly life and ministry remains unalterable. In fact, my existence as a man is inseparable from the priestly identity. It will ever remain so. I therefore cannot imagine any circumstance in which I would submit such a request.

With fraternal regards,

Rev. Paul E. Murray, Ph.D.
Catholic Chaplain and Visiting Assistant Professor of Religion

ARCHDIOCESE OF WASHINGTON

Archdiocesan Pastoral Center: 5001 Eastern Avenue, Hyattsville, MD 20782-3447
Mailing Address: Post Office Box 29260, Washington, DC 20017-0260
301-853-4500   TDD 301-853-5300

Office of the Vicar General
Phone: 301-853-4520
Fax: 301-853-5346

May 26, 2004

Rev. Paul E. Murray, Ph.D.
Professor of Religion
Bard College
Annandale-on-Hudson, New York 12504

Dear Father Murray,

I am writing in response to your letter of April 27, 2004 wherein you answered my letter March 31, 2004. For the sake of clarity, let me list the course of events since February 2004, which resulted in the removal of your faculties and the communication of the concerns in my March 31st letter to you. As a matter of record you were granted permission to be absent from this Archdiocese in order to teach at Bard College as of January 1998 and have continued on the faculty there and, until recently, served as Catholic chaplain there.

As of February 20, 2004, His Eminence, Cardinal Egan, referred to Cardinal McCarrick some significant and very problematic public forum information concerning your activities as a professor and Roman Catholic priest. Immediately thereafter, Cardinal Egan removed the faculties of the Archdiocese of New York, which had previously been granted to you and also informed you of this action.

Msgr. Michael Mellone then met with you personally at St. Thomas the Apostle Church on March 5, 2004. He made clear at that time that you could not minister as a Catholic Chaplain at Bard College, which does not automatically or necessarily mean that you cannot teach there. Msgr. Mellone also made clear that your listing on "Rent a Priest" was serious and unacceptable because it provides allegedly "Catholic Services" outside of juridical requirements. He made clear that you would no longer enjoy the faculties of the Archdiocese of Washington. You indicated the need for time to consider changing your mind on certain positions and abiding fully with Roman Catholic teaching.

228

On March 11, 2004, you wrote Msgr. Mellone asking that, in view of the "gravity of this decision," the specific points of concern be put in writing. In my March 31st letter, I responded by very specifically stating the concerns of the Archdiocese of Washington regarding your positions on certain matters. Your listing on Rent-a-Priest, your course description for "Same Sex Unions and Christianity," your role in the God and Sexuality Conference, and the "Innovative Worship in the Catholic Tradition" as listed on the Bard College website cannot be construed as in keeping with Catholic teaching. I was simply informing you of the concerns as you had requested and indicated that you are liable for certain canonical penalties unless you are willing to take public action to correct these matters.

Regarding your position on matrimony, it may be necessary to begin a process for declaration or imposition of a canonical penalty since your assertion of never having "denied church teaching regarding the sacrament of holy matrimony" is anything but evident in your course description. Moreover, your listing on Rent-a-Priest must be removed permanently and immediately. Your stated purpose of wishing to express "solidarity" with those in CITI Ministries as a means of "spiritual support" is neither a sufficient nor an acceptable reason to be listed on that website while you are a priest incardinated in this Archdiocese.

You have no faculties to function as a priest and should not offer your services as such in any public forum. As indicated in my previous letter, if you are convinced in conscience that you must continue in your current actions and positions, you certainly cannot function in priestly ministry and you cannot continue as a priest of this Archdiocese without eventual initiation of a penal process.

When you spoke with Msgr. Mellone it seemed that you understood the seriousness of your present circumstances and the consequences of your various choices. It was with this in mind that I urged you prayerfully consider requesting voluntary departure from the clerical state with the possibility of continued teaching at Bard College.

Page Three
Reverend Paul Murray, Ph.D.
May 26, 2004

Again, therefore, I ask that you clearly and publicly retract your public, heretical positions regarding the nature of marriage, that you remove your name from the Rent-a-Priest website, and that you provide verifiable assurance that you are not currently functioning as a Catholic priest on the Bard campus or elsewhere. I would appreciate a very clear reply from you no later than June 30, 2004.

In the meantime, I again assure you of a remembrance at prayer.

Sincerely in Christ,

+Kevin Farrell

Most Reverence Kevin Farrell
Auxiliary Bishop of Washington

Enclosure

June 29, 2004

Most Reverend Kevin Farrell, V.G.
Auxiliary Bishop of Washington
Archdiocese of Washington
P. O. Box 29260
Washington, DC 20017-0260

Dear Bishop Farrell:

I write in response to your letter of May 26, 2004.

You ask that I retract my "heretical positions regarding the nature of marriage." As I am unaware of having espoused any positions that are or might be construed as heretical, I do not know what you are asking me to retract. While you cite my course description for "Same-Sex Unions and Christianity" as the basis for your allegation, you fail to specify how its contents pertain to a denial of church teaching. I myself find nothing in this brief description of a course dedicated to the scholarly investigation of a subject would enable any reader to draw from it inferences regarding my religious beliefs.

You mention, as well, my role in the God and Sexuality Conference as somehow not in keeping with Catholic teaching. This conference is an organization dedicated to the scholarly examination of questions pertaining to sexuality and religion. I find myself at a loss to know how to respond to your nonspecific allegation regarding my participation in this conference. In any event, I categorically deny that my work with it in any way denies Catholic teaching, both because such work is entirely in the realm of scholarly inquiry and does not include professions of faith and because I categorically deny, in fact, that I deny Church teaching.

Regarding my listing with "Rent-a-Priest," while you may find my stated purposes for this association unconvincing, I recall that I posted my name in good faith while I still enjoyed faculties from the Archdiocese of Washington. The unwarranted removal of my faculties does not convince me that I should now remove this listing.

You seek, also, "verifiable assurance," that I am not "functioning as a Catholic priest on the Bard campus or elsewhere." While the priesthood remains an integral aspect of my identity and functioning as a person, you should know that I have communicated widely, at Bard College and elsewhere, regarding the removal of my faculties, so that there would be no doubt among those who know me or seek priestly services from me that I do not enjoy the status of having faculties from Roman Catholic officials.

Finally, for the sake of accuracy, I offer several notes regarding the chronology put forward in the first part of your letter.

You mention that as of Feb. 20, 2004, Cardinal Egan "referred to Cardinal McCarrick some significant and very problematic public forum information concerning [my] activities as a professor and Roman Catholic priest." I recall that in a phone conversation on Feb. 27, 2004, when I was informed by Monsignor Desmond O'Connor, Director of Priest Personnel, of the removal of faculties by the Archdiocese of New York, the only concern expressed regarded the appearance of what Monsignor O'Connor erroneously called an "ad" in *The Poughkeepsie Journal*. No other concern, including any regarding my activities as a professor, was communicated to me by him during that conversation or in his follow-up letter, dated March 1, 2004.

Regarding my listing on Rent-a-Priest, it is correct that Monsignor Michael Mellone reported objections stated by you during our meeting on March 5, 2004. He did not state the objections, however, in the terms that you now employ: "serious and unacceptable because it provides allegedly 'Catholic Services' outside of juridical requirements." Monsignor Mellone described your objections in narrower and more specific terms, namely, the attempt to solicit weddings. He made no mention at the time of any objection based on the notion that the service functions "outside of juridical requirements."

In addition, at no time did I suggest to Monsignor Mellone that I needed time to consider changing my "mind on certain positions and abiding fully with Roman Catholic teaching." What I requested and he granted was, rather, a brief time to prayerfully consider my response to the issues raised during our conversation. I wrote to him not long after, to ask, as you recall, that the concerns of the Archdiocese of Washington about me be put in writing and also that the question that I was asked to answer regarding my future with the Archdiocese also be stated in writing.

I note that the allegation that I hold heretical views regarding the sacrament of matrimony was first brought to my attention in your letter of March 31, 2004. This serious matter was in no way indicated, whether directly or indirectly, by Monsignor Mellone, when we met on March 5th.

With fraternal regards,

Rev. Paul E. Murray, Ph.D.
Catholic Chaplain and Visiting Assistant Professor of Religion

BOOKS

O books
O is a symbol of the world, of oneness and unity. In
different cultures it also means the "eye", symbolizing
knowledge and insight, and in Old English it means "place
of love or home". O books explores the many paths of
understanding which different traditions have developed
down the ages, particularly those today that express
respect for the planet and all of life.

For more information on the full list of over 300 titles
please visit our website
www.O-books.net

Wojtyla's Women

How Women, History and Polish Traditions Shaped the Life of Pope John Paul II and Changed the Catholic Church

John Paul II, the most charismatic and influential Pope in centuries, reshaped many facets of Catholic thought. Yet Church policy on women during his papacy remained deeply resistant to popular modern ideas on gender roles. Wojtyla's Women explores John Paul II's views on women, marriage, family and sexual ethics from both feminist and conservative Christian perspectives. Previously untapped sources reveal the influence of his upbringing in Poland at the outset of the Twentieth Century, a time when deeply rooted traditions collided with rapid social change and new ideas, against a backdrop of war, genocide, and political oppression. As the book reveals, women were a remarkable and unexpected influence on John Paul's understanding of gender issues and the Catholic Church's theology.

Ted Lipien has written an incisive and penetrating book on the role remarkable women, such as the Albanian-born nun and Nobel laureate Mother Teresa, played in shaping John Paul II's outlook on important and controversial issues that defined his papacy. Much of the ground that Lipien covers in his meticulously documented book is not familiar to students of John Paul II's papacy. He presents new information on the Pope's enduring relationships with women who had an enormous impact on his life, offers original interpretations, and makes a significant contribution in advancing the theoretical discussion on John Paul II's papacy. WOJTYLA's WOMEN's greatest strength lies in the author's impassioned analysis of astonishingly complex issues and events. Lipien's landmark book opens new paths for other scholars and is essential reading for specialists as well as the wider public. **Dr. Elez Biberaj**, author of Albania in Transition: The Rocky Road to Democracy

Extremely detailed research into a heretofore unexamined aspect of the beloved Pope John Paul II's life. This book is worthwhile reading for anyone interested in the personal network of highly influential women who shaped John Paul II's attitudes, particularly on the debate of women's roles. **Dr. Nancy Snow**, author of "Information War"

An important book. Few persons are as qualified as Ted Lipien to enlighten readers about Pope John Paul II's Polish roots -- and the impact that they had on his views on women. Lipien provides a stimulating analysis of the Pope's ideas on gender roles and how John Paul believed the Church should deal with sexual issues. While he does not agree with many of the Pope's stands on women, Lipien makes a laudatory effort to understand -- and explain -- them. This book is a must-read for anyone interested in the relationship between feminism and Catholicism, a key issue of our times. **Dr. John H. Brown,** former U.S. diplomat in Poland, editor of *"Public Diplomacy Press Review"*

9781846941108 **£14.99 $29.95**

Who on EARTH was JESUS?

the modern quest for the Jesus of history

A century after Albert Schweitzer's Quest of the Historical Jesus, modern historians with new techniques are back on the trail. In the most comprehensive survey yet published, David Boulton presents an engrossing account of the debate between contemporary scholars on what we can know about the human Jesus of history before he became the divine Christ of faith.

The best and most thorough account of the breadth and variety of historical Jesus scholarship. Lively, informed, fair, and highly recommended. **Marcus Borg**

Brilliant and timely... Everyone ought to read it, especially those with no sympathy for religion and its crazier adherants... David Boulton is an investigative journalist and the book is an enormous achievement, with its vivid descriptions of what scholars have uncovered... Apart from the excitement of the story of the historical quest, here is the perfect resource for people who want a one-volume guide to a multi-volume industry. It's all here, and it's as up-to-date as you are likely to get. **Richard Holloway,** former Bishop of Edinburgh, Primus of the Scottish Episcopal Church

A great place to start the search for the Jesus of the past and his relevance for the present. **Robert Funk,** Director, Westar Institute and the Jesus Seminar

If you know anything about David Boulton you will know how lightly he wears his erudition and with what wit. **Anne Ashworth,** editor *The Universalist*

A unique treasure. A fair, objective and exhaustive summary of historical Jesus discoveries... Scholarly, yet lucidly written for non-academic readers... A masterly achievement. **Lloyd Geering,** International bible scholar

9781846940187 **£14.99 $29.95**